T0304999

Chen

of related interest

Taiji Jian 32-Posture Sword Form
James Drewe
ISBN 978 1 84819 011 5

Bagua Daoyin
A Unique Branch of Daoist Learning, A Secret Skill of the Palace
He Jinghan
ISBN 978 1 84819 009 2

You Are How You Move
Experiential Chi Kung
Ged Sumner
ISBN 978 1 84819 014 6

Chen

Living Taijiquan in the Classical Style

Master Jan Silberstorff

Translated by Michael Vorwerk

SINGING
DRAGON

LONDON AND PHILADELPHIA

All images: WCTAG Archive

Originally published in 2003 in German
by Lotus Verlag
This edition published in 2009
by Singing Dragon
an imprint of
Jessica Kingsley Publishers
116 Pentonville Road
London N1 9JB, UK
and
400 Market Street, Suite 400
Philadelphia, PA 19106, USA

www.singing-dragon.com

Copyright © Jan Silberstorff 2009
This translation of Chen is published by arrangement with
Singing Dragon, an imprint of Jessica Kingsley Publishers Ltd.
Printed digitally since 2012

Library of Congress Cataloging in Publication Data
A CIP catalog record for this book is available from the Library of Congress

British Library Cataloguing in Publication Data
A CIP catalogue record for this book is available from the British Library

ISBN 978 1 84819 021 4
eISBN 978 0 85701 005 6

Contents

Part IV. Taijiquan in the Mirror of Medicine

Part V. Words by the Patriarchs of the Chen Clan

Acknowledgements

My deepest thanks go to my Shifu Chen Xiaowang who has accepted me not only as his disciple but assimilated me like a son into his family. Deepest thanks also go to Master Shen Xijing who made all of this possible. Without their tuition, there would probably be nothing truly valuable that I could contribute to the subject of Taijiquan.

For contributing their articles I thank Grandmaster Chen Xiaowang, Gerhard Milbrat (also for providing the long weapons for the photos) and Frank Marquardt; Anya Kurka for designing the family tree, and Almut Schmitz and again Frank Marquardt for the formal processing of the manuscript, and Max Fischl for the hours of telephone sessions on translation work. I would also like to thank Holger Neumeyer for the five-level-sketch at the very last minute.

I thank Claudia Mohr for her unfailing dedication in covering for me so that I could find enough time to complete this book. To my parents I feel grateful that they have brought me up in a manner which gave me the freedom to find my own path in life (and thereby to discover Taijiquan).

I wish to dedicate this book to all who have decided to make something real out of their lives, and to those who, despite all the strains and difficulties, have taken the path towards their inner selves. Finally, my dedication is to those who search for or have even found what we call God.

Figure 1 Calligraphy by Grandmaster Chen Xiaowang 'Gong Fu' – Great Skills by Great Efforts

Original preface

First, I wish to thank all the women and men among my students who during every seminar have repeatedly asked me to finally complete this book. I feel that without their urging there still wouldn't be any book on Chen-Taijiquan in this form in German and in English. This pristine style of Taijiquan was first established in Germany in 1994. There had been tutors for the Chen-style before, and as Germany's (and by now also Europe's) largest autonomous Taijiquan association, we are not the only ones representing Chen-style in Germany, but I think that everybody will agree that it was not until the World Chen Tai Ji Association Germany (WCTAG) was founded that Chen-style became popular in Europe. In fact WCTAG was the first to offer all of Europe a complete and authentic system of the original Taijiquan. It has restored to this art its integrity and its very essence. Even in the PR China Taijiquan is often dealt with just as a gymnastic health programme. Only a few organisations, such as our umbrella association, the Taiji-communitiy in Chenjiagou, are aware of the origins of this marvellous art. WCTAG has gained a reputation when it comes to health maintenance of body and mind, but beyond this it has also been successful in re-establishing Taijiquan among experienced circles of martial artists and philosophers as what it actually is: a highly remarkable and efficient martial art with a health-related and spiritual content. The gratitude for this is mainly owed to my Shifu Chen Xiaowang, who is not only and more than anyone else in the world an absolute master of this art, but who has also found a way to impart it systematically. During the year-long search for a true master, I met various men, all of whom were able to pass me something along my way. To all my teachers, women and men, I feel more than grateful for that. Even so, all the time something had remained somehow incomplete; I felt I was missing a part of Taijiquan, namely, the part that grants this artistry true profoundness. For my Shifu Chen Xiaowang there are no secrets, but instead an incredible openness and an understanding of things in a way I have never experienced before. And he is willing to share this knowledge with all.

I was first allowed to learn about this openness and skill by Master Shen Xijing. When I first met with him, being deeply moved by his mastership, I still found it hard to believe his claim of having learnt from no one else but Chen Xiaowang. This could have been a story told to impress a foreigner, but Master Shen Xijing did not wish to impress. On the contrary, the burden of proof was on my side. As in a Kungfu-film, over six weeks I knocked every morning at his door, being turned away by his wife with varying explanations. After six weeks he eventually opened the door himself. The training began. About six months later and after uninterrupted training, he took me with him to Chenjiagou, the birthplace of Taijiquan. Here I was not only introduced to the family of Grandmaster Chen Xiaowang – I was formally engaged to be his first Western disciple. From now on my path was clear: training, training, and training again. Actually this had already been the case before, but now it was no longer just up to me but also up to my new family, because from now on their reputation depended on my progress. Thus, to pay homage to my teachers is a main reason for this book. Without their consent, encouragement and support I would never have had the determination to publish it.

Another rationale for the book is the fact that although there are already a lot of Taiji-books, many of them do not deal with the subject in a serious manner. Most simply write down the sequences of the form and their descriptions. Taijiquan, however, is much too complex an art to learn in this way. A teacher who truly understands is absolutely necessary for one who intends to go beyond even the most basic level. Instruction books of this kind concentrate on the preparation and the memorising of movement sequences which are externally shown, offering benefit to beginners only.

This book aims to reach beyond that. Sequences of movements are explained only insofar as they may support the description of the actual exercises and their content. This book focuses on the explanation of the system itself. So-called secrets make way for well-founded explanations of the internal principle at work. Everything is based upon one principle, the Taiji principle: getting closer to it, making it comprehensible and creating a true understanding of how to transform this all-embodying knowledge into the subtle and refined texture and structure of Taijiquan movements.

The grandmaster of the *Yang*-style, Fu Zhongwen who passed away several years ago, once told me: 'There are three important requirements for learning Taijiquan. First: a good teacher, second: an intelligent student, third: open space for training.' I hope I'm able to draw nearer to the first of these requirements by way of my own teaching activities, of course through my teachers, and perhaps also by this book. The fulfilment of the other two requirements is up to you, my dear reader.

I wish you much pleasure and many new insights while reading this book. I'm looking forward to the many inspiring discussions on this subject which we will certainly be able to have together during our time of studying and training which lies ahead.

Jan Silberstorff
Sydney, February 1997

Preface to the first edition

The book presented here had been largely completed in 1997. That it is published only now teaches me that it is much easier to develop something in a burst of enthusiasm than to turn the initial product into a reality. With these thoughts I find myself once again deep inside my own training. The most important thing for me has always been to stand on the training site and to develop matters quietly while being all by myself. So for more than five years after their completion I had practically forgotten about these manuscripts. I wish to apologise for this by pointing out that I believe that without an adequate training enthusiasm, a qualified book can't be written. I owe it to my students that these manuscripts are finally published now. Without their continual reminders, I would have most likely left it lying there for even longer.

In order to gain something positive from the delay, I have added several articles to this book that were not in the original version.

My gratitude goes to my students and friends, but also to all Taiji-enthusiasts and martial artists of other systems seriously engaged with this subject, since all who follow their path with honesty, and who have crossed mine, have had a positive influence on me.

Jan Silberstorff
Hamburg, February 2003

Preface to the English edition

I am very happy that *Chen* is finally being published for the English market. Since the writing of this book was completed in 1997, and it was first published in German in 2003 (with Russian and Polish editions following in 2004 and 2006), many English-speaking friends and students of Grandmaster Chen Xiaowang have asked me about it. When I started my own teaching in England, Scotland and United States of America, I, too, hoped for an English version. However, this edition is not only intended for native English speakers; it will also be more accessible to our students around the world.

My personal thanks go to Jessica Kingsley Publishers and to my international non-German speaking organizers: Liana Netto, Oleg Tcherne, Jaromir Sniegowski, Marek Balinski, Ronnie Robinson, Luciano Vida, Svetoslav Somov, Khintissa, Bill and Allison Helm, Russel Deacon, Eduardo Molon, Mahesha Kodikara, Maria Bischet and Kim Ivy. These people helped me greatly and, together with others, do a lot to promote Grandmaster Chen's vision. To all of those helping Grandmaster Chen, I would like to dedicate this English edition.

When *Chen* was first published, the aim was to bring the essence of our great teacher, Grandmaster Chen Xiaowang, intelligibly into a Western language book. Around that, I tried to give some more general information about the art, mainly through recounting my personal experience. Grandmaster Chen Xiaowang and I also thought that it would be very useful to have the names of all the forms together with their figures at the end of the book as easy reference for students.

As the text was written 'last century' (but has not lost any of its actuality!), we decided not to update the pictures, in order to retain the flavor of that time. So Chen Yingjun (Grandmaster Chen Xiaowang's middle son) and I are very happy to be presented still as young boys...

I hope this edition will bring the same invaluable help to English readers as it brought to German, Russian and Polish ones. Grandmaster Chen Xiaowang has given us the principle and the system, there is only one thing left for us to do – practice!

For any shortcomings or overlooked out-of-date information, please accept my apologies and contact us so that we can improve the next edition.

Jan Silberstorff
St. Honorat, June 2009

Notes about this book

This book does not claim to be complete; on the contrary it is just a collection of thoughts about the various issues. I do believe that reading it will create a very comprehensive view on the system of Chen Style Taijiquan, but many questions will certainly remain unanswered. Taijiquan is a continuous process, without beginning or end so it would be a mistake to claim that anything written about Taijiquan was complete.

Some preliminary notes: throughout this book I have followed the Pinyin transcription.

For the single stances of the hand and the weapon forms as translated here, many terms just give the technical aspect of a movement. Many, however, have a background of myth and legend. The meaning of these terms is often not obvious to a layman without knowledge of the cultural background. Often both types of meaning apply to the same technique. We aim to give you a short, clear and compact exposition without neglecting the often marvellously beautiful and meaningful images. Sometimes further terms are added in parentheses.

What is Taijiquan?

Taijiquan (also written Tai Chi Chuan) is an ancient Chinese martial art and an art of movement. Its purpose is the cultivation of life, of health, and the wholesome evolution of body and mind as well as self-defence. It is meditative and physically strengthening, and it stimulates the development of internal energy, Qi. It therefore applies to both therapeutic and martial purposes.

This system, developed by the Chen family over centuries, utilises the philosophy of Yin and Yang, their changing phases as well as the harmonisation of body, mind and soul. In this way Taiji depicts man as between heaven and earth, thereby granting him reason (*dao*). It combines movements of self-defence (*wushu*) with the control of the internal energy, and is thus considered an internal martial art.

Since the mid-19th century, Taijiquan has been passed on to interested persons outside the Chen family. Various styles evolved, namely those of the families *Yang*, *Wu*, *Wú* and *Sun*. The Chen-style is the origin of all Taijiquan family systems and has spread all over the world. The movements are soft and flowing, full of expression, beauty and energy. Taijiquan goes far beyond usual fitness programmes, and due to its essential philosophy it may be accepted as a virtual path of life, or simply as a hobby. Its health-related value is acknowledged worldwide; health insurances partly refund tuition fees. As a martial art it is consistent with the history of traditional training methods, and is probably the most widespread Gongfu (or Kungfu) style in the world.

With inner energy being applied instead of muscle power, Taijiquan can be practised effectively by both young and old, man and woman, big and small.

I

The System
of Taijiquan

Chapter 1

Some Facts about the History of Taijiquan

'Taijiquan is a martial and moving art, thousands of years old.' Again and again this phrase pops up on flyers all over the world, even in the People's Republic of (PR) China. It is a slogan fit for advertising, and it also sounds good. I think it's time, however, to shed light on the myths and legends. So many people give up after the first years of their Taijiquan training because they get fed with wrong information or just get strung along. Yet things in fact are rather simple: Taijiquan by origin is a martial art. Nobody disputes that. But can it be that 20, 30, maybe even 40 years of training are required to bring a martial art into effect? That is at least what I kept being told. I imagined a young soldier who gets trained in order to be able to defend his homeland. Is basic military training to last until he is a grandfather? No. Taijiquan is an art of maintaining health and of self-defence that progresses through each training phase to the next. Only someone who does not know how to train will practise over decades without any effect worth mentioning. My Shifu keeps comparing this to a journey by car from Hamburg to Paris. Equipped with a roadmap I can reach my destination soon and be there within a day. But if I start without a map, and there aren't any roadsigns, I'll presumably be meandering all my life, reaching my destination somewhere along the way at random; more likely I never will. A large number of those who practise Taijiquan travel without a map. This is also the case in PR China.

Even with a good roadmap a whole lifetime is not enough to really fathom the profoundness of this art. This is the beautiful thing about Taijiquan: I can get better and improve the longer I live. This is a sufficient rationale for Taijiquan's effect on longevity too: that I'll have even more time for training.

When I was 18 years old, thinking that it was about time to accept the fact that the joys of life were soon to end – with many dreadful things awaiting me, like growing up, working, paying into pension funds and so on – I was struck by something astonishing: the older I get the more I can learn. Every day I can experience and find out about new things, I can improve and gain more insights. The path of wisdom, that's it! And in an instant I had overcome any crisis of puberty and, what's more, the midlife crisis by way of prevention as well. The only thing still missing was a method: an artistry that I could grow into. It had to be spiritual of course, and as I had always wanted to be Superman, it had to deal somehow with super powers and self-defence. It simply had to be something adventurous. During my everyday life it had to keep me fit and healthy. And full of sage dictums, with old masters with long beards like in those Kungfu films; in short: Taijiquan.

What I then experienced, however, didn't make it seem likely that I was to become a great guy, fit and firm, splendid and sage. As time passed I learned two things. First, not all that glitters is gold, and particularly, Taiji doesn't exist in everything with the word Taiji attached. And second: to become really great, one has to start really small. The first wisdom was born: within modesty lies perfection. Many hours of daily training were to follow in order to bring me a little closer, bit by bit, to the mastership I dreamed of. The Chinese call this *chi ku* – 'bitter eating', or *gong fu* – 'gaining skills through time and toil'.

Even the longest journey begins with the first step. In order to avoid a long way round, however, we shall obtain here a clear view on what Taijiquan is, and how it is to be taught. This is the purpose of this book.

So then, how old in fact is Taijiquan? As far as we know, Taijiquan has existed for about 350 years. It was a general from the 17th century who is believed to have laid the cornerstone for all we know today by the term Taijiquan in all its forms. However, we may wish to go even further back. We may imagine how man's first action after climbing down from a tree roughly consisted of smashing the coconut he still kept in his hand upon his neighbour's head. On the next occasion, however, his neighbour – who was not a fool – tried to evade the coconut, or may even have prepared himself with one as well. We may refer to this in terms of cultural evolution; what happens is the process of learning. Martial art in its most simple form is as old as mankind. Methods of health-preservation are part of living memory. It may have happened in this way: the first human wakes up in the morning, and what does he do? He stretches and pulls on his body. He finds that pleasant and cultivates it. One thing today is called martial art, the other is referred to in modern terms as gymnastics or, in China as a form of Qigong. Exercises of stretching and retracting that aim to lay open the meridians and allow the energies to flow were called *Daoyin* in former times. These movements were performed with conscious and deliberate control so that awareness, motion and energy would unite. Breathing techniques were then called *Tuna*. What since the last century has been called Qigong often is a merger of both techniques. So what is special about Tajiquan?

Every martial artist has always done something for his health. Let's consider a Japanese Samurai who is ready every day to fight for his life. Imagine that one morning he wakes up, and he doesn't feel good at all. 'Alas,' he sighs, 'I'm worn out today. I'm not in mint condition. I think today I'll go on leave.' Exactly on this day however he meets with the big challenge, his hardest fight. In short, a Samurai, willing at any time to surrender his life joyously during combat, will charge the highest possible price. Being a warrior, he simply cannot afford to have a day feeling off-colour. He'll therefore take to training methods that keep him physically and mentally fit, for example martial art and Zen, or martial art and Qigong.

General Chen Wangting, himself a grand and battle-hardened martial artist, served the Ming-dynasty for years, escorting travellers and combating insurgent forces. When around 1644 the Ming-dynasty was overthrown, and the Qing took power, all of his honours awarded for fighting were gone. He withdrew to his community in Chenjiagou. Chenjiagou emerged in the 14th century. It has remained a small village until today, and progress seems to have passed it by. It was founded at that time by Chen Bo who is regarded as the first generation of the

Chen family. He came from the province of Shanxi. This province allegedly suffered from overpopulation, and many families got evacuated to the neighbouring province of Henan. Due to war, the latter was more or less swept bare. When Chen Bo arrived there with his clan, the prior inhabitants of this swathe of land lay dead all across the country. The people around Chen Bo cleaned the area and temporarily founded the little commune Chen Bo Zhuang ('the commune of Chen Bo').

Two years later they relocated near to what today is Chenjiagou, the 'ditch of the Chen family'. Agriculture was more promising here. However, as may have been common then during the civil war turbulence, bandits kept the area under fire. Chen Bo purged the area of bandits. He and the martial arts cultivated within the family soon became famous in Wen County. At that time neighbours of the Chen family had already been instructed by family members in martial techniques. Chen Bo originally came from the rural district of the Shanxi province and moved from there to Hongtong. The city of Hongtong was renowned for its martial art (Hong) *Tongbeiquan*. It is presumed that Chen Bo brought this martial art with him to the new community, the Chenjiagou of today.

By now Chen Wangting of the ninth generation, because of his fall, recognised the vanity of secular fame. He noted that nothing is to last, that everything changes, and that there is no sense in holding fast to anything. He studied *Daoyin* and *Tuna*, being considerably influenced in this by the Daoist doctrines. He wrote:

> Looking at the years that have passed, how bravely I fought the enemy forces, and I have never been shy to face and all the risks; honours are no longer of any use to me. Now that I am old and weak I submit to the guidance of the book on *Huang Ting*. Life for me consists in creating boxing forms when I feel depressed, working in the field when the season has come, and during the remaining time in teaching the offspring so they shall grow to be worthy members of society.

He was the first to combine the idea of *Tuna* and *Daoyin* with martial art. He developed a system that combined both the health-promoting exercises of Qigong and the martial movements of *Wushu*. He took up the movements of self-defence and transferred them into a special type of Qigong he had developed. He called these *Cansigong*, the 'exercises of the silkworm'.

What before had existed as two domains had now became one. He introduced the teachings on the meridians into martial art and conceived the exercises of the 'Pushing Hands', *Tuishou*, which were not mentioned in the previously known system. Being a seasoned general, Chen Wangting had immense background knowledge and skill related to the martial arts that his family cultivated. He founded his system mainly on the work of a general from the 16th century. Qi Jiguang in his work *New Book of Recorded Effective Disciplines* (1561), Chapter 14 had assumed the main focuses of the systems known at that time. Chen Wangting took up 29 out of 32 stances from that work and modified them in relation to his theory. He created five forms which later became known as Taijiquan, a form of 'Long Boxing' with 108 stances and a form of *Paochui* (cannon strike). With the various weapon forms he created the 'Sticking Spear Exercises' and, as mentioned before, Pushing Hands. These are exercises which allow the training partners to learn in a 'soft' mode how to apply their energies without risk of injury.

While legends about the mystical origin of Taijiquan were disseminated during the recent centuries, it is today considered a historical fact that the systems known today as *Chen-*, *Yang-*, *Wu-*, *Wú-*, *Sun-* and *Zhaobao*-style are to be traced back to Chen Wangting. Reputable researchers including Gu Liuxin and Tang Hao were able to confirm this for the record. Here are some of their findings in brief. The book by Qi Jiguang mentions all the major boxing styles, but nothing in the sense of Taijiquan. Authentic evidence on Taijiquan has been the preserve of Chen Wangting, clearly referring to the works of Qi Jiguang. Furthermore, a relationship of all grand Taiji-masters of the styles mentioned can be traced back to Chen Wangting; this is illustrated in the family tree at the end of this chapter. Chen Wangting however cannot be traced back to anyone. Therefore Chen Wangting must be considered the primordial founder of all current styles. Moreover there are no records of the Exercises of Pushing Hands from before Chen Wangting.

Already Chen Wangting had disciples who did not stem from the Chen family. The story of Yang Luchan, who was the first non-family-member allowed to learn with the Chen family, resembles slightly the story of Christopher Columbus who discovered America. Columbus wasn't really the first, but he was the first to make it public. Similarly neither was Yang Luchan the first outsider who was allowed to learn with the Chen family. However, he was the first to teach Taijiquan in public, and earn his living from it. It was then that Taijiquan became known among wider circles.

This evolution in Taijiquan took place five generations after Chen Wangting, and after Chen Changxing (14th generation) had reduced the seven forms of Chen Wangting into two. He created the two forms which we know today as the first and the second form of the traditional Chen-style (*Yilu* and *Erlu Laojia*). The first form *Laojia Yilu* served as the basis for all the Taiji systems recounted above.

Chen Changxing later took in the house-servant of a family relative as a disciple. The Chen family at that time was running a pharmacy in the small town of Yongnian in Handan County in the province Hebei, which up to this day is the residence of the Yang and the Wu family. The servant's name was Yang Luchan (born Yang Fukui). He had come from a small pharmacy in his home village to the tiny village of Chenjiagou. While serving the Chen family, Yang Luchan was often present when Chen Changxing trained with his disciples. His dedication grew such that Chen Changxing soon accepted him as a disciple.

One has to bear in mind that the step of personally accepting some-one as a disciple required serious consideration, and still does today. Now it is common practice to raise a fee that allows the teacher to oth-erwise gain spare time in compensation for the time being sacrificed for teaching. The direct teacher–disciple relationship however had and has nothing to do with commercial aspects. Once someone has been accepted as a direct disciple, he is virtually taken into the family, in good times and in bad. It is as if the teacher taught his own child. Quite naturally he won't charge money for it. On the other hand, seri-ous teaching claims a large amount of time. When a pupil is taken in as a personal disciple, the teacher's honour is at stake in case the disciple should develop in an unfavourable way. The teacher in this way accepts a high risk for himself and his reputation, and he'll have to devote a lot of time to his disciple. It is quite understandable then that this step is reflected upon very carefully. Just imagine for a second that someone you do not know will be knocking on your door soon to ask whether you are willing to accept him as your disciple, designated to become your successor. You could start right off with teaching him every day, and while you're at it provide accommodation and catering as well! Would you spontaneously agree or wouldn't you rather shake your head and close the door? Well, things were more or less the same in ancient China, and in this respect the stories about weeks and weeks of waiting in front of the master's door or sweeping the courtyard over months are plausible. The master simply reassures himself of the disciple's patience, his virtue and dedication and his loyalty as well before he, if ever, will begin teaching him.

Yang Luchan by now was living inside the Chen family, but was of low status. He was a serf. Normally it wouldn't cross a ruling family's mind to turn a bondservant into someone akin. In the case of Yang Luchan, however, perhaps because of his great talent and his dedication, an exception was made. The legend of Yang Luchan secretly observing the training sessions or even creeping into the family as a servant pretending to be deaf and mute must rather be substituted by a more realistic assessment of the times. Being a bondservant he still could of course attend the training, but no one would have fancied the idea of granting lessons to a slave. Within the Chen family the story is told that Yang Luchan secretly and during silent hours had practised what he had seen. One evening in the half-light Chen Changxing had spotted a person in the distance practising Taijiquan. Unable to recognise the person as any of his pupils, he walked closer and identified him as the domestic servant. Impressed by his dedication to the training and the evidence of having learned so much without having even been taught, Chen Changxing without further ado took him in as his disciple.

Later Yang Luchan was even granted release. It was at that time that he went to Beijing and started teaching in public in order to earn his living. It was the dawning of a new era. Everybody could learn Taijiquan now. This was also the start of commercial dealing with Taijiquan as a kind of professional training. Times of upheaval had also arrived at Chenjiagou. Many new directions evolved, and here also teaching turned public. This development is to be considered positive, for otherwise we wouldn't have heard about Taijiquan till this day. However, wide dissemination also inevitably causes things to dilute. Quite obviously someone who has to fully give up the life he had been leading before will have to present a training attitude very different from the one shown by someone paying a couple of *Yuan* and attending the lessons once or twice a week.

The few able to undertake all the effort required in order to really learn about Taijiquan and make it their lifetime pursuit today are just as rare as they were then. Or just as many. While in former times it was a handful of people perhaps who really brought Taijiquan to a high level, there are the same number today, even though there are millions of practitioners. A little problem, however, is that of practitioners beginning to teach prematurely. A disciple of mine once said: 'In Taijiquan there are only beginners and teachers.' Many people who have hardly reached the first level, knowing only a bit more than the plain sequence of the form, unfortunately take to teaching too soon.

There may be various reasons: one is that by passing something on, I'm forced to reflect intensely on the things being taught and learnt. That provides the teacher himself with a reinforcement of his studies. Another reason might be someone's complacency, and he may simply like the idea of being a teacher. A third reason might be the seemingly good opportunity to earn extra money.

Many of those who register for so-called training courses for teachers don't really seem to care about the essentials, that is to make progress. They are simply concerned about being certified teachers. I often have talks with people wishing to become Taiji teachers. The majority haven't even really begun with Taijiquan. Still they already want to become teachers. How does this phenomenon occur?

How can they present themselves as Taijiquan, i.e. Gongfu teachers, without having to try particularly hard? Mastering Taijiquan beyond the elementary dimension requires the strongest effort. Most people seem to overlook this point. So those who teach should try hard, be patient and learn to understand the term Gongfu properly. If I should hand on a poor version of Taijiquan, the damage I'll inflict upon the reputation of

Figure 2 Chen exchanging theoretical treatises on Taijiquan

Taijiquan will be immense. Those who teach should always strive to bring out the best in themselves and definitely make an effort to understand this profession, thus paying this art the homage it deserves.

Back to our history again: it was the time of upheaval. Chen Youben (the same 14th generation) also created a new form which we know today by the term *Xiaojia*, Small Frame. The movements correspond with the sequences of the Laojia forms, but are conceived more narrowly. This version was then called *Xinjia* as well, New Frame. Chen Qingping, a disciple and nephew of Chen Youben, moved to be with his wife in neighbouring Zhaobaozhen. So the *Zhaobao*-Taijiquan today bearing the name of this neighbouring commune traces back to him. The form is mainly based on the first form *Laojia*.

Before going to Beijing, Yang Luchan first returned to Yongnian, and his artistry met with great admiration. By then he already had students. One of them, Wu Yuxiang, was so enthusiastic that he wished to study near the very source, and went to Chenjiagou. He studied with Chen Qingping, which brought a different character into the forms. Wu Yuxiang represents the source of the old *Wu*-style.

In Beijing Yang Luchan had a multitude of disciples. Even the Emperor's court asked for his teaching. Due to his numerous challenges, all of them confirmed to be victorious, he obtained a surname: the Invincible (Wudi). Only one story exists actually depicting him as not being victorious. He once fought against the founder of the famous martial art *Baguazhang*, Dong Haichuan. The engagement after two days ended in a tie – perhaps it's true, perhaps it's a highly diplomatic legend.

What Yang Luchan practised was still pure Chen-style. They say however that for purposes of teaching he had simplified several complicated and explosive movements. This is a move that continues today. As Taijiquan is spread more widely, the stronger are the efforts to simplify the form. This appears to be a necessity, as instruction tends to move away from individual teaching more and more. We can imagine that Yang Luchan conveyed the complete programme to his sons Yang Banhou, Yang Jianhou and Yang Fenghou. Changes were underway nevertheless, and starting with Yang Chengfu (1883–1935) who carried out further modifications, one speaks in terms of *Yang*-style. By way of another disciple of Yang Luchan, and of his son Banhou, named Quan

You and the latter's son Wu Jianquan, the so-called new *Wu*-style (*Wú*) emerged. This developed out of the old *Wu*-style, and through Hao (He) Weizheng the *Hao*-style and through Sun Lutang the *Sun*-style developed. Sun Lutang's prior experiences in *Baguazhang* and *Xingyiquan* were still incorporated within the Sun-style. Several other minor directions also emerged.

One should not imagine however that by now every disciple had a brilliant idea and founded a new style. Based on his status, his age and perhaps to his previous experience in other martial arts, everybody had his individual way of moving. Before there were books, photos and videos, the aim was mainly to convey the essence, the very principle by means of a movement pattern. The fact that movements appeared to be slightly different was not only normal but an absolute necessity as well. In accordance with the inner evolution, i.e. with one's personal progress, the movements change. If you see someone moving in exactly the same way year after year, you should not consider studying with him. He is not learning any more. Not to learn any more means regression. Students therefore should not be angry if their teacher once in a while deviates from the movement shown the other day, but instead should feel pleased about it. Unless of course it is the case of a teacher not being serious or doing it by intent or being forgetful…

From the times of Chen Changxing, public interest in Taijiquan had increased, and the Chen family willingly offered teaching. The 'new' students however no longer came just from Chenjiagou, and neither did they stay there. Following their apprenticeship they returned home or travelled in order to teach. They were distant from the sources now and left to themselves. As in those times there were no planes and trains and neither photos, videos or phones, the sequences of movement kept changing without any opportunity for the teachers to undergo correction by the masters. Further dissemination in this way caused an effect known as 'Chinese Whispers'.

A beautiful story about this is told by Ma Yuliang, the Grandmaster of the 'new' *Wu*-style who has now passed away: a disciple who had studied with Grandmaster Ma had been travelling for several years, and had now returned in order to deepen his knowledge. He demonstrated his form to the master and asked for correction. Grandmaster Ma saw how much had been distorted by the disciple during his travels.

As single corrections wouldn't have made any sense any more, he instructed the disciple to sit down. He wished to demonstrate the form himself to the disciple. He had hardly concluded the form when the disciple jumped from his seat, calling out: 'Master Ma, you changed a lot indeed while I was gone!'

Changes in this sense do not give a reason yet to talk in terms of different types of styles, and nobody did that routinely in those times. Even the very term Taijiquan appeared much later. Not until books depicting the sequences of forms by images and photos were published did people start differentiating and saying: 'This is *Yang*-style and that is *Chen*-style'. Now they suddenly began to distinguish, and when movements were no longer consistent with the standards being depicted, the word was and is: 'This is no longer the authentic so-and-so-style'.

The various Taiji-styles were defined from the outside. As far as I know, neither for the *Yang*- nor both of the *Wu*-styles, does anything exist like a deliberate laying down of rules for a particular system. In fact it was the observers from outside, disciples who at some point recognised the deviations as being so significant that they took to speaking in terms of different styles. Any known family style can be traced back to the first traditional form of the Chen-style (*Laojia Yilu*). Deviations actually can be recognised again and again within one and the same form.

My Shifu's only regular comment on that is:

> What's authentic alone is the principle. Taijiquan is a large family, no matter which style is preferred. If I'm able to transpose it, I'm doing good Taijiquan. Then it is authentic. If I'm not, it is poor Taijiquan. No matter which style. Regard a teacher on behalf of his knowledge and his skill, not because of the style he is associated with.

A disciple of Yang Chengfu, Zheng Manqing, modified the movements again and created a short form which was among the first to find larger dissemination abroad. In 1956 due to a government order the stances of the *Yang*-style were further reduced and the form of 85 movements cut down and simplified to the so-called Beijing-form with only 24 movements remaining. In this way Taijiquan, though in a rather cropped version, was able to be disseminated within primary schools, all across the land and also abroad. In recent years more forms evolved.

Competitive forms, for example, aimed to be presented during competitions, or mixed forms with the purpose being the presentation of all the main themes within one form. It's obvious that in this way the profound quality of Taijiquan is lost, but there were other evolutions too.

By the middle of the 20th century a modification was carried out within the Chen-style also. The movements of the first and the second form became even more spiral-like. While *Laojia* in principle consists of continuously slow movements interrupted only by explosive *Fajin* movements, the new mode named *Xinjia*, the New Frame, is marked by tempo changes of varied intensity. More leaps and more complicated sequences of movements were incorporated in the newer version. The course however largely corresponds to the *Laojia* forms, even though the first form here amounts to 83 and the second one amounts to 71 movements. As these forms are more difficult to perform than those of the *Laojia*, the latter is not at all diminished by these, rather it is enhanced. One should have a very solid foundation in *Laojia* to really be able to benefit from the essence of the *Xinjia*. As the movements visually appear more impressive than those of the *Laojia*, this version is often taught within modern *Wushu*. *Xinjia* is also the basis for the competitive form. In modern *Wushu* however aestheticism and sportive appeal dominate. It's thus not surprising that such presentations almost exclusively deal with harmoniously flowing, yet rather plain, outward and empty movements.

Despite the various trends within the Chen-style, the *Laojia*, being the original version – the forms after Chen Wangting are hardly ever performed any more – must be identified as the original and strongest source. From here the various branches emerge.

With Taijiquan already introduced in Beijing by Yang Luchan, finding great approval and dissemination by the beginning of the century, the genuine Chen-style in 1928 moved to the Chinese capital with Chen Fake, one of the most impressive masters from the Chen family. Chen Fake stayed there until 1957. He is one of the best examples of positive human development through a martial art. As a child Chen Fake was weak and ill; rumours were already going round in Chenjiagou that the coming generation would rather not bring forth a grand master. For the young Chen Fake this was depressing, being burdened after all with the inheritance of a great tradition. So he took to training more than anybody else and later was to enter history as one of the greatest Taiji masters. The stories about his victorious challenges are endless and soon made him become an extremely respectable personality. He paid all due honour to the term *Wude*, i.e. combining martial art with virtue. One of his three sons, Chen Zhaoxu, was soon likewise renowned as invincible. Success however made him a bit neglectful, and as time went by he rather took to favourite pastimes like music. Then a master of another martial art attacked him from behind by surprise, and Chen Zhaoxu was unable to be vic-

Figure 3 Chen Fake

torious. Stunned by this, the then still young Chen Zhaoxu turned to his father. The latter was upset about his son, asking him what actually he believed to have learnt at all. He inflicted a push on him so vigorous that Chen Zhaoxu is said to have flown upon a wall three metres high. Whatever altitude that wall may have reached in reality, Chen Zhaoxu was deeply impressed by his father's skill. So deep was his shame about this incident that he destroyed all his music instruments. Over three years he didn't leave the house, in order to dedicate himself to training exclusively (a similar degree of dedication can be currently observed in the middle son of Chen Xiaowang, Chen Yingjun). While still young, Chen Zhaoxu reached a very high level, and during a revenge confrontation defeated his challenger who meanwhile had taken to studying Taijiquan himself.

Chen Fake's other son Chen Zhaokui and his nephew Chen Zhaopi were to a large degree responsible for the dissemination of Taijiquan in the PR China. They too represented a very high standard. Chen Zhaopi first taught in Beijing, then from 1930 in Nanjing, returning due to the war with Japan in 1937 back to Chenjiagou, teaching the younger generation there. Many renowned masters of today like Chen Xiaoxing, Chen Zhenglei, Wang Xian and Zhu Tiancai have significantly learnt from him and from Chen Zhaokui as well. Chen Zhaokui held lessons from 1959 and later travelled across the whole country and taught. One

Figure 4 Chen Zaopi

*Figure 5 Chen
Zhaokui*

of Chen Fake's most famous pupils outside the Chen family is Master Feng Zhiqiang who still lives in Beijing.

Today the head and bearer of Chen-Taijiquan's family heritage within the 19th generation is Chen Xiaowang. A contemporary witness in his childhood years of Chen Fake, he studied for a brief period with his father Chen Zhaoku, then with Chen Zhaokui and Chen Zhaopi. By the middle of the century Taijiquan was quite well-known already, but Chenjiagou only to a few. Taijiquan had gained a name largely in Beijing. Very few wished to learn precisely where the art was actually from. That changed abruptly when the Japanese started taking an interest in Taijiquan. They didn't content themselves with simply learning Taijiquan – they wanted to know more about the sources and the origins of this artistry. So they travelled to Chenjiagou where they arrived at a village which the Taiji-hype had seemingly passed by. Chen Xian, Chen Zhenglei, Zhu Tiancai, Chen Xiaoxing, and of course Chen Xiaowang were introduced to them as the leading masters. Chen Xiaowang, together with Chen Xiaoxing the direct inheritor and, being the elder brother, also the successor number one in this grand tradition, found this worth reflecting upon. The Japanese themselves possessed a great tradition in martial arts, and he wanted to be able to prove the profundity of Taijiquan to them. Despite having trained intensely since the age of eight and being among the leading masters already, now at the age of 30 he once again increased his training enormously. He practised 30 routines a day, adding standing exercises, reeling silk exercises, *Tuishou* and the weapon forms. He no longer cared for anything but his training. He was later appointed to the position of chairman of the Province Henan's *Wushu*-department in Zhengzhou which had substantially supported him during that extremely challenging training period.

He decoded the system of Taijiquan in a highly refined and precise manner by making every single change within the body recognisable and comprehensible to the disciple. Thus, despite his mastery already being recognised nationwide, he again took another giant step forward, being duly considered today the greatest living Taiji-master. He continually emphasises that neither the style nor the inheritance make up true mastery, but one's own dedication alone and daily tenacious training under the guidance of a teacher who knows his craft.

Figure 6 Chen Xiaowang with his son Chen Yingjun

Grandmaster Chen Xiaowang travels to countless countries each year to nurture his disciples. For the latter purpose my Shifu Grandmaster Chen Xiaowang and I in 1995 founded the 'World Chen Xiaowang Taijiquan Association' (WCTA) which is now worldwide. Grandmaster Chen has four sons: Chen Yun, Chen Yingjun, Chen Pengfei and Chen Philip.

As pointed out above, besides the historical evolution, legendary myths of origins exist as well. For what, after all, is a renowned martial art without such a background?

There are tales about a Daoist eremite named Zhang Sanfeng who rose to be a national hero in China. However, his existence hasn't really been proved, and he is vaguely dated to the 8th or 12th century. Different from modern movie versions depicting Zhan Sanfeng as a great fighter for justice, the legend actually doesn't present him as a martial artist at all. He is said to have lived on the Wudang mountain, fully dedicated to his Daoist practice. Taijiquan he learnt more or less in his sleep, i.e. while dreaming at night of a legendary emperor. Or he allegedly received it as a present of the gods to the humans. True or not, the story shows the high significance attributed to Taijiquan in China.

The better known version however says that he watched a snake and a crane fighting with each other. Most Chinese boxing systems build on animal observations. While the snake preferred soft and round movements, the crane attacked with fast, explosive strikes – and the fight ended in a tie. Whether true or not, what's interesting is the symbolism of that fable, for the system is built precisely upon these energies, namely, soft, round, spiralling movements permeated by explosive

Family tree

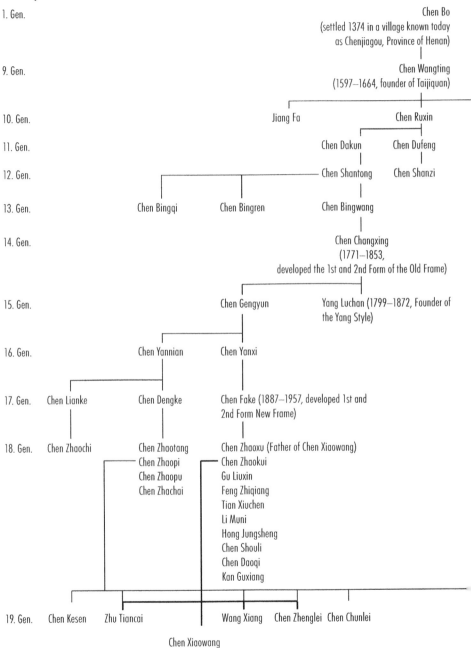

1. Gen.

Chen Bo
(settled 1374 in a village known today
as Chenjiagou, Province of Henan)

9. Gen.

Chen Wangting
(1597–1664, founder of Taijiquan)

10. Gen.   Jiang Fa   Chen Ruxin

11. Gen.   Chen Dakun   Chen Dufeng

12. Gen.   Chen Shantong   Chen Shanzi

13. Gen.   Chen Bingqi   Chen Bingren   Chen Bingwang

14. Gen.

Chen Changxing
(1771–1853,
developed the 1st and 2nd Form of the Old Frame)

15. Gen.   Chen Gengyun   Yang Luchan (1799–1872, Founder of the Yang Style)

16. Gen.   Chen Yannian   Chen Yanxi

17. Gen.   Chen Lianke   Chen Dengke   Chen Fake (1887–1957, developed 1st and 2nd Form New Frame)

18. Gen.   Chen Zhaochi   Chen Zhaotang   Chen Zhaoxu (Father of Chen Xiaowang)

Chen Zhaopi   Chen Zhaokui
Chen Zhaopu   Gu Liuxin
Chen Zhachai   Feng Zhiqiang
Tian Xiuchen
Li Muni
Hong Jungsheng
Chen Shouli
Chen Daoqi
Kan Guxiang

19. Gen.   Chen Kesen   Zhu Tiancai   Wang Xiang   Chen Zhenglei   Chen Chunlei

Chen Xiaowang
(today the chief representative)

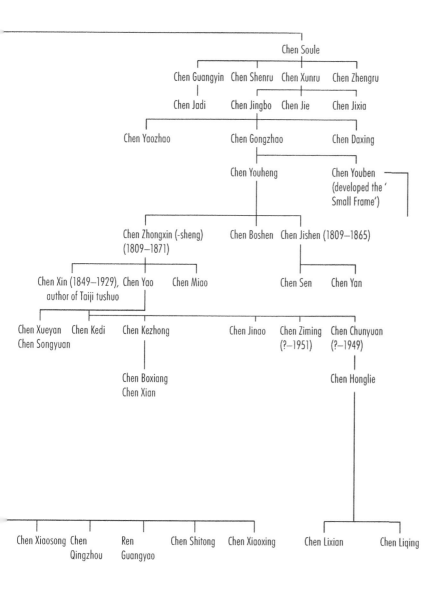

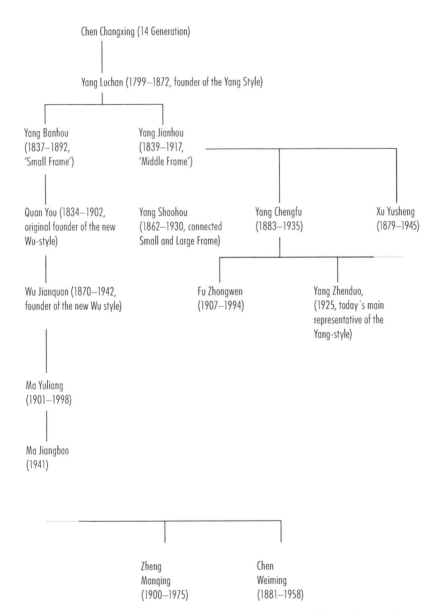

Chen Changxing (14 Generation)

Yang Luchan (1799–1872, founder of the Yang Style)

Yang Banhou (1837–1892, 'Small Frame')

Yang Jianhou (1839–1917, 'Middle Frame')

Quan You (1834–1902, original founder of the new Wu-style)

Yang Shaohou (1862–1930, connected Small and Large Frame)

Yang Chengfu (1883–1935)

Xu Yusheng (1879–1945)

Wu Jianquan (1870–1942, founder of the new Wu style)

Fu Zhongwen (1907–1994)

Yang Zhenduo, (1925, today's main representative of the Yang-style)

Ma Yuliang (1901–1998)

Ma Jiangbao (1941)

Zheng Manqing (1900–1975)

Chen Weiming (1881–1958)

In this Family Tree you can see once again the origins and the evolution of Taijiquan depicted from its very beginnings through to today. The Family Tree lists only the most important names and only the persons who are members of the now oldest still living generation.

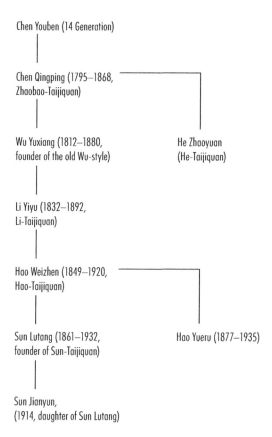

Chen Youben (14 Generation)

Chen Qingping (1795–1868,
Zhaobao-Taijiquan)

Wu Yuxiang (1812–1880,
founder of the old Wu-style)

He Zhaoyuan
(He-Taijiquan)

Li Yiyu (1832–1892,
Li-Taijiquan)

Hao Weizhen (1849–1920,
Hao-Taijiquan)

Sun Lutang (1861–1932,
founder of Sun-Taijiquan)

Hao Yueru (1877–1935)

Sun Jianyun,
(1914, daughter of Sun Lutang)

directness. Zhan Sanfeng investigated these forces and created the legendary Taijiquan. Sources appearing much later describe the master of inner alchemy as a martial artist. Originally reputed a Daoist, in the stories told through the centuries he ascended higher and higher in becoming a great martial artist with his roots of course in the Shaolin monastery. I'm quite curious to see what he will evolve into next in the future. Those enlightened by Daoism enjoy an eternal life in China, so it's not surprising that more and more heroic deeds keep emerging.

Yet every legend has a grain of truth. Of course Chen Wangting built upon the knowledge of his ancestry, and the origins of Taijiquan are deeply rooted within Daoist philosophy and inner alchemy. Connections here are quite likely to exist, and whether this can be tied to a person in an attempt in China to personalise historical evolution can be questioned. A link from Taijiquan to the Shaolin monastery is rather unlikely. In spite of the fact that both these cradles of Chinese martial art have a distance of hardly a hundred kilometres between them, and generals like Chen Wangting and Chen Zhongxin frequented the Songshan mountains around Shaolin for reasons of business, both sides unanimously deny any connection. The annals of the Chen family reveal nothing about any historical exchange. During my more than 20 visits to the Shaolin monastery, the inhabitants including my then teachers Shi Yongshin and Shi Yanhu each time explicitly denied a connection between the two systems. Yet both sides always emphasised their high respect for the system of the other.

So here we have the two great cradles of Chinese martial art: on the one side Chenjiagou (Wudang) for the inner school, and representing the outer course the Shaolin temple. These of course aren't the only origins of Chinese martial art, but rather the ones who have made a name for themselves. One should also bear in mind in this respect that by tradition each outer school has an inner aspect and each inner school an outer one. Naturally a lot more can be said about the history of Taijiquan.

Chapter 2

What is Qi?

This question engages everybody involved with Taijiquan. From our so-called civilised culture in particular, an understanding of this vital energy is presumably farther away than it is to most others.

Maybe this is why we are so fascinated by the image of a fantastic unexplainable super-force. What is meant by the term Qi is certainly a phenomenon not to be entirely fathomed within a lifetime, yet it is far from being unexplainable. In translation, Qi among other terms means 'breath'. The best translation here however seems to be 'vital energy'. While cautiously moving forward, we may vaguely draw a parallel to the term 'pneuma' as known from Greek antiquity. In most cases this term also refers to the 'breath of life'. Caution however is advised, for this is to convey merely an idea of something similar that had existed in our culture too. Wilhelm Reich with his 'Orgon' may be interesting on this issue.

We wish to stay with the Chinese model, however, as in its completeness and its effectiveness it cannot be compared to anything. Qi describes an energy inherent within ourselves that keeps us alive. It flows through the body, circulating on the designated tracks, i.e. the meridians. Many people who think they do not perceive or know this energy may find this explanation abstract and senseless. They can neither see nor sense this energy, so they don't believe in it. That their toaster functions simply because of the current coming out of the plug, flowing through the device on designated tracks, the so-called wires, seems to cause much less of a problem to them. 'Sure, electricity is something I can feel, with a nine-volt-battery for example I feel that faint prickle,' they'll reply. What's presumably intended with this may be a feeling similar to the one I have when a marvellously attractive person passes by. And what about the power current when the person turns around saying, 'Haven't we met before?'

Everybody senses Qi, even without training, but we are not conscious of it. What does it feel like when I'm on the threshold between waking and falling asleep, having this comfortable, warm feeling? We simply accept many of these every-day experiences without further questioning, without wishing to know precisely what it's actually like when I feel 'my hairs rising' and my entire scalp prickles.

Another example: Why does man move? What is it that causes a movement? The muscles? Going to a butcher's shop I find lots of muscles there, none of them moving, just dead meat. The muscles need a command in order to move, and this is transferred by nerves. Brain, nerves, muscles – all are available at a well-stocked butcher's. Back home I'm standing there with my purchased meat, but still nothing happens, nor when I lay the pieces upon each other. Because what is missing? Life. But what is this 'life'? What puts all those things into motion? Energy. Dr Frankenstein understood this well and inserted electric current into his pieces of dead corpses. This form of energy, however, bears no spirit within. It does derive from God, but it is not divine. No, what's needed is so-called vital energy. Without energy there is no motion, no thought, nothing.

They say that when energy is condensed, life comes into being. Through death it fades away again. Solar systems also emerge and pass away in a similar way. Why is it so difficult to believe that what applies to the universe applies to man as well? Energy is never lost, they say in physics; it merely transforms itself. We know many various forms of energy: thermal energy, motional energy and so on. Also within our body which is alive only by energy, this energy transforms itself. The Chinese distinguish between very many different kinds of energy within the body, and a good doctor must know them all. We want to engage here only in the four essential forms of this energy: with *Yuanqi*, *Jingqi*, *Qi* and *Shenqi*.

Yuanqi is the term that indicates primordial energy. Chinese medicine presumes that every human is born with a certain quantum of energy.

For various reasons this quantum is not equal among all humans. What everyone has in common however is the fact that this energy slowly gets consumed during life and that man dies when it runs dry. The timespan depends on the individual's way of living, and on how carefully he handles this energy. Comparing the situation with a car with the tank filled up, if we drive it carefully, we'll get much further with the same amount of gasoline than someone driving mindlessly and wastefully. We don't need to be stingy with our energies, however, for actually this *Yuanqi* is something like our reserve tank; it gets tapped when the general level of energy in our body is too low. This general energy is what we recognise as Qi, the living daily energy. We take it into ourselves continuously: in the air that we breathe, the food we eat, and by the sleep we need. The most efficient way to make use of my *Yuanqi* is *not* by doing as little as possible. This would be as if I drove my car as slowly as possible, or didn't drive at all. Instead I have to ensure that I exercise in a healthy and sufficient yet not excessive way, to have enough sleep and to breathe fresh air. When we lack sleep, when we're under stress, or whenever energy is weak, if the body lacks proper nutrition, all these situations have to be compensated for by the primal source of energy. When the shortage is no longer adequately compensated for, it runs dry. Then the person either falls ill or dies.

A method of reinforcing, cultivating and building up Qi is presented by Taijiquan. By way of training, Qi gets distributed within the body in a more efficient way, and all the organs receive an adequate supply. Blockages dissolve so that energy can cover all areas of the body. Moreover by way of improved breathing, energy can be additionally acquired with improved lung function and stamina. Anybody practising Taijiquan feels a kind of energetic field on his skin. This is like a protective coat lying over the skin to preserve the inner Qi and protect it from noxious influences from outside. It is the so-called Waiqi, or outer Qi. That is why one should not take a shower right after the exercises, because this protective coat would be destroyed ahead of time.

The Qi circulating within the body may transform into essential (sexual) energy, called *Jingqi,* bodily energy (*Qi*) and from there into mental energy. The latter is called *Shenqi.* We can easily imagine these processes. A simplified example: during sex we notice an increased concentration of energy in the related areas. Energy is being released across the entire body. This keeps concentrating more and more until during ejaculation the entire energy is discharged either genitally or involving the entire body. The mind during this phase is rather less active. We do not solve mathematical problems during the state of agitation within the plateau or the orgasm phase. Energy is withdrawn from the mind. Sensitive males after an ejaculation may therefore notice a strong loss of energy accompanied by mental weakness. Less sensitive males will not notice this as they have fallen asleep beforehand.

Someone who often keeps his mind busy, making extended speeches for example, may perceive a certain top-heaviness after a while, being followed by cold or shaky fingers. In this case energy rather concentrates in the head section while being withdrawn from the body. Energy always goes to where it's needed. Qi can transform itself into physical, sexual or mental energy. Blockages during this process cause many of the problems known to us, perhaps merely as a performance deficit, or more seriously, as illness.

Taijiquan not only helps in permanently creating a balanced flow in all areas, but may also transform energy just the way we happen to need it. This however requires a very good mastering of our Qi. One should ensure that a good balance exists during the natural or consciously induced (and thus still natural) transformations, so that one condition in turn is harmonised by the other. There should always be enough body-Qi circulating; this is the neutral condition. Continuous change between the transformations of mental, physical and sexual energy will create something like a break, and recovery becomes less and less important, for the change itself is recreation.

Sexuality is an important factor in life, but a 'leakage' quite obviously exists within the system. Sexuality should thus be performed in a way so that the energy thereby aroused is preserved within the system, otherwise it cannot undergo further transformation. Therefore after an ejaculation, a pause is required. In case of too many ejaculations, a generous refill from the reserve tank is needed. There are highly efficient techniques however of experiencing orgasms without releasing this energy, strengthening and further transforming it instead. This however goes beyond the range of this book.[1]

So energy does undergo changes, and most of all it can also be applied by deliberation. What a good acupuncturist does is something we can do by ourselves from inside. The more refined our studies have been on how to handle and master this energy, the more we will be able to apply it on all sections and subsections of our body and our life. This refers not only to merely physical issues but of course to mental and spiritual ones as well.

In the same way we can apply this energy for self-defence, and for the purposes of health and spirituality, or quite simply for the improvement of our life's quality. Whether this model of energy seems plausible or not is something that those who master it hardly care about. They see the results, and they feel the effects; Chinese medicine has been a science based on observation. Only the results count, and they are there, open to be experienced by everybody.

There are Western teachers who try to describe Taijiquan in merely mechanical terms. This approach is good because it is easily understood by Westerners, quick to be reproduced and applied. However, one should never make the mistake of remaining on that level. One would stay a performer only, without ever being able to discover the artistry and power in the practice. Taijiquan would remain limited, and it would lack spirit. Qi is not only a necessary energy, it also creates and transforms the entire spirit, the system's entire wisdom. This is the only way I can understand what is beyond imagination, into a limitless world that liberates the body and spirit with a depth of perception beyond measure.

---

1   Interested readers may directly refer to the author who offers seminars on this issue (Publisher's note).

Chapter 3

Taiji –
A Philosophy

The philosophy of Taijiquan is among the oldest in the world. The symbols of Yin and Yang, and what the Chinese call Taiji, have influenced Chinese thinking within living memory. Notations about the relationship between Yin and its counterpart Yang have existed ever since we are able to retrace the sources. All the classical books of China such as the Yijing, the Daodejing, the books of Dshuang Dsi or Confucius – everywhere the theory of Yin and Yang is found. This philosophy is thousands of years old. This is perhaps where modern Taiji-class organisers take their credibility from, advertising on their flyers a motional art that is thousands of years old, and which they believe they can teach us in a few weekends, certified by a diploma.

Today the philosophy of Taiji still very clearly permeates the Chinese worldview. Just as Christianity consciously or subconsciously determines our Western way of acting, a Chinese person will often act in accordance with the rules of Yin and Yang. However, that wouldn't give him the right to describe himself as a Daoist.

The Taiji principle that so many people in the West wish to claim for themselves – what is it actually? Let us consider: why do we so often hear in China a *yes* to our questions, while in fact we hardly ever receive a *no* if any answer at all?

One day I had travelled with Master Shen Xijing to a small place near the town of Xian because we wanted to buy so-called 505-health-belts. Sewed into these is a herbal mixture, and wearing them promises – like so many things in China do – a longer life. We wanted to ship them to Germany and sell them there. After a dusty day-long journey aboard a decrepit bus we arrived at the production company, signed a contract of purchase with a value of five thousand dollars, and went back with a box of sample packs.

On our way back I noticed that the Chinese description mentioned ingredients which had been missing on the English version, and which would have made them impossible to sell in Germany. 'Never mind,' Master Shen said, 'tomorrow we'll give them a call and tell them to tear up the contract'. Not even a discussion occurred. The company immediately agreed, and when I asked him whether he didn't feel misused – after all we had been on the road the whole day – he only noted with surprise, 'But why? Didn't we get to see a lot?'

I was granted the opportunity of joining many of these seemingly senseless excursions, and the limits of my patience were tested as we went. He however behaved as if every such occasion was the first ever.

Imagine you are en route with a group of Chinese, and you wish to buy yourself an ice-cream. Being a polite person, you ask whether someone else would care to have one too, and all say no. Being a connoisseur of China you know, however, that modesty is a societal keynote. So you ask once again, and again, and once again. Every single time you hear, 'No, thank you'. In accordance with Chinese courtesy you do however buy an ice-cream for everybody, and everybody eats it. And never in your whole life will you find out who in fact had wished to have one and who choked his ice-cream down for reasons of politeness. This issue is particularly interesting when the deal is about alcohol.

None of the Chinese people from either story would call himself an explicit follower of the Taiji theory, yet we find the roots of this behaviour to be observed a thousand times a day in China. One day when Master Shen's wife was in Germany, a friend of mine came in, took a banana and asked whether anyone else wanted one too. Nobody said yes. He then sat down with us, ate his banana and wanted to start a conversation with her. Master Shen's wife however wanted to depart – never before had anything so impolite happened to her. I asked her what had happened, and she replied: 'Your friend asked whether someone wanted a banana, took one for himself, and ate it up in front of my eyes.' 'But what was your answer when he offered bananas?' I wanted to know. 'Of course I declined!'

What had happened? My friend had not been impolite at all. He had asked politely and acted in accordance with the answer. The way he acted is the consequence of a religious–ethical foundation just the same, but in this case our Western one. Our culture knows the One (God) and his counterpart (the Devil) just as well, or in another way of putting it, Good and Evil. Our way of thinking searches for a decision between the two poles. The Chinese way of thinking does not recognise this sharp definition. Its vocabulary doesn't even contain a clear *yes* or *no*. Chinese thinking does have the part and its counterpart, yet it searches for the connecting link between both extremes, the integrity within contrasts. This way of thinking is not straight; it is rather circular.

That brings us closer to the issue. To know that inside everything there is both a part and its counterpart and to seek harmony therein describes Taiji quite well.

But where do the two contrasts come from? Where do the One and the Other come from? Back to Adam and Eve? No, both parts already existed there, i.e. the male and the female principle. So then, even farther back. Back to the original, the One, the inseparable, back to nothingness. Towards a condition that cannot be described, for it cannot be distinguished from anything. Ahead of the Big Bang. In Daoism, and Taiji ultimately arises from Daoism, this state of being is called *Wuji*. It is symbolised by an empty circle. Inside this nothingness something emanates in an instant. So here we have the nothing and the something that is potentially contained in it and practically emerges out of it.

And here we are with the Two. And with the Three, that is the connection between both and within the counterparts of the substantial. And out of this the Ten Thousand Things emerge, Laotse says. We have the non-substantial and the substance. Out of this occur Yin and Yang, the part and its counterpart, in all forms ever to be imagined.

Everything is permeated by the Dao, that which holds together all, that which is, and still is not. What is omnipresent and still cannot be conceived. It does expand, and it creates all things that we know and all we do not know. This state, the symbiosis of all things, is called Taiji. We should not commit the mistake, however, of considering *Wuji* as the one and Taiji as the other. Both are deeply interwoven with each other.

Wuji is regarded as emptiness. Inside of it a thought emerges in an instant. It takes to motion and decomposes into itself and its counterpart. Out of this, all that exists comes into being as well as all we do not know. Taiji arises out of *Wuji.* Everything clear?

All that remains to be done by me, then, is to transform it into motion. That's how easy Taijiquan is, the teachings of motion in accordance with this principle. Or perhaps not? Here we find the reason why the novice at the beginning of his Taiji training actually doesn't understand anything at all, even if he thinks he does. When I'm teaching novices and ask them: 'Have you understood this?' they all nod, and I know that they don't lie, even though they haven't understood the faintest thing. And neither am I better off, for I am standing in front of their faces which are full of expectation, starting to describe something to them that cannot be described. 'He who speaks does not know – he

Figure 7 The Wuji symbol (above) and Taiji symbol (below)

who knows does not speak,' Laotse says. Am I to hold my lectures in a speechless mode? That would be really mysterious and might even entitle me to raise the seminar fees.

'Why,' says the Chinese poet Pai Chuyi from the ninth century after Christ, 'did someone who knew write 5000 words then?' Our attempt is to make an undescribable issue understandable. The path is the goal. In order to get ahead I have to let go of my intellectual approach and realize my insights in a holistic way instead. And I must be able to transcend. Body, mind and soul – all that is flows together, together towards integrity. Out of this integrity a sentiment will arise. A feeling for the subtle. Out of this, awareness will arise. Now we are getting closer to Taijiquan.

Without day there is no night. Without illness no health, without good no evil. The particle is defined only by its counterpart. That's the way it is.

The idea follows the acceptance of these seemingly contrasting poles. The idea wishes to understand these, to permeate them and to harmonise them with each other. Inside every human there is not only good, there is evil as well. The point is not, however, to suppress either of the two or to abhor them. We should instead gain an understanding of these matters in order to improve our conduct with them. Harmonising these relationships does not mean allowing them both fifty–fifty, but integrating them instead into unity and being aware that neither will get out of hand. It is the same thing with nature. Humans have a desire for sunshine, but sunshine exclusively would make everything wither and the soil would bear no fruit. If we wish to enjoy sunshine, we will have to accept rain as well. In the case of uninterrupted rain, however, the land gets flooded, remaining unfertile. The balancing middle is required, but not an exact, static middle, rather, sun in the morning, rain in the afternoon. There are times of sun, and there are times of rain.

I remember an incident when I was with Master Shen Xijing in Chenjiagou, and we wanted to return to the large city of Xian. On the day of departure it started raining, so I put on a raincoat, but he came and told me not to worry, we would simply wait until the rain was over. Exactly that however did worry me, because we could wait the entire week.

I recognised at that time how much this philosophy fits together with the socialist system of labour. Apparently it was not significant whether one was late for work. My first teacher Sui Qingbo from the Shandong province did not appear at his workplace for years because he lived in Germany for some time. After his return his working place was still there as it had been before.

Back to the subject: the better we understand the principle, the deeper we can delve into the matter. The Taiji-sign describes these conditions precisely, with its two aspects flowing into each other, as a symbol of occurrence, of extension and disintegration, with its two small dots likewise indicating that the One always bears something of the Other within itself. In order to enlighten this with more accuracy and to be able to mark scales which are more subtle, the Chinese use the symbolism of continuous lines (for Yang) and interrupted lines (for Yin). They are usually presented separately, as tri- or hexagrams, aiming to observe every single phase of change with more and more accuracy.

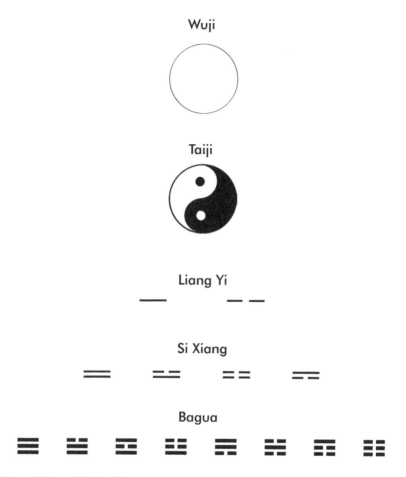

Wuji

Taiji

Liang Yi

Si Xiang

Bagua

Figure 8 From Wuji to Bagua

It is the base for the Yijing (also: I Ching), one of China's most ancient books.

The better we understand things, the more we'll be able to describe them in depth and illustrate their contexts. Within Taijiquan this means that we can integrate the body in a more and more refined mode, being able to gauge it with more subtlety, and being able to direct energy with more intensity through our mind and body. This philosophy of *Wuji* and of Yin and Yang is not only the foundation pillar of Taijiquan but of all the other arts in China as well, such as geomantics, fortune-telling, astrology, calligraphy, music, even science and medicine.

Following the natural course of affairs, not to intervene but to act spontaneously instead means *Wuwei*. *Wuwei*, mostly translated as 'non-acting', doesn't necessarily mean to lie back and view things from outside. Neither is it something like ignorance or sufferance, a sort of refraining-from-defence. The soft defeats the hard – every human knows it, but nobody acts on it, Laotse says. The reason is that wrong images on this issue are epidemic. If the concept of *Wuwei*, of non-acting, according to the Daoist view is pure passivity, then Taijiquan as a martial art as well as for healthcare is hardly worth its reputation. How am I to protect myself from something, be it aggression or illness, without any reaction? And here precisely is the answer. One principle of Taijiquan is to give way, receding however without losing personal stability. This is not like a piece of cotton flying away, but giving way on the basis of a strong centre, a strong root with a powerful trunk and flexible branches. It is also described as iron wrapped in cotton. It involves yielding out of a strong structure, without having to abandon my own centre. It's the centre that I find within oneness, within *Wuji*. Out of this, of *Wuji*, Taiji will arise, the change, and with this the choice of being able to give way. To yield without having a foundation would mean to stray off the path.

With *Wuwei* another important point is introduced. Non-acting indicates a condition of spontaneity, namely, acting in accordance with the actual situation, backed by all my expertise, but within the here and now. Therefore my actions are never rigid, not following any stiff dogmas established in the past; instead my actions rather grow afresh within the situation they arose from. Therefore *Wuwei* does not represent an ideology, but the wise and not predetermined spontaneous action which is part of the great whole, adapted to the course of nature from where its decisions evolve. Or even better: spontaneous action depicts acting out the nature of things. The same goes for one's personal nature as well. Knowing about my nature, perceiving it and being able to understand my inner voice in a clear and lucid way means that decisions are no longer determined by results. What remains is merely to flow side by side with our own naturalness. The only thing required is just to follow, following being the only thing that happens. Determinations do not have to be taken until a relationship with one's own nature no longer exists, namely, when the inner voice cannot be perceived. Then

I do have to determine an action out of a certain argument. In this way, however, my intuition would most likely result in a random hit. *Wuwei* however turns it into an extremely reliable source. Within a deep level of meditation 'non-acting' literally means the way of reaching the spiritual experience of emptiness.

Every cause has its effect, as does every action. Everything is within continuous change. Nothing ever is the way it has been a moment ago. That is why our action, if it is to exist with the situation and be reasonable, must be spontaneous and natural, and merely passive in the sense of not being pre-determined. The sage will therefore act in the way the situation suggests him to. He is one with nature and with himself. In this way he evolves harmony and peace with himself and all other creatures, all things and conditions.

Things aren't done however by taking all decisions on an ad hoc basis and by gut instinct. Feeling certainly does play an important role, yet there are two kinds of spontaneity: the right one and the wrong one. Taking the right action spontaneously means being able to trust a feeling and to follow it. In order to do so I have to stand inside my centre, holding a large treasure of knowledge and expertise about the context of matters. Being not centred means I cannot be unbiased. When I'm not within my centre, my judgement must remain subjective. Right away my feelings will rather tell me what seems to be good for my ego, but not what in fact is the right thing to do. If I don't know about myself and the world, if I still have to surrender to so many illusions and run after them, how will I then be able to create a liberated spirit that will do right from its centre?

Taijiquan centres our body and our mind; it creates a strong centre and harmony within. It gives us the knowledge and the feeling that enable us to act adequately by intuition.

Wuji, Taiji and *Wuwei* are not abstract terms estranged from worldly matters. They are conditions of unending harmony and a joyful life to be lived and experienced by every person. To achieve these, however, takes more than a good conversation. Integral practice of self-discovery is required. Taijiquan is eminently suited to this, since it is the vital, liveable and direct access to these old teachings of wisdom.

Taijiquan is the exercise. Taiji is the goal.

Chapter 4

Taijiquan –
A Martial Art

The water is clearest at the spring. Fu Zhongwen, grandmaster of the fourth generation in Yang-style (1907–1994), had this in mind when shortly before his death he once told me: 'Jan, if you wish to truly understand Taijiquan, you must drink the water straight from the spring.' He meant to say that I should take up my studies directly at the original sources, that is, with the founding family itself. Fortunately I had already done that anyway. But another aspect just as important crossed my mind while I was listening to his words: learning Taijiquan not only at the spring, but also understanding it at its origins.

The origin of Taijiquan lies within martial art. Far into this century Taijiquan in fact mainly gained its reputation as such. All the excellent grand and legendary masters of Taijiquan have made a name for themselves because of their martial abilities. Its founder Chen Wangting was a general. In Beijing Taijiquan became known through Yang Luchan and Chen Fake, not only because of their physical skills, but mainly because of their reputation as being invincible.

This is not of course to diminish the great health-related merit of Taijiquan; it shows that Taijiquan was at first famous as a martial art. Not until many martial elements were removed, as happened during the evolution of simplified styles and forms like the Beijing-form, did the martial aspect slowly lose ground in the practice of Taijiquan. High goals are not consistent with rapid popularity, and are not quickly realised. Taijiquan as a martial art however requires a profound understanding.

Another point is the fact that the Chinese government considers Taijiquan convenient as a health promoting form of movement, not as a way however of spreading martial skills among the civil population. Therefore, not only Taijiquan but the entire field of Chinese martial arts had their traditional values curtailed. We know this today by the term of 'modern *Wushu*'. As a partial section of the whole, this is valid in its own way. In the sense of a true art, however, it lacks the connection with its roots, and in being spread in this way it can neither grow nor prosper. It is satisfying for those who enjoy moving themselves with beauty and expressiveness. However, what about those who are fascinated not by sports but by the artistry itself, those who wish to get in profound contact with it, indeed to study hard and understand? Those who wish to tread it as a path of life? I mean those really interested in the immeasurable profoundness of Chinese martial art? Those who are honest with themselves and keep searching with their whole heart? Their task is to go all the way back to the source, tracing the roots in order then to grow up near it.

How am I ever to reach the state of being one and integrated if I start by curtailing my method, in this case Taijiquan?

Taijiquan is a martial art, there is no doubt about it. And all who do not care to know about this are fooling themselves. Whatever other excellent exercising methods there are, whether Indian Yoga or Chinese Qigong, if I decide to do Taijiquan, I have chosen a martial art, and a very good one, too. Any attempt to remove terms like striking or fighting or likewise from the Taijiquan vocabulary is inappropriate here, which does not mean that Taijiquan is a matter of militancy. Quite the contrary. No real Taijiquan master lives with the reputation of being a bully, but avoiding the terms of martial art doesn't make a man more peaceful. Deliberately facing the issue perhaps will, because only he who knows his aggressive energies will be able to control them.

Taijiquan is Qigong. Its movements however stem from martial art. Martial art and Qigong always belonged together, though nowhere as closely as in Taijiquan. Within Chinese culture, and this is the one thing we have to consider if we do want to recognize the treasures of this art, there has never been a clear distinction between peace and confrontation with violence. Grand martial arts have evolved out of monasteries. Any movement in Taijiquan applies to self-defence in a very obvious way. The first form alone has 41 various movements showing an average of ten basic types of application. That would bring us to some 400 techniques. Adding those of the second form, the new frame and the weapon forms, we come up with many thousands of applications. All techniques are to be understood however as the water-drops of one big stream, and by forming an integrated whole, they realise their enormous potential. All techniques and movements are based on one and the same principle, the Taiji principle.

All movements imply applications. What's essential for me is to recognise the common element therein. There is no use in learning techniques and counter-techniques as if the point was putting the right key into the proper keyhole. During the tension of a standoff we would find it rather difficult to insert a key properly at all. And what after all if I first had to sort out the right one from a thick bunch of keys?

Taijiquan thus works by intuition. This means that we learn to (re-) act automatically and adapt to the situation, recognising the opponent's intentions before they can turn into action. The aim is to counter the force before it really has unfolded. How does that work? By way of the Taiji principle.

With the exercise of the Standing Post we learn to make our body permeable, making the centre of our mass sink downward (*wai san he*, see Chapter 8, on the Standing Post) as well as connecting all energies with each other and centring them. By way of the Silk Exercises we learn to maintain this condition while moving. That way the disciples learn about one of the most essential aspects of any martial art: to really maintain balance and on a level that is far beyond imagining a sense of an equilibrium.

By opening the meridians and with the heightened sensitivity of our body we learn *ting jin* – 'to hear the force'. We perceive movements of the person opposite before they really take place, not only during the approach, but in the very first moment that comes prior to a move: while it is still emerging as an idea. What is required next is '*dong jin*' – 'understanding energy'. This means we must learn to perceive force not only during its emergence, but to find the right interpretation by intuition as well. All this happens on fine-tuned levels and not really consciously, and because of this it happens very fast. Paradoxically we obtain these abilities by moving and researching very slowly. Once we see through the opponent's energy, we re-direct it (*hua jin*), adding our own force (*fa jin*) when the opponent's force has run into a void. These four scales are closely connected and provide a consolidated compact movement, keeping us inside our centre while uprooting the opponent. Considering the Taiji symbol, we can see one energy emerging and being dissolved again by the other, just as during the procedure described before. We learn about this in depth during the *Tuishou* partner exercises, Pushing Hands.

To sum up:

Ting jin	to hear force
Dong jin	to understand force
Hua jin	to re-direct force
Fa jin	to add own force

To hear force, to understand it, to re-direct it and to add one's own – this is the key to all. Technique as such is secondary and will naturally evolve during this process.

Another important principle states: 'The last will be the first. The opponent does not move, I do not move. The opponent moves, I am already there.' Many will have heard the story of the two Samurai facing each other for hours without moving, eventually ending their fight undecided. Each of them feels he'd be dead the moment he moves. Sometimes this can be observed in nature when a wild animal is hunting a weaker one. Sometimes both remain in silence. Once however the animal being hunted shows even the faintest attempt of a movement, it is lost.

It is often said that the assailant has immense advantage on his side because the defender has to be much faster. The assailant, they say, has the reaction time of his opponent at his disposal, as well as the time the latter needs for designing and executing a counter-technique. This is true however only as long as the defender allows himself to be forced into this pattern. I do not start the fight, but neither do I react to what my opponent does. As long as I react I must indeed be too slow. The word itself gives an adequate description. No, I act from the outset as well, but not until the assailant has begun, which he has to do if he intends to attack me. The moment the action ahead is detected, I shoot forward, thwarting the fight before it has really taken place. At this moment the opponent has not only started, he has even – perhaps without realising it – committed himself to a certain move. That makes him stiff, and I am flexible. In Taijiquan this is also called catching the right instant. It should however not be mistaken for timing or having a good eye for the opponent's 'gap'. This way of proceeding doesn't really work by way of mental reasoning, of recognising and analysing a movement; instead it is a subconscious, utterly sensitive action. Good fighters explain that not until after a fight had they recognised what had actually happened. This way one can be incredibly fast while the mind remains in complete calmness. In reality it isn't even fast. We do not need speed-training in order to master this level. One could almost say that mastership in this technique lies between time and space, because I am countering movements before they have taken place, without any hectic rush, with greatest calm, and yet so fast that I am not conscious of it until it is over.

In the same way they say: 'While looking right, don't forget about the left; looking upwards don't forget the bottom, and in trying to see all you won't see anything.' This has a variety of meanings as well. One of them is to not direct my attention on a distinct part of my opponent. Looking into his eyes can be deadly if I don't match the opponent mentally. Looking at the right fist may cause me to miss the action of the left. If I do try to keep all in sight, my mind will be in chaos, I'm over-concentrated, totally uptight and much too slow for action. Therefore I rest my view roughly on the solar plexus of my opponent, unfocused and calm, just like a seasoned car driver will drive through a narrow tunnel without bumping against either side. He looks forward in an unfocused and calm way. While not seeing any detail clearly, he still has everything within his field of vision. He is not constricted, but open to all. In this way I take my opponent into my sight with calmness. He appears to me rather by shape, but that's precisely why I 'see' everything, so that I can perceive every single move. The slightest attempt at a move is enough for me to shoot forward and take control of my opponent.

In Taijiquan, kicking, beating, wrestling, levering, ground fighting, no matter over what distance, or by which means – in self-defence everything is allowed. There are no limits to the possibilities because no limits are set to the situations. You can do whatever you want to – one thing alone is important: the principle. Without the Taiji-principle any technique is close to inefficiency. Let's look at this in terms of a levering technique. A disciple may work hard year by year practising his levering technique. However, he often finds that it doesn't quite work. If someone resists, perhaps being stronger than he is, it simply doesn't work. And why? Technique is not a guarantee for success; what is important is the principle that the technique is based on. To anticipate force, to understand it, to re-direct it and to add one's own, that's the answer. Dull execution of a technique cannot result in success. I must be sensitive and gentle enough to be able to sense technique from the inside. While applying a levering technique as in *Tuishou*, I must be able to track my opponent's centre and to likewise direct my energy into the place in him where pain becomes sensitive. If the opponent tries to escape the lever, that is if he applies force or tries to evade, the gateway towards his centre of pain or rather the gateway itself will change position. I have to follow accordingly and must not lose control over the centre.

In brief, the fight will be won by the one whose mastery of sensing energy is better, not the one who repeats the technique learned during training. Generally, I do not have to learn all the techniques of levering in all their variety to apply them in any situation. Understanding the principle and the energy of a technique enables me to transpose it to any situation, and according to the situation, the techniques evolve by themselves. Knowing one leverage, I know them all. If I don't know the principle I know none.

There is another reason why repeating techniques continuously does not necessarily determine a successful action. Once again our story about the key: just imagine that you were hounded by a bunch of fearful potential opponents. You arrive in panic at the door of your house, anxious to unlock it, but you just don't make it. The key won't enter the lock. Feeling extremely stressed, you keep missing the keyhole or you may even drop the key. What would now be the logical training to find a remedy for this? Putting the front door key into the door lock a hundred times a day? Certainly not, as under normal conditions I manage that with no problem at all, I'm a master of this technique. The reason for failure is due to my mental state. We must learn to stay calm in stressful situations.

An important basic formula in Taijiquan is *nei san he* – the inner three harmonies:

Xin yu yi he: 'The heart connects to the awareness'

Qi yu li he: 'The energy connects to the force'

Jin yu gu he: 'The tendons connect to the bones'

Within the Standing Post we find the source for a serene mind and for mental power. During the silk exercises and the form we combine this with movement. Concentration, energy and force will emerge. Everything is involved: mind, concentration, imagination, energy, muscles, tendons and bones, organs – in brief, all that we have.

'Heart and awareness join with each other' – this has many meanings. Let's for a moment see it this way: to do something wholeheartedly is to do something 100 per cent. If I apply a technique only halfheartedly, the result will be unsatisfactory. My teacher always tells me: 'Either you fight or you don't fight. There is nothing in between.' It is ambivalence that must be avoided. The heart says: do this, the mind says: no, I'd rather not. For example in self-defence, your mind perhaps tells you: 'Oh, I'm being attacked now, I'll have to strike back.' But the heart is whispering: 'Oh, I'd rather not, I am afraid!' Here there are two opinions working against each other. The counterstrike in that case can't but be 'halfhearted', i.e. unsatisfactory in its result. *Xin yu yi he* therefore means to conduct will, emotion, mind, feeling, i.e. our entire inner life, towards union. In this way 100 per cent of mental power and force can evolve. Within our form this means that our thoughts and emotions come to rest, and emptiness sets in. Out of this emptiness, the condition of *Wuji*, a consciousness, arises that merges completely with the movement it has initiated. In the ideal case, a consciousness of only one direction will evolve, concentrated without any distraction, a consciousness not only controlling the movement, but being the movement itself.

Qi yu li he means that the energy flows in absolute accordance with the physical, the external power. In this way inner and outer energy flow together and do not work against each other. The inner force, our Qi, is collected and channelled by our consciousness. It is maintained in a way that connects to our muscles, and movement begins. Qi impels the muscles, and hence the movement, and at the same time it merges with the muscles within. It cannot be separated from them, and still it goes ahead of them to improve their actions.

Jin yu gu he means that the tendons and the bones not only stand for themselves but for the entire connective tissue, for nerves and organs and the rest of our anatomy. They too work together in the same way.

This entire process is called the inner three integrations, *nei san he*. It ensures that everything within the body is permeated by the leadership of spirit. Everything flows together towards integrity and can no longer be separated. This provides a deep, permeating sense of being whole and complete. In addition to the effects upon energy and health, this results in a condition where worries and fears are absent; a condition of genuine release.

In this way we may attain 100 per cent of our entire physical and mental energy. It is like a rope; all the single threads are entwined into one strand, so that it cannot be broken. This phenomenon of absolute power can be applied universally. Whether it be on the occasion of negotiating a salary increase, a case of love or during a rough bar-room fight, with the entire physical system working together as one, a level of presence and performance will evolve that actually cannot be countered. Furthermore, efficiency is greater than the theoretical sum of all the ingredients involved. The reason for this is that by the combination of body and mind, a third entity appears: the power of unity.

We will gain true insight on the processes just described here, however, only by way of our Taijiquan training. Words can never explain precisely the reality. Neither is it the purpose here to repeat techniques continually. The principle underlying them must be experienced by practice, and thus one may move ahead from theory to reality. In order to really understand this principle we have to train a lot, and even once we have adopted the principle in its entirety, we have to train continuously. It's like boiling an egg. After I've heated the stove and placed a pot on it, brought the water to boil and added an egg, I still have to wait some four or five minutes until the egg is boiled and ready. Just like the egg is being boiled slowly, the body and the mind will slowly develop by continuous training. In the classics we read: 'The Qi is entering the bones.' That means that the body is gradually taken over and permeated by this intensity. Eventually the inner and the outer structure will change; something comes into being that has not been there before. What evolves is *Gongfu*.

The spiral movements being practised during the form are an essential part of the Taiji-combat. Circular movements will divert a force much more easily than a linear movement. Someone who may not be clear about this should take a look underneath his car – he will find wheels there. A look into space as well will make him recognise that stars and planets are round and their orbits are round and elliptical as well. The moons are circling around the planets, the planets are circling around the suns, the solar systems have a joint axis. All is interwoven in a spiral way. A straight direct movement indeed takes the shortest way, yet it cannot 'flow'. The wheel had to be invented. Light, radiowaves, all abide by this principle.

We can check this quickly and easily by way of a partner exercise: two partners are standing opposite each other, their forearms leaning against each other. One person now tries to push away the other's arm and vice versa. With two opponents being equally strong, this is very stressful, as force is working against force. If one of them however determines to move the entire arm into a spiral movement, a kind of rotation, he will find that not only will he win, but that it is much easier for him, too. He will feel this even more clearly the more this spiral movement occurs from the entire body being controlled by it. In the beginning such movements are still rather large, but with increasing skill the spirals become more and more internal and more and more compact. Being external during application, they keep getting smaller which actually makes them appear as straight-lined and direct movements, while in fact they are full of internal windings and spirals which take up power, divert it and pass it back to the opponent, as for example in the technical sequence shown in Figures 9–14.

My hand can take the shortest path towards the opponent, and being rotated, it will also arrive.

The types of application in Taijiquan can basically be subdivided into four categories:

1. **Lun zi bian yan de li** – 'The force from diverting a wheel'. Like a stone hitting a spinning wheel and being thrown off, the opponent's force is diverted by the rotating arms of the

Figure 9

Figure 10

Figure 11

Figure 12

Figure 13

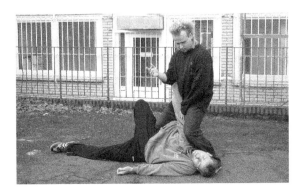

Figure 14

Figures 9-14 Counteracting a fist attack with a throw: Jan Silberstorff and Frank Marquardt

Taiji practitioner. We give way to power while not losing our centre.

2. **Lun tiao de li** – 'The force from blocking a wheel's spoke arm' or: 'Laterally breaking the force'. We stop the opponent in the same way we put a stick between the spokes of a spinning wheel. The wheel will seize immediately. It is important that we do not confront the force head-on, but intervene instead crossways to the force's origin. That way it becomes possible to easily counter even a considerable force.

3. **Zhuan tou de li** – 'The spiral force'. As mentioned before, we absorb an attack into our network of spiral movements. Within these the force gets lost, the direction of energy turns around, and we add our own force. The better our inner network is developed, the better and more compactly will we be able to apply this principle. Round, spiral-like movements are hard to follow, and someone who tries to do so will easily lose his own balance. Once mastered, these spiral movements are actually experienced only internally; therefore one should not imagine these as wide, circling movements. On the contrary, the movements are hardly visible or not visible at all, and the opponent seems to be defeated by himself.

4. **Bao zha li** – 'The explosive force'. Similar to a real explosion, force can be emitted from any part of the body, without any warning. Just as suddenly as it appears, it will again disappear. Master Shen Xijing says:

> It is like a lake. It lies there, quiet and smooth, nothing can disturb its peace. Suddenly the silence is torn, an overwhelming floodwave occurs, tearing everything away. Then again, as if nothing had happened, silence and harmony will prevail, the lake before us lies calm and peaceful.

But how is this so-called *bao fa jin*, that is, the handing out of force explosively, accomplished in reality?

Yin-energy from the earth and Yang-energy from heaven merge within the *Dantian*. The body is relaxed and sunk, calm and collected.

Then – when Yin and Yang merge – this force jointly erupts. By way of the Taijiquan-form we learn to develop inner energy and make it circulate inside our body, but we learn also to release it to the outside in various ways. During a fight such as *bao fa jin*, three is an explosive movement. This is mainly practised in the 2nd form. During an explosive movement, energy is concentrated within the *Dantian*. This is similar to a pot with boiling water inside being tightly closed by a lid. When the pressure caused by the steam is sufficient, it will tear the pot apart. In the same way we are creating a pressure within the *Dantian*, and we can then release, set free and channel this energy as we wish (and as we can).

Carrying out force in a purely energetic way is called *fa qi*. This also applies to the transfer of energy onto others, for example for stimulating healing processes. The entire energy and power of the body are collected in the centre and become transferred jointly to the point from where they are to be released. This may be done with calm or with explosiveness, hard or soft, slow or fast.

As we will see in the chapter on martial techniques of Taijiquan, Taijiquan in the meaning of self-defence does not have any basic position. Energy and weight have sunk. One is calm and relaxed, yet ready any time. A confrontation may occur by surprise, either because I am unprepared, or because I fear an escalation may occur, being unable however to determine the exact time, because being the 'good guy' I'm not the first to attack but will try instead to avoid a physical stand-off. If then, however, things do escalate, I have no time to prepare my actions, and any previous planning beyond proper awareness would be fatal. A situation hardly ever takes place due to my prior judgement. Here again the principle of *Wuwei* occurs, the non-planned spontaneous action. Each situation is new; even a straight punch with the fist is always somehow different. Thus I have to rely on my natural reflexes and my feeling for my opponent's energies and my own. That's exactly what I train for during Taijiquan, and that's why during training I don't have to waste any thoughts on speed. For on one hand I train that in my explosive movements, on the other hand I ask myself: how fast is a reflex? Isn't it so fast that I do not become aware of a movement until it has happened? Thus I am fast enough anyway. What I have to learn however is to carry my reflex and its energy in the proper direction.

Once during my morning training in the park I was attacked by surprise: a man, all dressed in leather and with tattooed arms, believed his own martial system better than Taijiquan. A classic situation. He got into conversation with me, and we talked about Taijiquan. In the middle of our talk, without any warning, all of a sudden he attacked me. I did not really become aware of the attack before the opponent lay on the ground. With great pleasure I recognised that without any speed training and though I had started as a defender, I had still been the first to arrive at the finish. That's why the saying goes: what is slow during training is fast during combat. It is energy that controls movement. As mentioned before, the classic says: 'The opponent does not move, I do not move. The opponent moves, I'm already there.'

In a similar way, it is also said:

Being protected on the right, I'm open on the left, and vice versa.
Being protected at the top, I'm open at the bottom, and vice versa.
Being protected at the front, I'm open to the back, and vice versa.
Being protected everywhere, I'm open everywhere.

Whichever way I'm trying to protect myself, I'm always leaving a gap. Even while positioning myself in trying to cover my body all over, I am again so limited in my manoeuvring space that I'm open to being attacked everywhere. So I would rather stay with my natural and relaxed attitude – yet centred and aware.

Taijiquan as a martial art is a tremendous research issue. With advancing skills, a steadily growing comprehension will evolve. For realistic self-defence it should be mentioned that there are no rules. Anything is allowed. There is no 'This technique is Taijiquan, and that one is not Taijiquan.' There is only good and bad Taijiquan, depending on how efficient the moves are. This again depends exclusively from mastering the inner principle that is within all movements – the Taiji-principle.

Chapter 5

Taijiquan –
Teaching for Health

Taijiquan has an all-embracing health effect. True. But why is this the case? In a time when doctors and hospitals here in the West appear increasingly impersonal, many look to the traditional health methods of the East. Modern China in turn is interested in the technical achievements that Western medicine offers. That way a sensible combination of both systems in the East and the West slowly evolves.

Taijiquan abides by the principles of Traditional Chinese Medicine. Chinese healing procedures apply in a holistic way, and over time they have matured into being a genuine profession. Understanding an art however requires knowledge about its historical backgrounds. Most Taijiquan enthusiasts suffer a tremendous shock when, feeling unsatisfied with the rose-tinted narratives of their teachers, they travel to China. What they meet with initially is a terribly loud, over-populated country full of peculiarities that initially they don't feel comfortable with. There is hardly anyone who is not glad to return home after two or three weeks. Then, however, he wants to go there again at the next possible opportunity.

As for myself, I have been to China some 30 times through the years, having guided travel-groups to China as well as having shown Germany to visitors from China. The impressions on both sides are more or less identical: fascination, pride at having been there, and relief at eventually being back home. This is followed by a strong desire to return. Things weren't different in my case.

After my first journey – it lasted two months and took me to the family of my then teacher Sui Qingbo in Qingdao – I thought I had learnt about the country. During my second journey I slowly started feeling doubtful. During my following journeys, each of them spanning several months, I began to feel that I still had a lot to learn about China. Following another year in China, I began to feel apprehensive. I suddenly felt that I didn't understand anything, and that all my assessments were wrong. The Chinese instead seemed to understand everything, and at least they seemed to have a full grip on me. So I got duped at any takeaway snack-place, cheated by any cab driver, and betrayed, used and fooled by so-called good friends. I was quite helpless. Until she came: Changhui, my girlfriend at that time. She understood everything and knew everything, and at least she understood me. In this she was my ally.

So I launched a terrible campaign of vengeance. When someone out of 'old friendship' (in most cases we had known each other for a few days) invited me for dinner, in fact because his boss was sitting at the table nearby, and he hoped to get a better position due to his 'foreign friends', I knew the score now. When someone gave me shoes or any kind of technical gadget, I knew that later they would wish to chat and persuade me into some trading contract with Germany. Everything was different now. While having been unnerved initially because these apparent courtesies stole my precious time for training, I now accepted dinners and gifts, and frequented the best tea-houses in town, but this time on my own terms. I had got the message that something was expected from me as well. Invitations for dinner were agreed at times when I too was hungry, and not, as before, when I was just stepping out of my favourite noodle place. I allowed myself to be endowed with anything I could use, and what I could not use was put in the gift-box and was passed on whenever the occasion arose. I was encouraging during business discussions and enjoyed watching someone making every effort to get a better job. I even allowed myself to be conned by my dear cab drivers, because for the first time I realised that the add-on charge for me as a European amounted to only about ten cents. Actually the cab driver was almost right, it suddenly seemed to me. Generally, the behaviour of travellers in second- to third-world countries is peculiar; as soon as they've packed their rucksack they seem to become like Uncle Scrooge. Of course I don't like to carry much money with me while travelling for months, but the average globe-trotter is all too complacent in the role of being 'a local', that is, he does not want to be seen as a tourist. After some tough rounds of bargaining, a jeans vendor looked at me with scepticism and asked: 'Does it really make such a big difference to you paying in your own currency five marks and ten or five marks and twenty?' This hadn't occurred to me before.

I was sitting once in front of my then favourite hotel, one I had until then considered the cheapest and most modest hotel in Xian, the Victory Hotel. Two travellers came by, asking for the prices. I answered: 'Twenty Renminbi'. 'Is that true? That much? Well, they're not gonna screw *us*, I've been on the road too long for that. There's one at the other end of town, they charge eighteen!' And off they went, with a quick turn on their heels. I watched them getting lost with their gigantic rucksacks among the pedestrians at rush-hour. They'd be walking for about one and a half hours, just for an amount worth about 20 cents. A tourist acting native is about as senseless as a native acting as a Westerner. For example, my girlfriend, knowing that abroad people are free to touch each other and even kiss in the open street, was determined to introduce that to China as well. There, however, such manners don't work at all, and even less with foreigners. I guess I learnt the major part of my repertoire of Chinese expletives during the times of our walks together through the public parks. I'm still uncertain today whether the Chinese passing by were indeed concerned about morals or just realising that some 'long-nose' now had a custodian. He would be much harder now to rip off…

Later I noticed that nothing actually happened as a result of my socializing. Hardly anyone received a better job, and no business deals were signed. Nobody really seemed to be interested. However, an enthusiastic business talk would establish a harmonious atmosphere that lasted over the following weeks, and then it was time to go out to dinner again.

Not long ago we were travelling with a TV team producing a documentary film on Taijiquan and Daoism in China. Some companies approached us and asked to have their factories filmed. We have always generously compensated with their products. The deal was about soft drinks and spirits. As was anticipated, there was grumbling from the

Western team, claiming that God knew how much they had to do, and that it was impossible anyway to present booze as part of the film. But as had been the case before, the 'quiet rule' applied, and nobody really expected the factories to appear in the film, even though it had been earnestly discussed. It was simply great having had a foreign TV team there. The mayor had seen it, and crew photographs were taken. And us? We had beverages piled up to the roof which enabled us to supply our hired guns during parties. A magnificent result.

While having been nervous and stressed previously and consequentially sometimes even ill, I felt great from now on. Health, it seemed to me, consists of understanding the nature of things, the inner and outer conditions we are in, and the ability always to create the space we need for our physical and mental well-being.

It's just the same with Taijiquan. The very understanding of the health aspect requires profound introspection and sensitivity. Taijiquan is healthy because in a gentle and careful mode it keeps the body moving, so that it won't stiffen up, but does not wear out as occurs with other types of sport. The entire body and mind will relax and find relief, the blood circulation is improved, physical, mental and energy blocks clear, and all organs are supplied with sufficient amounts of nutrients and energy. Illnesses are prevented; existing ones are less severe. The body can thus work at its optimum, with all of the organs, muscles, tendons, nerves, blood and bones working together in harmony. Thus, the body becomes forceful and strong, it will become resilient and unassailable. The person will then live for their full lifespan and will die peacefully.

Taijiquan brings us back to our natural balance, but a genuine connectedness must grow between Taijiquan and the life I'm leading. Simply training in Taijiquan can remain a very technical and thus limited process. It should enter into all of our daily life. If I lack sleep, if I'm under stress or have emotional problems or I'm physically ill, I slip out of my natural balance and off my centre. It seems a sad fact that today just by socialisation and being on the treadmill, one is separated from one's natural anchorage. I think how many people have to get up and go to work while it's still dark, getting home (especially in winter) in the dark again; this is no quality of life. Just to think of having to get up day by day with the help of an alarm clock makes me feel uneasy.

Whatever the case may be, I easily slip out of my natural equilibrium, so that I'm out of balance, and I do not feel well. Having the opinion however of not being able to change anything about my external conditions, I seem to have no other choice, so I've got to do something to create an artificial balance within my imbalance. For the early-to-rise that may be coffee, for the physically ill, medicine; to decrease stress we may use alcohol, cigarettes, drugs, sweets, or whatever. Indeed these things do help. I feel better having created an artificial balance. The only problem is, I'm depending on support from external aides, and I become addicted. Since these sources supply me with an artificial equilibrium only, granting me only limited happiness, they are usually unhealthy. This puts a downward spiral into motion that makes us more and more unhealthy. Because of the habit, we feel these alien helpers are enjoyable. But honestly: whose first cigarette ever did taste good? Who hasn't thrown up having been drunk? Who doesn't get sick from lots of cake? The body knows quite precisely what's good for it and what is not. With the connection between body and mind being forcibly interrupted, finding myself in permanent deficit, the body will surrender and bid these drugs welcome.

Taijiquan training will not only restore the sensitivity for one's own body that has been lost, it will even raise it appreciably. The connection of body and spirit is being rebuilt, and unity will be established. Thus, we're slowly heading back to our natural balance. The closer we get there the better we learn: sugar results in a sore throat, cigarettes cause nausea and dizziness, coffee tastes terribly bitter, causing nothing but a pounding heart. Because that's the way these aides work: when the body is unbalanced they seem to help by providing an apparent well-being. For anyone living within his natural balance, however, these things hold not attraction.

So the more I approach my natural balance, the more these dependencies will cease. Leaving negative habits behind is almost like a spin-off from training.

When a youth I started my training during a period of heavy drug taking. I was convinced that whatever benefits the training would bring, my excesses were the most beneficial of all. Nothing and no one would take them away from me.

After the first couple of training sessions, however, while sitting with friends drinking lots of beer as was usual in those days, looking from a rooftop over the city of Hamburg, I said 'Well, I've only trained for a few sessions, but if that physical feeling I get continues, I'll definitely quit smoking and drinking some day.' 'Great!', the others replied in unison, 'so you can be the car driver now!'

It had never occurred to me that I needed to quit drinking and smoking, and the whole process of withdrawal took some two years, but since then I have not smoked a single cigarette.

Many of my students have regained their health, even though they had been advised never to practise any type of sport again; they've recovered from vertebral disc prolapses, serious drug addiction or serious depression. Much is within reach if only we try!

Whether it's hard drugs now or just one piece of cake too many, nobody need be dissuaded from anything. One thing is clear, however: Taijiquan is a healthy process of practice that will contribute to your good health, for the body and for the mind, inside as well as outside.

The processes described here will only take place if I allow the training access to my entire life, being ready to surrender my old ideas.

In order to achieve comprehensive health, and even to go beyond, a profound introspection of Taijiquan's theory, practice and philosophy is required. This forms the basis for what is most important: a deep sensitivity for the personal spirit, one's own body and its mechanisms. Out of this understanding I learn to understand myself – only then do I get to know myself at all. The better I get to know myself, the better I'm able to listen not only to others, but to myself as well. I realise what's good for me, what adapts to my nature, what my goal is and what will inflict damage on me. However, as the saying goes: health is more than the absence of illness.

Body, mind and soul need to be nurtured in order to work harmoniously, but this does not mean through the extremes of extravagance and affluence, or through asceticism or self-sacrifice. Instead, it is through an all-comprising evolution corresponding with our destiny as connected to our own personal path. Recognizing this, however, is very difficult for many. However, one who has found himself, having developed this knowledge, will lead a happy and healthy life independently from birth, illness and death. This is the true health I can preserve through Taijiquan.

We seem to feel the importance of health most clearly once we've fallen ill. How soon however is this ordeal forgotten once we've regained health again? We should create a different mindset towards ourselves and our body. Especially in times when we're doing well, we should value this condition and be conscious of it. During these times we should behave in a way that enables us to maintain this state as long as possible, as a precaution. Once we've fallen ill, our level of energy rapidly declines, together with the motivation to rehabilitate by our own effort. During healthy times, however, we have enough power and motivation to turn health into a sensitive experience. It's fascinating being able to sense every single pore of the body, being able to sense discomfort while it is still approaching, and to adopt preventive measures. We can learn so much during this about ourselves and our body. While we are healthy we feel good, and it is enjoyable to ponder about life. Small obstacles can put a tremendous restraint on the joy of living. On one occasion I was in Thailand, going by a very small boat to one of those paradise islands. Actually I had planned to get a conch shell there for my beloved girlfriend and to use this heavenly place for meditation, hoping to absorb a big dose of wisdom. Unfortunately I was taken over by nausea which lasted for two days. The only wisdom I was granted at this time was that there didn't seem to be any piece of food that didn't smell somehow unpleasant! With a long face, I sought out one of those marvellous conches and then went and hid myself under my mosquito net.

The human body is so incredibly fascinating, so fine-tuned, that its capacity for resilience is amazing. With all the complexity of the body's construction, it's a miracle that it functions for so long and so miraculously. Any automobile's design is incomparably more simple, and yet still breaks down much more frequently. Thus we should be grateful when we are healthy, instead of being resentful when we are ill. With my computer I'm having similar experience, and I think many will know what I mean: WCTAG's office was in need of a computer installation. We know, however, that these devices frequently crash; a serious challenge to our bank balance, our peace of mind and our calmness. Then I found out what a miracle it is that computers work at all.

I'm sitting at the moment in the mountains of Tenerife, writing on my laptop. It's so small, yet everything works, so let's enjoy life whenever possible when things are running smoothly.

Unfortunately, even small states of pain are enough to affect our quality of life. However, we should thank God for the incredible design of the human body, and resolve to care for our body like a treasure, for only then may our spirit grow. The spirit must be in good shape in order for us to feel good; a healthy body with a good feeling inside is the best condition to be in.

Taijiquan is applied in therapy all over the world. In China it's nothing strange when patients do their sword-forms in the hallway of a hospital, just as in Germany our Chen-style ball form is successfully applied in various rehabilitation clinics. Taijiquan is eminently useful both in prevention and rehabilitation, and the practitioner feels good.

For the same reason it is wise to work cheerfully and with motivation on the body and upon oneself during times of good health. The training creates real strength and wisdom; I'm creating a reliable basis for preventing illness or better overcome an existing one. If I don't start Taijiquan until I've fallen ill, it can be a gentle form of rehabilitation.

In general terms, however, Taijiquan should be understood as a way of education for living. Taijiquan is not intended for fighting illness; it serves for health maintenance. It's the mental attitude that makes a difference here. Taijiquan is an education for a healthy and conscious way to live. To care about my life. To show me who I am, to learn what is good for me and what I should avoid. It is a way of maintaining and keeping health, and not just a defence against illness. In ancient China, doctors were paid as long as the patient stayed healthy. A case of illness was a doctor's failure. While Taijiquan is successfully applied in fighting illness, one should also seek symptomatic medical care. It's here where I obtain the medicines to combat the symptoms of illness. In serious cases this is by all means reasonable. However, this is not the duty of Taijiquan. Fighting symptoms is not a way of life, but a temporary necessity. Taijiquan is a way of life, to preserve health. The cause of illness is being removed, not the outcome. This is an active process. It includes growth and wisdom, and it is the means of my personal maturation.

Chapter 6

Taijiquan – A Spiritual Exercise

Taijiquan creates a strong body, keeps one youthful, protects us from ageing and keeps attackers away. Everybody knows this and it is known as well that the mind plays the greatest role. However, Taijiquan can also be a very good psychotherapy. Surprisingly, this aspect isn't treated with much significance in China. My Shifu Chen Xiaowang once said to me: 'In the West I've noticed the great significance and importance of Taijiquan is as a mental therapy. People here seem to have many more mental problems than physical ones. Fortunately, Taijiquan can serve as an effective remedy.' A pupil of mine from Belgium (he is a psychologist) told me during a stay in Hamburg: 'Throughout all the time I've studied psychology I haven't learned as much about the subject of spirit and life as during my Taijiquan training here.' I studied sociology myself for some years, then dropped it somewhere between pre-degree and diploma, because my experiences were similar. Taijiquan enabled me to progress faster, even with sociology. Not that social theories embroidered by science fell from heaven during my training, but it did add to a deeper understanding of the nuances of human behaviour, so that suddenly – and that's the big advance – I could also sense them. Of course I do have to study various subjects if I want to have a theoretical overview, but if I'm interested in understanding the world, its various contexts and my role among them, Taijiquan can help me. It's the same in medicine. Of course my Taijiquan won't suddenly enable me to quote all the meridians by heart, or fix a good herbal tea. However, I know how to keep myself healthy, and I am aware of the inner relationships of being, the ability of a transfer to the outside, of understanding the world. Taijiquan leads me to a deeper understanding of its principle, and as the rationale of Taijiquan puts all things in this world into a context open to understanding, it is no longer surprising that I may gain so much.

Taijiquan is fundamentally based on the philosophy of Yin and Yang. Out of this the *Yijing*, the *Daodejin* of Lao Tse have evolved into the entire Daoist and Konfuzian philosophy of life and much more. This dualism also plays an important role in ourselves, though somehow in a different form. To the Chinese the term 'both' has always been more important than 'either…or'. Again I'm contemplating my laptop, this time in a marvellously beautiful suburb of Sydney. The laptop too is based on the principle of Yin and Yang, that is to say the one of 0 and 1.

Looking at myself, my inner life, my relationship with the world around me, myself as a being between heaven and earth and as part of society, looking at my environment, nature and eventually the cosmos and genesis itself: all this is a long sociological, psychological and philosophical process. What's really profitable with Taijiquan is not that I'm intensely dealing with it during my training – I virtually live these studies. I sense them. I perceive them and try to sense deeper and deeper into this matter. Perceiving matters with consciousness is far ahead of any intellectual and theoretical dealing, because it leads towards understanding in terms of entirety. Why are Eastern religions – much in contrast to some of the Western ones – booming? A religion that annunciates its truth in authenticity should neither be better or worse than any other doing the same. The differences on one side lie within the related cultural background and the theological aspects; in reality however it differs within its ways of being practised. Religions and spiritual doctrines such as Buddhism can be lived in reality by any aspect. There are meditations, physical exercises, teachings and a peaceful and most of all a positive way of expression that does not spread fear. Something can be understood here as an entirety, to be lived and gained, as in Daoism. As long as I feel nothing but the power from the lectern with a finger raised and pointing, having no spiritual and physical exercises to really make me aware of God, then my religion will in fact stay a belief, a hope. Then I can't but believe and hope that everything will be all right that way. I believe in God myself, but not because as a child I was baptised Protestant and later received Confirmation. Nor do I believe because the Bible has convinced me in any way. No, I believe in God because I can perceive Him every day, because His power is flowing inside me, and because I feel how fate, destiny and divinity flow together and are present inside me and my fellow human beings.

Generally spiritual development is highly connected to physical and mental training, for not many people are assaulted by the Holy Spirit while walking round some corner! Neither will enlightenment in most cases come overnight. We must learn to experience spiritual development not only by thought, but in a holistic way that also includes physical exercise.

There are many different religions, philosophies and views upon of world. Every population tries to obtain an understanding of matters from out of the world it experiences. Every tribe searches for understanding, searching for a path towards inner peace and eternity. That way all people arrive at results related to their mentality, which they then search to establish in the form of religions, philosophies or worldviews. What they all have in common is the search for the beginning, the genesis out of which all has evolved and the eternity into which all will melt, and the attempt also to describe permanent change and to find ways of breaking out of it. The essence of all religions, philosophies and worldviews eventually appears to be identical, at least when they try to express the truth. We can therefore listen within ourselves to appreciate the divine, instead of continuously searching for fulfilment by external means or having to be coaxed there as in politics.

Who can tell what is the truth? Some find this political party is the right one, others find it's that one. Some revolutionaries revolutionise this, others revolutionise that. Some propagate this religion, others that. Which of them is actually right? Some readers will say: these. Others will say: those. Others again will say: none of them, the truth lies in between.

In my opinion the truth is not to be found anywhere here; it stands high above all these matters. These are all but external phenomena evolved from out of one and the same essence. The only thing we can state with certainty is that all is subject to change, so there can be no firm dogma, no ideology, no policy that always fits. That is unless it was the non-dogma, the non-ideology, the non-policy; this may mean that now this policy makes sense, in another time another one may. The non-dogma depicts matters in transformation. Activities and thoughts adapt to the times. They are spontaneous. They are like *Wuwei*, the non-acting (see also Chapter 3, Taiji – A Philosophy). They abide the change and adapt to it at the same time as they are changing themselves, so harmony can be kept. Truth is the motor of all these matters; it is what keeps everything together, and it permeates all. It is the energy that makes all things work, whether we now call this Dao, existence, nature or whatever. For can it be named after all, the Dao? Can I make myself an effigy of it, one of God? Microcosm is macrocosm. God's realm is inside you. All is one, and yet all exists as single and separate.

We should not attempt to convince others of anything but rather take to the path ourselves, to the path where we fathom the contexts, where we feel them in depth. In short: we must understand the divine within ourselves and within all things. And a tip for the novice teacher: the more you find, the more the people will wish to know from you. But what are you going to tell them when you have not found anything yet yourself? Taijiquan is one way among many to really find, if we earnestly strive for it.

Taijiquan however works just as pragmatically and directly as an enrichment in daily life. For those who are not searching for instant divine wisdom, but are just doing some gentle exercises, Taijiquan is a marvellous therapy for the minor ailments. It calms the mind and brings it back to its original condition. The training won't make mental problems disappear in an instant, but it's a help in recollecting one's own centre. If the mind is mellow, the body weary, a round of Taijiquan often helps to bring it all back to the point of rest. Body and spirit may recover. Suddenly a more objective view on things is possible again. The answer to a problem is often very near then.

To me, Taijiquan has always proven to be a good friend in times of hardship. It has kept me together, has given me advice, calmed me and given me the power not to give up. It is something that is always there. Everything in life changes, the ambience around us, the people we are in contact with – yet my Taijiquan is always there. It's right in place in case I need it. This in turn is the reason why I have never given up Taijiquan. It is like a treasure that I'm harbouring, a treasure not subject to transience. Nobody can take it away from me, and neither do I have to tow it with me, but still it is always there. People often wonder why during my distant travels I hardly ever carry more than three kilograms of luggage with me. My most important and most voluminous baggage is Taijiquan, and it weighs nothing. No matter where I am, I never get bored. Last week I spent eight hours waiting for a train from the little village Champun back to Bangkok. Time passed by in a moment; I trained Taijiquan. If I'm seriously tormented by mental problems, I always have my psychiatrist with me. Taiji always gives me comfort and advice. Doesn't that sound fabulous? And indeed, it is so. Taijiquan applies to any domain of life; one only has to find the adequate approach. We get supplied with this by training.

Through training I learn to be patient. Out of patience calmness will slowly evolve, and out of this in turn relaxation will set in. A calm mind is very important for a harmonious life, as out of this a centred way of being will evolve. We develop our spiritual centre. Here we feel at home. It is like a castle open on either side; anything can enter, and still it is my shield. I do not lose my centre. I am open and flexible and still cannot be assailed, always at rest, always calm and centred. I begin recognising my very ego. I discover love for myself, and out of this love for all beings. Developing calmness doesn't necessarily mean leading a secluded life. Whether it's abdicating from the world or venturing into the stock-market, what's important is being at ease inside, having a settled mind. Given an adequate physical structure, the energy can sink down to the *Dantian*. We sustain our centre. Creating and keeping our centre inside ourselves, not depending on what's happening around us, is a true condition of release.

On the other hand, when I move off-centre, everything around falls down upon me, everything becomes too much for me. Being able to maintain my centre no matter how hectic things are will keep the situation from turning into distress. Then it is just action, and life is a joy.

Taijiquan as a spiritual exercise offers a marvellous form of self-education. Through the effort of daily training, and development of one's own personality, martial teaching is raised to an art that involves the discipline of one's own ego as far as its complete abandoning.

No matter whether we are a *bon vivant* or hermit, Taijiquan fortifies our centre, our whole equilibrium. The exercise of standing provides me with the structure required for developing a settled and centred condition. The silk exercises train my ability of keeping this centre and the inner texture during motion, during change and alteration. Within the form I learn to develop this further to a high level. I learn to adapt to all types of change without losing my balance in all situations of life, and I recognise the origin and the effectiveness of all things. This is the spiritual exercise in Taijiquan – and its limits are beyond estimation.

Chapter 7

Techniques and Principles of Taijiquan

TAIJIQUAN AND ITS MARTIAL TECHNIQUE

Taijiquan abides by a very distinct principle: the one of naturalness. This is of utmost importance, and it follows the principle of the silk-exercises: learning to understand Yin and Yang, being able to cultivate the energies. This is the way to achieve real naturalness. The fighting techniques of Taijiquan work with the principle of naturalness also. However, even naturalness has to be (re)learned by us; that is what training Taijiquan is for. Achieving naturalness consistent with the principles of Yin and Yang during my movements evolves a technique all by itself. People always wonder why 'Taijistas' practise nothing but the form – since fighting can be carried out all by itself, without ever having been rehearsed by them. Well, this isn't completely true. Most people training Taijiquan have no skills at all related to self-defence, as their knowledge is often too limited. Many aren't really interested in a deeper knowledge. Those however who are and those among them who are fortunate to have a good teacher will soon learn how efficient Taijiquan is. The main part of essential progress however lies within my training of the form. This is where I work out my body structure, my sense of force, intuition and adaptability of my (re)action as well as subtleness towards the situation. You simply (re)act. And afterwards you realise: 'Oh, that was like the Crane posture.' Or: 'That was like the Single Whip.' Or: 'Oh, that went wrong; keep training.'

In earlier times I had always been interested in basic postures. I kept asking: 'But there must be some type of a stance that keeps me ready to respond in case of danger.' 'Just take the preparational stance if you absolutely wish to have a basic posture,' my Shifu Chen Xiaowang replied, 'Silly answer,' I thought in total ignorance. Totally impractical, that's what it seemed to me. Hands down, in front of the opponent. Not until much later I learnt that it's much more unwise to move myself into an adventurous posture just because my counterpart raises his voice a bit. And in the case of a surprise attack, there is no time anyway to take any basic postures. During an open stand-off, it's not only provocative and dangerous, it is absolutely unnecessary as well.

Maintaining naturalness while being fully concentrated, with calm, sensitivity and respect for my counterpart, I am prepared for all. It's the situation that decides. This is my basic posture: the Qi being sunk, the mind being clear, all is relaxed while being sensitive down to the last pore. Body and mind united, the body contained and at ease. I am able to say: 'The opponent does not move, I do not move. The opponent moves, I am already there.'

Later my Shifu told me: 'Just be natural, the rest will happen by itself.'

In this way, Taijiquan has no martial technique at all. That's why many find it so difficult to visualise Taijiquan as a martial art. I've found that almost all martial techniques, i.e. the applications I have seen by now in Taijiquan, occur in the same or similar way in other systems too. In turn there are basically no applications in other systems that Taijiquan does not have. It is not the technique but the principle within which turns it into Taijiquan. Technique as such is something external and is of no significance to the essence of Taijiquan. When Chen Wangting created Taijiquan he took the movements from the boxing systems known by then and combined them with the teachings of inner energy conduct. It is the mode or the Gongfu of performing these techniques that makes the character of Taijiquan, so it is not surprising that Taijiquan practitioners rarely ever train in techniques of self-defence. In most cases the reason is regrettably the lack of interest in understanding Taijiquan as a martial art anyway, while in fact the very masters in this ancient treasure of culture are routinely seen again and again training the form. And that way it is good.

The statement: 'He who knows the other is prudent, he who knows himself is sage,' is to be taken seriously. I cannot defeat the opponent until I've overcome myself, and the same goes for a fight happening in reality. The point is to achieve such a fine adjustment within the body that the opponent no longer can reach me. He can no longer intrude my centre, no longer break my space. In turn he can no longer find his own space any more. If my body is capable of moving without waste, without inner resistance and blockages, I'm able to transmit real force. As long as I keep permanently blocking inside my body, continuously breaking off my centre, only a fraction of my energy will be enforced anyway, and push-ups won't help me out of it.

Any real mastership initially takes place inside myself only, coming towards application from there. That's why form training is so important. Because this is where I learn to move without any loss of energy and force. Of Chen Fake it is said that rehearsing the form was 95 per cent of his training. He remained forever undefeated.

Let us focus on the question of self-defence afresh. Let us leave aside at this point the general question about the senselessness of physical violence. The greatest enemies of man are and will remain illness and death by accident. Taijiquan as a preventive for healthcare and training of consciousness is an incredibly efficient martial art, which means it is effective in counteracting the existing dangers which are frequent in today's society.

Let us stay instead with the issue of physical confrontation, dedicating ourselves purely to the incident of physical violence at the moment it occurs. What happens when the tremendous forces of two irate humans collide head-on? Or when the mighty uncontrolled force of any human impacts on the harmless and peaceful nature of a person like ourselves?

I remember my early initial period in my study of Taijiquan. I had been training for only three months, it was Friday night, and as was typical of my youthful exuberance then, I found myself drunk at a party. The host had just been instructed by the police to suspend the party as neighbours had complained about the noise. He asked us to leave his premises quietly. A friend of mine had driven by car. I wished him well for his journey home, jesting that he honk the horn just one more time.

However, I was horrified when he did just that. It was very loud. I was about to look around to see whether the host had observed us. However, not only our host, but his spontaneously hired defence squad of three, were standing right behind me. While turning around I sensed a hard fist approaching my face. I stumbled back. One of them pursued and attacked me. Then a miracle happened: drunk as I was, I first warded off the assailant's one arm, then the other one more strongly. My knee came up into his abdomen, the guy flew aside, and I stood there in an almost perfect Crane stance! I was so pleased with my rapid training success that I didn't realise that the remaining three would then give me a good beating.

One is advised best when one has learnt not to enter perilous situations or else to overcome them without resort to violence. This may be achieved for example by not encouraging anybody to sound the horn at night!

Let us now focus on the most significant point. It doesn't matter what we've done right or wrong beforehand: what is important is the moment of stand-off. With the fist already flying towards us head-on – nothing else matters. At this moment of real conflict, the outcome is usually determined by being tough, by weight advantage and by chance. Despite all the fantasies, it is a sad fact that martial art as we know it from films has to stay right there. In most cases a real stand-off is much clumsier, not choreographed, and most of all, it's much shorter, so short that nothing but endurance matters. Things are different during a tournament. There I can find that I'm out of breath after the first round if I haven't prepared myself properly. The 'round' in a real situation hardly ever goes beyond five seconds, and I'm so driven by adrenaline that I'm not aware of that anyway. That doesn't mean that strength is not important, quite the opposite. Weight being applied is very effective, and difficult to counter by technique. In most cases the race is run before I'm able to realign. No time then to learn about the opponent's weak points, create tactical strategies and so on; all this belongs to competition. During a real stand-off it's simply two forces exploding upon each other, and in most cases that's it; velocity is of secondary importance. I have witnessed someone being smashed with a bottle from behind, and it broke into a thousand pieces. The attacked person turned around unhurriedly, and boxed the assailant's ears, just like Bud Spencer! In a real case only a proper blow will succeed, and furthermore, only one which results in a knock-out. Anything else is easily overcome by adrenaline, which will make the assailant even more aggressive and he will not feel the impact until the fight is over. I have learnt by my own experience that sudden kicks into the abdomen provoked me into nothing but a panicked straightforward attack, while a few minutes back I would have still been ready to negotiate. In football they call this an own goal. However, hitting the abdomen is favoured in all the books dealing with these issues. We should absolutely respect the difference between theory and practice. Most schools of martial art rather resemble a university that has long lost the relationship with reality. Here we also find the reason why one goal is common among all traditional martial arts: bringing so much power into one blow, there is no need for any further action, because who knows whether I'll get a second chance at all.

Modern systems often suggest many minor strikes. The question is, however, whether enough time is left or whether I will not have been overrun long before. Reviewing my numerous observations of real confrontations I consider an evolution towards 'quick and painful' as being much more effective. It's fascinating to witness again and again what a large number of strikes a human can take as long as these aren't final, and once the person under attack isn't fully in control of his mind any more. He seems to simply ignore the strikes. That's why street bullies are often much more dangerous than martial artists. They have no stylised technique, but lots of real expertise, and they do not care about pain. What should also not be forgotten is the unfair inequality of mental attitude. For such an assailant his intentions always go with some sort of pleasure; he is the initiator of the whole thing, even though he may sense my fear that he is much more at home in this than I am. To me being a peaceful man, it feels alien, and I don't feel enthusiastic about it at all. In reality, I just don't feel like it. As with all things, the one to succeed in most cases will be the one who enjoys it the most. How, after all, can I defeat a dangerous man while feeling halfhearted? And aren't things much worse when I'm paralysed by fear?

Does that mean now that I have to enjoy violence? Or gulp down tons of fodder like Bud Spencer does and measure six feet four at least? For that type of an attack, it certainly wouldn't be the wrong thing to do. Sumo wrestlers whose life consists of fighting know this quite well. But I have goals beyond this, and staying healthy is one of my aims too, because, as mentioned before, this is the most efficient way of self-defence. And besides that, such a readiness for violence cannot be really ethical, so I'll have to find a way that can cope with the heavy weight, power and mental determination of my opponent.

Taijiquan eventually rewards the serious practitioner with a physique consistent with the physical optimum. A well-structured body encountering a heavier yet poorly conditioned one can well compensate for the weight. With Taijiquan I additionally learn to make my body receptive. This is the consequence of an optimised structure that enables the body to open up; therefore I must no longer withstand the pressure – it simply flows through my body and into the ground. This allows the Taijiquan expert to keep standing effortlessly. Out of this balance it becomes possible to re-direct considerable forces, and to make them veer off the targeted centre. Another important point is that with an optimised inner and outer structure the parts of the body collaborate in the very best way, retrieving the maximum of force from out of my body. In this way I can succeed in releasing the entire energy from out of my body mass, an effect never achieved by plain muscle training.

Just imagine please that you give out a punch with your arm as powerfully as you can. Or that you are able instead to bring your entire mass into this punch, performing it with faultless inner closure, body and mind perfectly attuned as one. A heavy man has weight, but he may not be able to apply it. Again it's not *what* but *how*. Once I'm able to bring out my joint forces without any resistance of either mental or physical kind and without any blockages, with my body being receptive and centred, I will not only be able to counter even the most massive force; moreover, it's going to feel as easy as child's play. A new pupil weighing 120 kg (I am 70 kg) during the first lesson asked me for a test, saying that he had heard something of my power of stability and he wished to try to bring me off balance. I agreed, and he reached for me. I have to add here that we were just about to take some photos, and my fiancée who stood on one side was busy adjusting the new camera. So while we were standing there, I explained to her the workings of the camera. In between I told the pupil: 'OK, get started, please.' 'What does he mean, get started?' I heard him ask the people around in amazement. I looked at him; his face had turned red and sweat was pouring from his face. I hadn't realised that he had started long before; I hadn't realised the very meaning of the term.

When the power of someone flows through me and when I'm able to position my centre and my balance over the opponent's, even the strongest impact feels as gentle as a breeze.

So the foundation is a structure able to be not only resilient to all, but also able to ward off or re-direct and bring an enormous amount of force involving the entire body into any movement. However, this is not achieved by resisting or by huge efforts, but instead by being open and by being centred. Thus I am capable of applying these techniques with efficiency. Without this foundation, any technique remains insufficient. Provided with a firm foundation, all techniques may be applied with much more ease. Locks don't need to be opened by force; they are sensed. It is just the same with a good punch, a strike, a wrestling manoeuvre or similar. You just flow through.

The nature of a conflict is thus determined by man himself, that is by his structure and his mental condition, rather than by the techniques he has learned by heart, otherwise the trained fighter wouldn't be able to foresee the outcome of a fight. He does not focus on his opponent's set of technical variations, but will rather sense the reactions outlined by the parameters named above.

Mental attitude is very important. Untrained street bullies – I'm talking about people who have never seen a martial arts school from inside unless it was in trying to beat up the teacher – are so dangerous partly because they share an attitude. They aren't shy of violence, they want some action, and they are fully engaged. The self-defender is routinely reluctant to engage with violence, he doesn't invite the situation and he feels uncomfortable. In most cases he also feels great fear. In contrast to the assailant he is not wholeheartedly involved. In Taijiquan this reads: 'Xin yu yi yu qi yu li he', which means to say: 'The heart joins with awareness (imagination), this creates energy, and this will create the force.' (See also Chapter 4, 'Taijiquan – A Martial Art').

This means in turn that if heart and mind are in conflict, I will be ambiguous inside and too weak to defend myself against an undivided force. This maxim is of profound truth and basically the most important rule, i.e. constitutional secret of any self-defence. Within my mind I have to achieve clarity and oneness with my inner nature if perfect efficiency is the goal.

The form is also essential for this. It's the form that develops a calm mind and clarity in observation; then I can face situations with a neutral attitude. By way of training I go deeper and deeper into my physical and mental balance. Only with body and mind being balanced will the latter gain calmness as it no longer is too busy with re-balancing. When the mind is at ease it can become receptive and transparent to myself, and in the course of time I may then understand myself and all other matters. In this way I will achieve a profound self-confidence, and fear will decrease. I can then approach challenges much more confidently.

We once did a test sequence by asking several test persons to take a normal standing position. Under a sudden surprise attack they reacted with a shocked movement, in most cases in a passive backward move that brought them off balance. Again we placed a number of test persons; this time however we corrected their posture carefully and aligned them to their centre. Again another surprise attack. This time hardly any shock could be observed, neither could it be called a *reaction*. What took place with calmness and clarity in a progressive mode adapted to the attack was *action*.

The body knows itself much better than we think we know it. Sensing a threat, it reacts with a kind of emergency braking. That is, it searches for a passive shelter, being unable however to address the problem. Being within its strength, however, it no longer needs to take cover and can instead do what needs to be done. Balance is very essential.

Initially this is mainly achieved by practising the Standing Post, and after that I build up all that follows: the concept of the silk-exercises is the path to fully unfold my internal energy within the proper structure. Beyond this and with an advanced understanding, I then become capable of 'reading' the opponent's energies, and most of all, to adapt myself to them.

This means that on the basis of my centred structure, I learn about the opponent's motivations and attacks before they have been realised. I'm already on my way to the point where my opponent is still planning to get started, but he is so involved in his action that he can no longer retreat. So he is preset, and I have parried him before he becomes aware of his action. His attack in a way builds up a bridge for me. This results in another crucial saying: 'The last shall be the first', namely, I'm the last to start and the first to arrive, and not even by way of speed.

These mechanisms are really understood only by way of one's own advanced training; at least they become clear once they have been practised. I'll try and explain:

A traditional image would be: the opponent lashes out at me and I react, being so fast due to prior speed-training that I can outclass the attacker's speed and counter-attack. This may serve as an approach, but not in Taijiquan. I have often demonstrated myself how even very slow punches could not be countered any more. What if they come at me fast and without warning? Another concept is required if I wish to reach a high level. Also as I get older, my speed is unlikely to improve.

In the Taiji-form I work to make body and mind unite. That is, I bring body and mind so close to each other that they merge. This creates a new form of consciousness, opening areas where the non-expert can no longer follow, which is why he cannot anticipate my movements any more, whether they are fast or slow.

The more intensely the merger between body and mind results in unity, the shorter the transmission path between the instances will become. We feel the wish for a movement and want to perform it. This requires us to cover a time-span: from catching the thought through to the determination of the act and its transfer to the related nerves and muscles, followed by their contraction up to the movement being executed. So it is awareness that stands at the beginning, followed by movement and the path of transmission and execution at its end.

The closer the approach between body and mind becomes, the shorter this distance will become, up to the ideal situation where the mind controls the movement while being suspended within. Then there is, so to speak, no difference between mind and movement.

The following drawings illustrate this:

Figure 15

If I react inside the same dimension of movement as the assailant does, I can't help being too late if I just copy my opponent's move starting only after he does. Our drawing now looks like this:

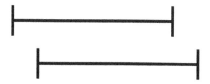

Figure 16

The second line shows my reaction, and consequently I'm too late.

I have to anticipate and analyse the attack (how will he hit out? Or will he kick? Which leg...etc.) I have to choose a proper counter technique, and my response will be disproportionately late:

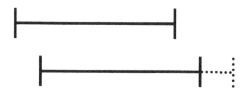

Figure 17

And this is how the drawings look when body and mind are more and more becoming one:

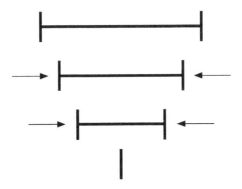

Figure 18

The less of a separation distance I have here, the more space I will gain for moving inside the opponent's attack. Not only does this imply a large amount of freedom, it even seems as if I 'saw' the attack before it has taken place. Therefore even if I start from the last position, I'll arrive however in the first. In fact I move inside an intermediate range unknown to the opponent and which is thus invisible to him.

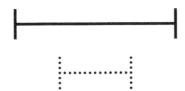

Figure 19

This enables the expert to fend off even a sudden attack with ease, for this range of perception is no longer coupled with consciousness and not subject to mental reflection.

What is further added is the moment of 'becoming one' with the opponent's energy. The classics call this: 'The opponent moves slowly, and I move slowly. The opponent moves fast, and I move fast.'

In the complete sense this means that in a way I join with the opponent's energy. I move precisely within the same intention as my opponent does, yet I'm always ahead of him. If the opponent attacks slowly, I'll handle it slowly. If he's fast, I'll be fast. So this also means: if the attack is serious, my response will be likewise. If it is just the action of a friend playing around, I'll move incorrectly so that my response will be deliberately ineffective.

Two examples of this: whenever I'm aboard a car in the passenger seat and the driver performs a frightened and sudden braking manoeuvre I find myself immediately in a combat posture with my fists clenched. The other passengers are always enthusiastic about my fast reaction skills, but I am not. Because what's supposed to be great about it? If we were sitting in a car and almost had a crash, and someone came flying through the windscreen, I would certainly not have wished to box him. Neither can I fend off glass fragments in this way either. I judged my reaction unsuitable. One day, I was aboard a taxi, and a little boy suddenly leapt right in front of the vehicle, leaving no time for braking. He had jumped out of a parking bay in front of our car because he wanted to get to his friends on the other side of the road, and he hadn't seen us. He smashed against the windshield, flew from there across our car and landed between two others. He stood up, shook himself and told me (I was already by his side): 'Darn stupid, I'm going to be in trouble with my mum!' Fortunately, nothing had happened to him; the windscreen however was broken. What's interesting about it in relation to our issue: again there was no room for considerations, again the movement was spontaneous. However, this time I had not taken up a boxing position; I rather covered my face with my hands as in the Crane posture, which was probably the best move for such a situation.

On another occasion I was at a bank filling in a payslip. A lady friend of mine saw me and crept up from behind wishing to pretend a surprise attack. I only heard a loud scream and felt something coming closer. Before I knew what was happening I heard myself scream out loud and had already stepped up against her. Not until then did I realise that she had stopped. Everybody in the bank was startled; we however burst out laughing.

It was always the same with duels: when friends were kidding me or when I found myself in a friendly sparring situation, I did make mistakes. In the case of a real challenge, however, or a surprise attack, I did not.

This is the meaning of the statement: 'The opponent moves slowly, and I move slowly. The opponent moves fast, and I move fast.' I'm acting within the set of facts given by the situation. The result is major control as it eliminates the error of over- or under(re)action, which is the reason why Taijiquan training includes so very little of punching the sandbag. The form, however, must be practised and corrected properly, and abiding with the principles, otherwise it lacks substance.

Finally the training of the Pushing Hands and of combat, which are the preparation for a real situation, aren't insignificant, but they are of secondary importance and are thus given less space. Moreover, in Taijiquan they are rather soft because of the reasons mentioned before, because this is the best way of accessing these energies. Subtle adjustments require calm, not a hectic pace. These aspects essentially contribute to a martial artist's healthcare. During the training sessions of many other fighting systems, more injuries occur than the average civilian will ever suffer during his entire life. Would we call that effectiveness?

Chen Wangting had objected to this as early as in the 17th century when he created Taijiquan. Let us conclude again with the wise statement of Zhen Manjing: 'Properly applied, Taijiquan is the best martial art, poorly trained it is the worst!'

TAIJIQUAN AND ITS 13 TECHNIQUES OF MOVEMENT

Understanding the basic pattern of the 13 techniques of movement is an essential step in understanding Taijiquan. The 13 techniques of movement are:

Peng	balance in all directions, ward off
Lü	to yield
Ji	to press
An	to push

Cai	to bring down
Lie	to separate
Zhou	elbow
Kao	shoulder
Teng	to strike from bottom to top
Shan	to yield from top to bottom
Zhe	to turn, to wind, to fold
Kong	empty
Huo	to stay within the principle, being lively, agile

Peng, the first concept, quite reasonably stands at the beginning. Mentioned in books often as 'forward defence', it appears in the dictionary as 'inflating', and that is quite the right term. It is the basis for everything. No matter from which direction and in whichever way an attack may happen, I can take up the force and pass it back, standing inside my centre – nothing will bring me out of it.

It's like a balloon. The more it becomes inflated with air, the more it billows from inside to the outside synchronously in all directions. If I press it on one spot it will give way, if I let go it goes back to the shape it had before. This is exactly how we wish to be, but much more resilient and well-rooted. The better our stance, the more resilient the balloon will be as with our roots. It can be compared to a circus tent being equally stable in all directions, adjusted around the centre pole.

There is a very good film entitled 'Pushhands', about a grandfather of a family travelling to join his emigrated son in America. He is very traditional, and of course he is a master of Taijiquan. His Americanised family doesn't really get along with him any more, and so he runs away and even though he is old, he starts working as a dishwasher. When he is no longer welcome there he refuses to leave. First the restaurant staff try to push him out, later even the firefighters intervene, yet nobody is capable of moving him off the spot. This is a way to express *Peng*. *Peng* means being able to hand back any attack and to dissipate it without losing one's own structure. My Shifu once told me: 'The mountain comes first, then comes everything that bounces off it.'

Lü, as all further techniques, requires *Peng*. Only someone standing inside his centre can apply techniques in a convincing way. However, *Peng* means more than just centre. This 'inflating' creates a centred counter-pressure that destroys the assailant's balance by way of his own attack. *Lü* means to give way to the impact forced upon me, be it a punch, a strike, a kick or similar. The point is to surrender to this force in a way that I can make the force run past me while still being in its control. This is called 'sticking', which is in contrast to the normal evasion. Contact with the opponent enables me to get out of the force's way and to still control it.

The third technique *Ji* is translated by the term 'press'. There are many interpretations. The most pragmatic and thus most frequent is that of bringing the opponent off balance by way of soft pressure. This doesn't mean a friendly slap, but an action preparing the one following by a soft forward pressure. This forward pressure is soft but determined. The opponent normally doesn't perceive that or doesn't take it seriously, therefore it is very effective. A comparison: bar-room bullies routinely open their action by pushing the victim. This is often accompanied with words like, 'hey dude', 'are you scared?' or similar. It's not important what is being said at this moment; the important thing is that something is spoken, in a way as a bridge. The meaning of the ritual is: first, the bully assures himself of his predominance, which becomes obvious when no adequate response from the 'opponent' follows, when he is intimidated. The second reason is that a push brings the victim either off balance or to step backwards, which makes an attack easier. What seems natural behaviour to the bar-room warrior is a veritable principle in Taijiquan. No, I don't mean pushing someone on a Saturday night! The principle consists of staying aware of one's own balance and pushing the other slightly off his own. This is preparation prior to real discharge of energy, so its effect is similar to *Lü*, bringing the other off balance. Both techniques of course can also stand alone. Giving way at the right moment (*Lü*) can bring the opponent to the ground. Pressing at the right moment (*Ji*) can mean that the opponent is bounced off. Often however they serve in preparing the actual technique. This actual technique is not separate however from *Ji* or *Lü*. The discharge of energy is accompanied by 'pressing'. Hence, the purpose of 'pressing' is to deprive the opponent of anything he may counter with at that moment as he is busy trying to regain his balance. Furthermore he has no comparable energy as he is no longer able to move from his centre. *Ji* is often used in a diagonal setting, which makes it easier to deprive the opponent of his balance, as I'm not pushing against his standing leg.

An is the push. Here (basically as well in all other techniques) a large amount of energy can be released. It is very hard on the outside, soft and adaptable inside. It follows in most cases a previous action and is performed after the opponent has already lost his balance. *Ji* and *An* are different insofar as *Ji* is applied diagonally, while *An* aims direct or rather downward first. *Ji* often follows the opponent's attempt to make us run empty; it prohibits that. *An* in turn often undermines *Ji*.

When it is applied without a previous action, *An* can be divided into two phases. In phase one the opponent is uprooted; in the second phase he gets thrown off or downwards.

Cai means 'to bring down'. The term means that all energies are aimed at directly grounding the opponent. *Lie* means 'to separate'. Energy is applied in such a way that the other's body is deflected in at least two different directions synchronously, so that he will no longer be able to continue and will lose his balance. Both techniques are often carried out with leverage.

Zhou means elbow, which includes all techniques performed with the elbows. *Kao,* 'shoulder', describes all shoulder techniques. If my fist gets intercepted, I don't stop but keep flowing; this makes the elbow rise. Should both hand and elbow be blocked, I keep flowing again, and what appears is the shoulder.

Or I can re-direct the opponent with my hands past my centre only to hit him hard with my elbow or my shoulder at his weak spot where he is unbalanced. Elbow and shoulder are used not only for striking or pushing, but just like the hands for deflecting, giving way or pressing as well.

Elbow and shoulder are synonyms as well for medium and close combat distance. Hands and fists cover the long distance, elbows the entire space between hands and body; thus the knees are involved as well. *Kao* depicts the close range, thus also applications of the hip, the chest and the entire trunk region.

In Taijiquan all techniques can be performed with any part of the body. We don't have just two fists; our entire body is in a way made of fists. It is possible to discharge energy from any tiny section of the body. While practising the form in a calm way, energy flows continuously through my whole body, through every single part of it. From any point however where energy is flowing I can emit it and bring it out explosively. Here, the flow of energy is rapidly and compactedly directed at a focus point. Whether this happens with the hand, the lower arm, the upper arm, the shoulder, the chest or wherever else is therefore basically of no importance. It depends however on the level of training. The second form and special exercises are required to do this. Accordingly, all techniques can of course be applied with the elbow (*Zhou*) or the shoulder (*Kao*). Taijiquan's shoulder punch in particular has become very famous.

'Striking from the bottom to the top', *teng*, can be identified well with the stance of *shan tong bei*, 'protecting the back and turning around'. The moment I've swerved downward (*shan*), my elbow is moved to strike from bottom to the top. This is an example of *teng*, that is, combined with the next, the tenth technique, *shan*. During the sequence described, I therefore dodge downward, giving way to the opponent's push in a way that forces him to follow down. At the moment he loses his balance, my elbow jolts forward and beats him. Both these techniques *teng* and *shan* can be applied together in manifold ways as well as separately from each other.

Zhe is a term I'd like to translate here as 'twisted' or 'wound' respectively together with 'guiding downwards in circle'. The opponent is led downwards along with his force, and his entire body participates. In this way his body slumps to the ground, comparable to the swirl in the bathtub when the water is sucked into the drainpipe.

Kong, 'the emptiness', describes the phenomenon of not being there, at least not where the opponent suspects us to be. By learning this technique I do not intend to call for a *Ninja* job training where we dissolve into haze and suddenly appear behind the opponent. Still, he who has the ability shall be blessed...

The true meaning of *Kong* is very subtle and not only describes the external 'not being there'. The meaning is to be understood rather in a subtle context. Intending to push or beat someone implies having seen him and that's what the entire action is usually built upon. If the opponent moves, that is if he changes his position, I perceive this and can adjust myself. What am I to do however if I feel the person is still standing there while in fact he or she has already moved? All of a sudden the point of attack is empty, there is nothing, and the bridge I have built to reach my counterpart collapses. I fall into a hole and thus lose a large part of my balance. Within mastership such processes happen on a highly refined and textured level, so that the master no longer even needs to swerve. He may even be touched, and yet where the body, the intuition (and the mind as well) suspect substance, there is emptiness, and where emptiness has been suspected there is suddenly substance. Tremendous punches can be performed in this way with little effort, and great power may suddenly turn against the initiator where he encounters emptiness when he had expected substance. The body reacts on a reverse path, and this may cause the attacker to be suddenly thrown away a distance of several metres. Encountering *Kong* is a profound philosophical moment. It's like stepping down a stairway in the dark. If there is one step more than I expected I instantly fall into nothingness and lose control. If I'm being pushed aside in the same instant, things do get dramatic...

In order not to 'grab into the void' I have to learn to control all my moves from my centre, and only from there. If I align my moves, whether physical or mental, with an image or an expectation depending on anything else but myself, I'll lose my balance because I've been counting on something external. Once again, Push Hands is like real life: if I lean on the counterpart, forming a kind of a bridge, I depend not only on him being there and moving the way I expect him, I'm fixed in my own movements as well. However, moving from out of my centre and retaining this I'm free and independent within my moves. Then it is no longer important how the other acts, and I can fully accept him. Briefly: if I depend upon myself I don't need to depend upon others. If nobody can be dangerous for me, I can virtually withstand (i.e. 'stand') them all. This means I can afford to feel sympathy for these people. I don't have to do anything negative because I feel fear of being left without power or control. That's why defying the inner enemy first is so crucial, and it's the rationale of the saying: 'He who knows the other is prudent, he who knows himself is wise.'

The last technique is *huo*, agility, liveliness or adaptability and staying inside the principle of movement. Just as *peng*, this technique is part of all other techniques as well. It means that body and mind can perform their techniques with velocity and intensity. No matter at which speed or activity a movement is being performed, the essential aspect of *huo* is never to infringe the principle of movement. It also means that body and mind are capable of adapting to any speed or movement that an opponent may show. 'The opponent moves slowly, and I move slowly. The opponent moves fast, and I move fast', as the classics teach us. This means I can adapt to him at any instant and encounter him the way he leads me to, from the deepest calm to the most tremendous aggression. It means that I can counter and withstand any energy and apply it against the opponent. Therefore, in anything I do, *huo* never abandons the principle that lies within movement and spirit.

All 13 techniques flow into each other, and they result from each other. *Peng* is always present. *Huo* must never get lost. Neither of them can be without the other. A move with the shoulder can have the quality of *Lü*, an elbow can correspond with *Cai*. *Cai* and *An* can be applied at the same time and so on. Often several of these concepts have to be applied at the same time and combined with more so that the opponent cannot follow.

To give an example: the opponent wants to push me, I yield (*Lü*), and in a controlled way I make his force run empty. If I have no structure, my arms get entangled with his, and I stumble backwards. If my structure is good however and *Peng* is developed I can take up the force, re-direct it and give way to it. I remain inside my strength. If, for example, I turn right to make the force run past me, my opponent may identify my intent and resists me. Because he senses when things don't work the way he wants them to, he will try to correct himself. Again this may cause me to lose my balance. It's like someone running away from someone else. If he turns right, the pursuer will turn right. If he turns round the corner to the left, the pursuer will turn left as well. This, by the way, is the Taiji principle as well: adequate pursuit will drive the opponent into the corner out of which he cannot free himself any more. If I'm skilled, I work in a three-dimensional mode in several directions. I'll direct his pushing hand downwards and sideways as well. That means *Cai* and *Lu* work together on the base of *Peng*. Now it is as if an attacker pursued two escapees: they separate and flee in various directions: who is the pursuer to run after? He cannot catch both of them. As in this case both are one he'll be no longer able even to reach one. Due to this lack of orientation, the attacker falls into a hole and loses his centre. In this case a shoulder punch (*Kao*) would be adequate. This aims directly at the opponent's weak spot, because in the line of attack he has no leg to parry the force. This makes it easy to see how 'four ounces can defeat 1000 kilograms'. So therefore with little force I can push someone far away.

Modern Taiji literature and more modern Taiji systems often subdivide the 13 techniques of Taijiquan into the five lines of movement and the eight techniques (energies) of movement. They are mostly taught in this way in all Taiji systems outside the classical Chen-style. However, the last five techniques have been neglected.

Traditionally the eight moving techniques consist of 13. The five types of stepping are not a part of this; they represent a centre pillar of the system and are not part of the 13 movements. Why the five techniques later became lost in more modern systems is to be explained later in the book.

On the correlations of the 13 movements alone a thick book could be written.[2] The 13 movements can progress towards a very profound understanding of Taijiquan.

At this point we will focus for a brief moment on the beautiful transfer of the 13 basic techniques into the modern and more intellectual understanding of Taijiquan. It is composed however at this point of only eight techniques and the five directions.

The five directions of movement stand for the five elements: wood, fire, earth, metal and water. Each direction is attributed to one of these elements. In China the five elements traditionally represent the five primal materialities out of which all other phenomena can be deducted. The five elements in turn can be traced back to Yin and Yang, and these again evolve out of *Wuji*. The first eight techniques of movement refer to the eight trigrams that represent the single changing phases of Yin and Yang in the never-ending circle. So we have all things and their

---

2   In fact, the author has since written this book in German, entitled *Schiebende Hände*, published by Lotus Press (publisher's note).

changes: the five elements and the eight trigrams give a basic description of all that is in life including the changes and the course that things may take. And it is the same in Taijiquan. A true master of Taijiquan realises things the way they are and knows about their provenance, their changes and their re-appearance. He knows not only the mechanics of duelling but of life in general. Mastering Taijiquan also means mastering Taiji, which in turn means knowing the Dao. A beautiful goal – and a long trail, yet even the longest journey begins with the first step. As always, the path is the goal.

Based on the beauty of this philosophical cross-over we may perhaps formulate an explanation that accounts for the abbreviation of 13 techniques down to eight. In the times of upheaval, the times of Yang Chengfu, when Taijiquan was transposed from its military background to the civil population (the Chen family changed from an uninterrupted line of commanders of war to a social community of martial arts), much work was done on the philosophical structure or its consistency with the Daoist worldview as well. It was not until then that terms like 'Taijiquan' were used. Inside the Chen-clan the only terms to be used were 'The way of the fist' (*Quanfa*), namely, 'Boxing art of the Chen family' (*Chen shi*). Yang Luchan still called it 'soft boxing' (*ruan quan*), and it was now recognised intellectually, discovered, classified and systemised. However, all the talking and discussion about Taijiquan will not replace even one minute of training if I haven't taken to the right path. Being on the right path, however, I will learn all the philosophy during my progress anyway, via my own body.

Taijiquan was thus adopted by the intellectuals during the first half of the past century. One should not condemn this, however. It is here that nowadays the most widespread type of theoretical Taijiquan is rooted (talking a lot, training a little), but without this way of dissemination it may never have reached us here in the West. By way of the philosophical presentation, it gained access to wider circles of the population, including those who reject martial arts as such because they wrongly believe them to be violent. The gates were thus opened wide for Taijiquan to spread across the world, and simplification of the training issues were another natural consequence of this process.

Martial art is not violent; indeed it is the opposite of violence. Elementary questions about the nature of being human are found here, of life and death, of power and being powerless. It is the direct reason for life itself, and the pursuit of absolute freedom.

In truth this deep philosophical knowledge has been the mother of Taijiquan ever since its inception. As already mentioned, Chen Wangting created Taijiquan in the middle of the 17th century, based on the experience of the decline of all living things and their continuous change. He accomplished this philosophical basis using the techniques of martial art so that these truths could be studied in the living organism by way of movement. Chen Xin (Pinsan, 1849–1929) described the theoretical and philosophical–spiritual foundations of classical Taijiquan in his unique work *Chen shi taijiquan tu shuo*.

Whichever way interests may shift; all that is has always been before. We only have to search for it in the right place.

TAIJIQUAN AND ITS FIVE MOVING DIRECTIONS

The five directions of movement in Taijiquan have a symbolic meaning as well as a pragmatic one. They consist of:

qian jin	front
hou tui	back
zuo gu	left
you pan	right
zhong ding	middle

The middle is clear: my place is where I stand. As a symbol it means that I don't just stand there, but that I am also rooted; my Qi is sunk into *Dantian*, my spirit being calm and concentrated. Middle means that wherever I am I remain within the best of my structure, relying on myself, on my own centre and nothing else. Now I can act from out of myself remaining independent from outer influences. This allows me to view things without any bias and with objectivity. This is the same within *Tuishou* as it is within life itself. This way of being centred does not only imply that we must not lean on the opposite person during *Tuishou*. We would plunge if the substance we held on to suddenly changed into emptiness. The same happens if we apply too much force, so that it goes beyond our own centre. In this case we lose our centre just as the point we rely on, in this case the opponent, doesn't act the way we anticipated. This means in general that loss of balance occurs whenever when we go beyond our centre, anticipating something which then doesn't happen in the way we thought. Even during the form we routinely rely on external things. Our eyes continuously adhere to outer appearances, so defining our body in its balance. A simple test will prove this: just stand on one leg. Now close your eyes. Your balance increasingly wavers. What it lacks is the outer brake. 'Centre' in this respect really does mean being inside my middle. Out of this balance I then make contact with the outside, yet without getting stuck. This principle of the centre makes us realise how much we do rely on outer things in all fields of life, being unable therefore to act without bias and out of ourselves. This becomes very obvious in *Tuishou*. If we lean on another person in order to compensate by some sort of a bridge-function for his weight and his pressure, we succeed only at the cost of our own bias and attachment. My movements themselves are fixed, and I can no longer move freely. Moreover, I can easily be knocked sideways. Things are different when I am able, despite even considerable pressure from outside, to stand within myself and balance that pressure, without adhering myself to anything coming from outside. This way I remain free and 'invulnerable', since I am never really reached. My centre is never occupied. This enables me to accept everything, because it can flow right through me without endangering my centre. Stress falls from me, and I no longer need to stiffen; instead I can rather yield.

The preparation stance, i.e. the concept of the Standing Post, pervades the entire form. Its structure reappears in every movement. It is the same in self-defence. No matter what I do, no matter where I move, I will not give up my centre. It is the energetic connection going across the meridian-points *baihui* and *huiyin* that connect and unify heaven, earth and man as centred and aligned on one line.

We should try not to interpret the preparational stance in an external sense, moving into meditational stances everywhere and any time. When I was a youth I got teased at parties for trying to stand that way.

Not even in situations of self-defence do we stand exactly as during the exercise, because, as the word itself tells us, it's an exercise. In fact we seemingly stand normally, but using all the advantages we've gained from this exercise. The higher the level, the less important the outer form becomes, so that with increasing skill the question of how to stand is no longer relevant. I must be able to transfer what's inside, and when I'm able to maintain that, things from the outside lose their importance.

How strange would it look if someone set out to give a demonstration of his rooting power, needing to get himself into position first or perhaps complete a round of Qigong? It is either there or it is not. So we are centred and, according to our level, within our middle. All we have to do now is to follow whatever may come.

'If the opponent pushes forward, you shall withdraw', say the classics. That does not mean to flee from the scene in despair, but to open space backwards for an intruding force in order to intercept it at its dead point. 'If the opponent withdraws, you shall push forward', they also say. When the opponent has reached that dead point with his attack, he has to withdraw for a short time to start a new one. This should not be imagined in terms of distinct time intervals but rather as acting within the here and now. Right at the moment of my opponent's withdrawal, I push forward. I apply the same principle if the opponent raises his arm for a punch. His fist moves back a little for a moment. It's here where I push forward, the opponent's centre lies open, and I can capture it. When I'm able to align with the opponent's energy, flowing along with him, all these processes take place by themselves; the opponent determines my motion. As my centre is the stronger one, my movement of 'following' him is not only superior to his, I'm also the first to arrive, in line with the classical sentence: 'The opponent does not move, I do not move. The opponent moves, I'm already there.'

I can also directly cut the opponent's action and stop him by forward thrust while he is still approaching. This thrust however never goes beyond my own centre.

'If the opponent pushes forward, I shall withdraw. If the opponent withdraws, I shall push forward.' To complete our classical quotations: 'I stick to it'. That enables me to intrude into intervals of time which I can sense but not measure. As for me, I am flowing circular and moving in spirals. Push forward, move back, just as my opponent suggests, keeping him under steady control, so that I don't need to re-coordinate and use a pause to recharge. The opponent cannot intrude into my centre, but centre control remains important, for my own of course, but also for the opponent's course. This means I'm not only standing perfectly balanced, but also by positioning I keep targeting the centre of the opposed. Neither his hand or foot, nor necessarily his centre, but rather the spot where I can destroy his centre. That is the point I cross and so reach his centre. Whether it's a knock-out blow, a throw, a punch, a mental or a physical control or whatever, is determined by the situation. Wherever my movement may go, it always aims at maintaining my own centre and controlling my opponent's centre. In this way I will neither be distracted nor lose my tranquillity, and I'll never lose sight of my goal. The movements of my opponent (physical or mental) provide a connection for me in order to gain control over his centre. It's like the image of the snake coiling around one's neck. With any attempt at a rescue move it will close in on the emerging gap, coming closer to destroying the centre in its attempt to strangle me.

The body is never at rest; it moves permanently. Even while we believe we are at rest there is always motion, because we live. That's why motion must not be imagined in large forms only. The micro-movements are intended as well, and since these are steady, an enormous tempo emerges. In the instant of the beginning, the end is already determined. Therefore in an ideal case a fight does not even take place, because in its very beginning it has been overcome, decided and finished.

These basic principles go for frontal movements, those at the back, as well as for those going sideways. What the five directions of movement depict are the various options (including all directions in between, all diagonals) of moving myself or giving way in all directions and consequently following my opponent. The combinations of all these choices are also practised during Tuishou. With its stepwork during partner exercises it almost resembles an old-time folkdance. One might assume of course that it may have been a secret training method to keep the ruling authorities from finding out about the dangerous nature of Taijiquan. All jokes aside, during the Cultural Revolution period it was extremely difficult and dangerous for the Chen family and certainly many others to train Taijiquan or other traditional arts. In Chenjiagou as in many other places there was hardly anything to eat, and the political situation was in fact so tense that death was feared if one appeared in public with Taijiquan. Often training was impossible simply because of the famine, and because of the political situation, the Chen family preferred to train covertly behind closed doors, only answering detailed inquiries in the basement. Interestingly the current government is trying to make a simplified version of Taijiquan popular.

Back to the issue: once I have mastered the task of following my opponent through any of his actions no matter which direction they take, I'm able to control him. Following him this way in all directions may appear to be achieved by covering distances and taking steps, but it is also achieved while standing or by subtle movement.

Once I have this control there is only one who will win – and that's me. So the five moving directions not only depict the stepwork, but any type of direction the opponent may choose in order to get a hold over me. Control does not mean to intercept any opponent action 100 per cent; that would be impossible. It means to continuously control the opponent's balance. I can achieve that by bringing him off his centre no matter what action he may take, and by not allowing him to find the way back. That's the meaning of the word control.

The moving directions can of course work together. If the opponent strikes me I can, for example, take in the punch, let's say, to the left and give way while coming forward in the same instant on the other side and launch a strike myself. If the body moves in its entirety this is one enclosed movement. If I'm giving way on the left my left shoulder will automatically move backwards. This is released from the hip and the *Dantian*. This will bring the right shoulder forward, and I only have to allow the motion to flow ahead into the arm. In the same instant I have not only secured my balance and intercepted the attack, but performed a very efficient counter-attack on the other side. This is what moving forward and back at the same time means.

'Looking left and looking right', as it is often described, also includes circular steps which enable me to walk around the opponent and make it very hard for him to get hold of me. There are many reasons for applying circular steps. They appear as various concepts of application as well. In *Baguazhang* the circle-step has become very famous. Setting the steps at angles as well as combinations of diagonals and straight

CHEN

lines (triangles for example) in order to get out of the way of an attack may be adopted to access the opponent's weak spot, or take him up into a spiral, be it externally by steps or in a minimised mode by impulse – all these are variations of 'left, right, front and back'. The centre is the basis of it all.

Beyond this, the five directions of movement also conceal many different symbolisms and martial principles. They are represented by the Five Elements. A short note on them may serve at this point:

1. 'Front', *qian jin*, stands for the element metal. It characterises going to the front, to enter and intrude (the opponent's centre for example).

2. 'Back', *hou tui*, stands for the element wood. It characterises stepping back and warding off the opponent.

3. 'Left', *zuo gu*, stands for the element water. It characterises awareness, perception, recognising (the opponent's intention).

4. 'Right', *you pan*, stands for the element fire. It characterises willpower, acting in reality and truthfully, 'to move like the Seven Stars' (in closure and entirely in one direction).

5. 'Middle', *zhong ding*, stands for the element earth. It characterises the genesis, the maintaining of the centre.

ON BREATHING

Respiration during Taijiquan should be calm and natural. It should not be artificially attuned to motion. By and large, rules like 'raise = breathe in; sink = breathe out' rectify it, but they should not be overemphasised.

The body itself takes air for breathing. We might forget our keys, our appointment, yes, perhaps even our training, but we never forget our breathing. Even while we're asleep, we're breathing. Except for extreme conditions of shock or literally breathtaking moments, we don't need to worry about our breathing, or its intensity. If the body requires

106

a lot of oxygen, it will take a lot of it; if it needs less, it will take less. We only have to allow it. Respiration adapts to the circumstances.

If our body posture is imbalanced or stiffed, the breath will correspond by being shallow. If our body posture is good and relaxed, the breath can flow deeply and calmly. The breathing we prefer in Taijiquan and the one approved as the healthiest is profound abdominal respiration. Correcting our body as described for the Standing Post makes our respiration flow naturally and in depth. The body in a way has no other choice. If the body for example is leaning backwards too far, the belly's muscles harden up in order to maintain the position. This will block the ventral area, and air cannot enter. It remains higher above, and a shallow pectoral breathing sets in. If I keep forcing the breath downward the condition gets still worse, because in the ventral area there is no room left. Tension and hardening increase, and pain may occur. If instead I correct my physical posture so that the *Dantian* may relax, with hips and chest released and unconstrained, it would be an unnatural feeling to keep the breath in the pectoral section not allowing it to flow downwards. That's why the saying goes:

- Improper physical posture, proper respiration = two mistakes.

- Improper physical posture, improper respiration = only one mistake.

- Proper physical posture = proper effortless respiration.

A natural and correct motion initiates a natural and correct respiration. This way our breathing will always be in tune with our moment, and the better our structure in motion is, the deeper and more relaxed our breathing. This means that breathing is corrected by the inner and outer physical structure.

Just imagine this: you have learnt your Taiji-form, and in an artificial way you have adjusted your breathing to it. With extreme scrutiny you make sure to inhale while raising, to exhale while sinking and so on. You are used to training under normal conditions, at sea-level for instance. However, for a holiday you've gone to the mountains, let's say at an altitude of 3000 metres, and on your first morning there you start your Taiji training. What happens? Your entire system collapses. You become breathless; your heart may even start thumping and laboured breathing will occur. Why?

The oxygen pressure in the air is considerably lower than in your home town. According to your practised breathing method, you maintain the same breathing structure and thus take in much less oxygen than you need.

Imagine now that you allow your breath to flow naturally all the way and in tune with your motion. What do you feel now? Nothing at all. Despite a change in the aerial conditions, your breathing will naturally adapt to your moves, gaining the oxygen it needs. Consistent with the level of your moment, it is calm and deep.

I have had that experience myself. I started my Taiji-training in Germany and was initially very strict in trying to maintain exact breathing control. Raising = inhale deeply, into the belly of course. Sinking = long exhalation, all naturally with ease. This created difficulties at first, almost bringing me close to the perils of choking. After a while however it was OK, and I felt quite well doing my form. Then I made my first excursion to China. One day I found myself in the province of Xinjiang, high up in the 'Turkish' part of China near the marvellously beautiful Tianchi, the Lake of Heaven. That is West of the Gobi desert. There lives, at an altitude of about 3000 metres, an ethnic Chinese minority, the Kasaks, in their yurts, a kind of tent. For a short time I was their guest. Early in the morning I was standing there doing a little round of Taiji, and suddenly and all over again it was like at the beginning. Forced respiration, fear of suffocation, and then I noticed the mountains around me which reminded me a bit of my former days when skiing, how short of breath I was when I dragged myself on my skiis to the ski-lift, and then it entered my mind that something was going wrong. I had to fully re-choreograph my respiration.

Later, when I began my apprenticeship under Master Shen Xijing in Chenjiagou, nobody told me anything about respiration any more. I was puzzled, having heard that breathing is the most important thing about Taijiquan. 'That's exactly why we don't bother about it,' he replied. 'Typically Chinese,' I thought crossly, and stopped worrying about my breathing. As time went by and after several corrections my feeling during the form got deeper, and my entire body now seemed to breathe. One single energy seemed to be flooding my body, guiding and feeding it. Indeed it felt as if all turned into one. And so it continued, more and more.

I met Nuria, my fiancée, at that time. She is Spanish, and I started teaching the natives in her country. One day, while with a number of students on the Teide, the famous volcano in Tenerife, we wished to train there of course. The Teide is more than 3700 metres high, and yet the feeling in its entirety remained. Not until it was over did I remember the experience from Heaven's Lake. It was not to be compared. Respiration now remained calm, deep, discrete while still being profound and powerful. I can say now that the better my physical structure is, the more will my breathing be complete, deep and calm, in an entirely natural way. (You may also relate that to the philosophical aspect of *Wuwei* as described in Chapter 3, 'Taiji – a Philosophy'.)

During a more profound level of Taijiquan training a feeling of an intense respiration evolves, as if one is simply gaining oxygen through every single pore of the body. It no longer feels like breathing through the lungs. This condition occurs once you are able to merge with motion increasingly, slowly blending body and mind towards wholeness, allowing respiration to flow along naturally. All becomes one: body, spirit and breathing. A feeling of absolute wholeness evolves which would turn any attempt of deliberate breath-control into an obstacle. Even the paradoxical ventral respiration comes by itself just by the structure of motion.

Of course there are some exceptions. For example there are some breathing exercises of their own outside the forms, or the breathing characteristic of the complicated small movements within the *Xinjia*, the New Frame, or on deep refinement of motion, or further ahead during explosive movements. Here indeed the point is to regulate the breathing in a distinct way. This is of importance however only for advanced practitioners and at higher levels of Taiji-Gongfu. Once you are among the advanced, you already know by instinct and expertise how to breathe during the related sequences. An intervention is rarely necessary at this point. That's the beautiful thing about Taijiquan: one's got to learn it all, yet everything comes by itself.

ON STUDYING AND TEACHING

Taijiquan after Grandmaster Chen Xiaowang is built up logically step by step. Still questions keep being asked again and again, about how the training and also the teaching should be performed. After all, everybody eventually finds his way of learning Taijiquan if only he or she takes to training with enough enthusiasm. However, in order to offer help, I wish to point out a general concept.

Learning as well as teaching can be divided into three sections. These three sections cannot be separated.

The training of motion

I understand this term in the sense of learning the basic exercises and the training sequences that then follow. First it takes a trained eye in order to copy all the movements properly. The point is to master the correct positioning of the single body parts. Which leg is carrying the weight, which hand points to which direction, where do the eyes look to, when does the weight get shifted, and so on. This process of learning promotes an 'outer' perception of one's own body. No matter that we may be amused by it, it still happens frequently among beginners that they think they have more weight on the right leg while in fact it's the left one. Or that the right hand has to be high and the left one low – the beginner may be harbouring this idea while indeed he is holding them the other way round. In brief, the first thing to learn is to tell right from left.

When later we manage to memorise and perform the course of the single sequences we have achieved a certain ability of an external motor body control. The training which follows after that resembles soft gymnastics. Eventually the movements become soft and relaxed. This corresponds more or less with the level that may be reached during average courses offered in evening classes.

Having performed the form as being studied, the movements are recorded inside the cerebellum, and the cerebrum is open again for further information. We will then proceed to the next stage.

The centring of movement

We now seek to attune all our movements to our centre. The body is aligned in a way that its point of balance together with its energy centre is coordinated at one and the same point: the abdomen. Now we attribute each section of the body to its neighbouring one (for example the upper arm to the forearm), then aligning both internally as well as externally to the centre, the *Dantian*. We try to maintain this during all our movements. In each stance we actually produce the conditions of the Standing Post, carrying it through the entire form without destroying this condition by movement.

It's necessary to understand that this stage deals with a process of continued improvement. Whenever I have mastered this within a certain sector I discover yet another, deeper area that is of a texture even more refined, which in turn is still fully uncoordinated. In the same way it is clear, of course, that the domain of stage 1 continuously develops together with the one of stage 2. And as stage 1 forms the basis for stage 2, they can no longer be separated.

Out of both these stages the basis for the third one is built:

The inner movement

During Standing Post, my inner and outer body can merge. Internal energy is released, and the *Dantian* becomes the centre of movement. As I do not lose this condition any longer during movement, the flow of energy is induced.

At first I learn to initiate this by way of the external motion with corresponding awareness. After I have succeeded in this sufficiently, another important change can take place: the internal motion takes control. Now I no longer move my outer body directly; I am directing the inner energy, and the body follows accordingly. This means that motion becomes real. This requires largely avoiding twists and 'collisions' between the internal and the external body, the goal being eventually to dissolve them completely. This is depicted by the image of the silk-threads. In case of an incorrect movement they either rip or clot. Mistakes during stage 1 and stage 2 naturally impose restrictions on the range of success. Progress however will take me to a state of lightness and ease, in contrast to the 'empty', i.e. the useless movement. This state of relaxation takes a lot of effort to reach, and is therefore all too often misunderstood.

If I have in fact reached inner movement through these processes, the goal is then to keep refining them in depth over and over again. If this takes me to a fully integrated coordination, I shall reach unity.

II

The Chen Style
of Taijiquan

Chen Taijiquan is a logically structured and complex system of martial art and health maintenance. In its own way it is complete. It mainly consists of the following sections, building upon each other but only representing the cornerstones of the system:

1. *Zhanzhuang:*   Standing Post

2. *Cansigong:*   The Silk Exercises

3. *Taolu:*   Forms

4. *Wuqi:*   Weapons

5. *Tuishou:*   Pushing Hands

6. *Fangshengshu:* Applications

As we've learnt in the philosophical section of this book, Taiji evolves from *Wuji*. *Wuji* is the primal state of all that is. Inside *Wuji* the power is concentrated out of which everything comes into existence. The course of practical exercises follows the same path. First the apprentice must learn to experience and practise the state of *Wuji*. He must learn to display his body and bring it into the proper structure so that the energies of the body can fuse, and a unity of body and spirit can be achieved. In this way we can find and develop our centre (Dantian). This is the condition prior to all that follows.

Laotse says: 'Out of one there will come two, out of two come three, and the 10,000 things.' We are amidst those 10,000 things, but they are alienated from naturalness and its destiny, so the training aims at returning to the primal state first, to the beginning. The aim is to then re-develop everything anew in its own direction. The final goal however, after the 10,000 things have found their proper positions, is to find the way back again to the One. This time, however, it is not in order to reason and to re-shape our life, but to turn back against the streaming current to the primal state of being.

The basic exercises will be described in detail on the following pages. Figures written in parentheses indicate in each case when a step during the exercise has been performed.

Chapter 8

The System
of Chen-Taijiquan

ZHANZHUANG – STANDING POST

The purpose of the *Zhanzhuang* exercises is to recreate our personal and natural state of being. We learn to be centred as one with body, mind and energy. *Zhanzhuang* is thus characterised by the state of *Wuji*.

We begin by putting our body and mind at ease. We are standing upright with our feet closed. Top of the head, ears, shoulders, hips and ankles should be aligned as on one line. The body becomes relaxed from top to bottom and held with natural ease. The tongue should touch the palate. In order to calm our mind, we focus and listen to an imaginary point behind us which will detract our attention away from the forebrain. The energy combines with our awareness so that it can flow down the spine. In our mind we're becoming empty and relaxed. Inside our body also we sense a line, a 'thread', along which we release our body and which holds our body together (1). After we've

Figure 20 Chen Xiaowang exercising the Standing Post

Figure 21 *Figure 22* *Figure 23*

Figure 24 *Figure 25*

Figure 21–25 Zhanzhuang: Jan Silberstorff

reached this condition we sink our body a little. We bend our knees a bit in order to relax a bit more, and to be able to open our energy channels. A comforting and pleasant feeling sets in (2). As we are calm, relaxed and the body is slightly sunk, we can shift our weight onto the right leg and raise our left heel without losing our balance (3). We can now safely perform a step to the side. By a distance as wide as our shoulders we first touch down the tip of the toe, then the entire foot in parallel to the right (4). The weight is equally distributed on both legs. All this contributes to the essential correction of the body (5):

Starting from the top of the head: The bodyweight sinks down. Our starting point is our zenith (*Baihui*), down from which we 'release' our entire body. In this way the point of balance can shift downwards.

Relaxing the spine: The practitioner concentrates on every single vertebra one by one, from the top to the bottom and tries to leave each section relaxed. In this way the spine regains its natural shape and becomes ready to absorb the energy.

Emptying in the chest: The practitioner relaxes his chest, without forcing. This will free the chest, making it 'empty', and the energy can sink down. Together with the spine the body gains its naturally upright form, *kong xiong ba bei*.

Relaxing shoulders and hips: The practitioner concentrates on the shoulder region, releasing it while he seeks to go deeper into this area for further release. This way of 'releasing' applies for all kinds of loosening in Taijiquan. Weight and energy will sink. One should bear in mind that all phenomena in Taijiquan require a certain amount of exercising. In the same way, we loosen our hip area including the lower back area around the *Mingmen* point, waist, pelvis and abdomen. Releasing this area makes it open, so that energy can flow into the legs and feet, joining with the upper and the lower part of the body. If the hip area is blocked and the connection between the upper part of the body and the legs is weak, the body is not contained, and no unity can be established. Many difficulties in *Tuishou* have their source in the hip area. Vital functions are seated here including the centre of our sexuality.

By way of opening the hips, the metabolism and the circulation of blood and energy are considerably improved while toning up the organs in this region. When both the shoulder and hip areas are open, they can join in fluency. This is also described as: 'shoulders and hips draw towards or float into each other'. This requires the upper part of the body to be naturally upright, with the thorax and spine released and open, and the shoulder and hip region also open. We are trying to make the energies of these two regions join and attune. It may feel a little like magnetism. The image of clouds of mist rising and sinking between these points as they do along a mountainside may help. This unites and contains the upper part of the body, and a feeling of compactness sets in.

Relaxing elbows and knees: As with our shoulder region, we try to loosen and relax the elbows and the related areas as well. At first, this may appear to be a bit more difficult than with our shoulders, yet a similar effect can be felt after a time. The joints become pervious, and we learn to maintain this perviousness while extending ourselves, which may make leverages performed against us less efficient, or it may heal bruises faster. More exercise is needed if we wish to produce this condition in our knees. We have to understand precisely what the term 'release' in the Taiji-sense means. It's our legs that carry the body. The practitioner tries to loosen them while he keeps standing. Increasingly the body will start to contain itself through its structure, and the muscles may relax more easily. That is what opening up and becoming receptive means. We conclude by making a connection again between the elbows and knees. The points draw to each other, and energy between both points is connected.

Relaxing hands and feet: This refers to the entire area from the wrist to the fingertips, from the ankles to the toes. First the hand area is released, then that of the feet. The central points of the palms (*Laogong*) and of the soles (*Yongquan*) can open independently of each other. In most cases this is not required, as it normally happens by itself during the course. After that, hands and feet seem to float into each other again, drawing to each other.

Now that we have established a connection between shoulders and hips, elbows and knees as well as hands and feet, a feeling of utter compactness will spread. The necessary condition of course is a naturally upright and open spine and an emptied chest. This may be checked again and the process repeated.

The containment of shoulders and hips, elbows and knees, hands and feet is also called *wai san he*, the 'three outer containments'. The body is contained through the connection of these areas. It gains stability. And if the consistency of the 'silk threads' is not being torn, neither can the structure be broken; also under high impact of an external force we maintain our centre. The aim of training is to develop these 'silk threads' and to supply them with more and more force until they cannot be separated any more. Yet *wai san he* not only refers to these three essential points. In advanced work the disciple notices that to every point in the body there is a corresponding one in another place. These must be joined in order to produce stability. Once I succeed and make these innumerable points all over the body join with their corresponding points, it becomes easy to imagine the unassailable stability the body achieves. During *Tuishou* at the level of mastership, I no longer perform by thrusting my hand or my elbow; my entire body is driving. Any target area within myself finds its analogue area, then unites and pushes forward.

An example: I'm grabbed by my upper arm and wish to repel the assailant. From the arm alone, this can't be done. However, I can move my arm from inside my whole body. This is perfected if the corresponding area, in our case the upper leg perhaps, in a connection with the upper arm and controlled by the *Dantian*, pushes forward. Eventually all points are linked to their analogue points and under the control of the *Dantian,* so that the body is contained within, and during a movement appears entirely as one. Now I am able to 'fill up' (yang) the single point and its analogue. For this I consequently need two shares of yin from the body that are related to those points. I can also link a yang-point with its related yin-point. That way, for example during *Tuishou*, I may liberate myself from an area blocked by my opponent through releasing another one in a different place. In the same way I can treat areas of the body afflicted by illness, while working on corresponding ones located in different positions.

If I am brought off my centre, *Dantian* can no longer be my body's point of balance. I have lost my strongest force. Now I have to realign the entire body to this new yet worsened situation. That means I have to re-define all points and their corresponding points to this new condition. In this way I still can make the best out of my weaker position and retain the chance of being highly superior to someone who is of lesser sensitivity.

In therapy the approach is the same. If a body, be it due to illness or physical injury of whatever kind, is not within its natural centre, I can either try to place it back there or re-define the centre in relation to the physical state.

Let's take the case of one leg being too long: if that is caused by misadjustment in the hip or pelvis area I'll correct and release all points towards the *Dantian*, and the body will eventually return to its natural, proper and healthy stance. If indeed the leg itself should be longer than the other, everything else inside the body will shift accordingly. I'll therefore decide to re-define the natural condition and correct all points and their analogue points to this 'new' centre. The *Dantian* remains the energy centre; what's new however is the overall arrangement, so that the alleged weakness is transformed into a strength. This however requires a profound understanding and a precise 'vision' of the situation and its options for re-definition.

Here is *wai san he* again in summary:

Jian yu kua he:	shoulder and hip conjoin
Zhou yu xi he:	elbow and knee conjoin
Shou yu zu he:	hand and feet conjoin

Since we have performed the five points of correction as mentioned above, the *Dantian* can relax and fill up with energy. The entire body is released, calm and naturally upright. All channels of energy are open, energy is accumulated in the *Dantian*, and it spreads out equally through the entire body. The mind is calm and relaxed, body and mind are unified. Our awareness concentrates inside the centre of energy and spreads through the whole body. We reach our condition of *Wuji*.

Now the requirements are fulfilled to start with the actual exercise of the Standing Post. From out of the preparational stance, we slowly raise our arms while continuously correcting and releasing our body. We maintain our condition of *Wuji*. The hands should not be held above shoulder level. The exact positioning of body and arms develops through the years of training and forms the basis for any further level to be reached. There isn't more to be described within the limits of this book. Any improvement in physical stance is individually different and depends on the level of training. A book will never be a substitute for a teacher. Corrections are never achieved by following a fixed pattern, but are different for every individual. They must always be provided by a sensitive teacher. Their direct aim is to relate the energies inside the body with each other and to keep refining this process. The more I succeed in re-composing the body, the more the adjustments are refined, the more energy I will be able to release and apply for my health, for self-defence and much more. It is never enough simply to copy the position and hope that through the years something may happen. The corrections required are much too complex for this.

In this position we remain standing, in the beginning for five minutes perhaps, later it may be half an hour, or more. At first it may be hard for you to keep your mind at ease, and the body may not be comfortable standing for long and may even hurt. This is quite natural and will decrease eventually. All discomfort gives way to a feeling of rest, warmth, of being harboured, and with unity and compactness of body and mind. The better our ability to correct the body and to release the body and mind, the closer we will get to this condition. The time-span for exercising is flexible. More important than duration is the appropriate standing, otherwise many years of training are spent without ever making any significant progress. Let's give ourselves a little time to discover all these things step by step. In this way we will in the course of time reach from an 'outer' *Wuji*-condition to levels deeper and deeper towards a true condition of *Wuji*.

Closing exercise: While lowering the arms we should be careful again to proceed with this very slowly, in order to be able to adjust and re-adjust according to any change in our body. After this we are standing again in our preparational stance and correct our physique again as pointed out above. We concentrate within our *Dantian* and put the central points of our palms (*Laogong*) one over the other over the *Dantian*. Women put the right hand first, men do the same with their left. This way we keep Yin and Yang in balance. Both *Laogong* points merge into one with the *Dantian*. Awareness and energy are collected here. After a while we start conducting the *Laogong* spots around the *Dantian* in small circles by way of shifting our weight. In one direction first, then in the other. Eighteen times for each direction is an adequate number. With the passing time, a *Dantian*-movement evolves until the *Dantian* eventually takes control over motion.

Finally we recollect inside *Dantian*, release the hands and correct once again. The centre of energy is *Dantian*, yet energy is always distributed within the entire body. Slowly we open our eyes keeping our view inside first and slowly re-adapt to the outward view. Finally we slightly stretch our legs again, pulling the left leg back close; the exercise is completed. Light massages may follow, and a little break for contemplation is recommended.

CANSIGONG – THE SILK-EXERCISES

Cansigong, literally the 'Exercises of the Silkworm', forms the essence of Taijiquan. All movements, exercises, applications and techniques have their rationale here. *Cansigong* ('reeling silk'), composed by Grandmaster Chen Xiaowang, builds exercise upon exercise and initially serves as a basic exercise for beginners. Soon however it becomes clear that the key for all that follows is to be found here, and that training *Cansigong* should become one of the most important training sections, particularly for the advanced student. During Standing Post we learn to centre ourselves, bringing the energies to life, collecting them inside the body and merging them to unity. Precisely this is the required condition for the silk-exercises. Without losing this way of being centred and the entire energy context, we begin to move. Energy is carried through the whole body in a very distinct way. The movement is to be as entire and accurate as possible, so that our basic condition will not be destroyed while at the same time the flow of energy contained in this movement can be generated. All the body's limbs shall be harmonised. The mind must not be negligent. A little too much motion, a little loss of awareness, and the energetic flow is disturbed, interrupted, 'torn apart'. It's comparable to reeling off a silk thread from a cocoon. If I pull a bit too strongly, it will rip. If I pull a bit too gently, it will stick. That is where the name is from. The classical texts say: 'moving a thread through a ninefold winding hole of a pearl'. The aim is to make awareness and motion join so softly yet in a distinct and coordinated way that the thread will not block but find its way – this image should clarify that the thread is being pushed, not pulled. It is just the same in our exercise. If we are able to translate this, the body will be free from blockages, the movements being soft but full of structure. The flow of energy is released.

The movements are composed so that energy will flow through our body in a distinct way. We learn not only to raise our energies and enrich them, but also to control them. The latter is of essential importance if we wish to achieve an advantage. Because while wishing to cultivate them for reasons of health, self-defence, or for whatever other reason, we must learn to control energy. Not before this is achieved will we be able to apply energy in a specific way.

The setting of the exercises is simple: after Standing Post we begin performing single-hand movements while standing. When we are mastering these, to realise the *Cansigong* principle, the same will follow with both hands and with taking steps. For the second time in our life we learn to stand upright and start our first attempts in walking, this time however with a principle: the Taiji-principle.

The Single-handed Silk-exercise: We are standing upright with our feet close together. Top of the head, ears, shoulders, hips and ankles are again aligned as on one vertical line. The body is at ease and relaxed. The mind is calm, the hearing is focused to the back. We place the left hand's gap between the index finger and the thumb on the hip (1). Then we slightly sink our body to allow it to relax and open further. The energy of the *Dantian* increases (2), so we can shift our weight onto the left leg and raise the right heel without wobbling (3). We are taking a step to the right now that should go beyond shoulder width and touch down with the heel. After that we unroll the entire foot (4). Together with a weight-shift we're leading the right hand in a circle over top left to the right. The weight is now more on the right leg, the right hand's palm turned outward, together with the elbow at shoulder level. The arm is curved in a bow at an angle of about 135 degrees. This is the starting position (5).

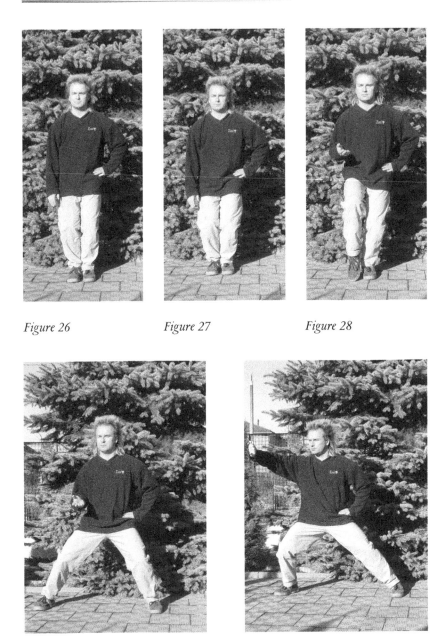

Figure 26   Figure 27   Figure 28

Figure 29   Figure 30

Figures 26–30 The Single-handed Silk-exercise: Jan Silberstorff

With the body centred and all body parts relaxed and accordingly in alignment, we start leading the arm downwards in a semi-circle. At its end the palm points half upward. No weight shift happens during this place. The energy runs from the fingertips across the shoulders back to the hip. This is a whole-body-movement, that is all parts of the body, even the smallest ones, are connected, and all is being coordinated in unity. The movement is being guided from out of the *Dantian*. Here it has its source. In general terms, all kinds of movements in Taijiquan are initiated by the *Dantian*. It makes no difference whether it's about rising or sinking, opening or closing movements; it always begins in the *Dantian* and is permanently controlled from there. Sinking movements starting at the top of the head have their origin in the *Dantian*; this does not become obvious until the exercises have been performed for some time.

When the energy has arrived at the hip on the same side as the arm and the movement is thus complete (1), we smoothly start to shift our weight by about 60 to 70 per cent onto the other leg. Arm and hand follow, and the hip area is released, so that the energy can flow from the side of the hip to the *Dantian* (2). Movements (1) and (2) are considered Yin-movements because energy flows back to the centre.

The first movement generates Yin, the second makes it complete. Energy flows back from the extremities to the centre, that is, from outside to inside. Now we slightly turn our hip outward and let the arm and hand follow, whereby the arm rises and the palm is turned in towards the body first and then slightly to the outside. Thus the energy can rise from the *Dantian* across the *Mingmen* area up the spine. Here we have rising Yang (3).

We finish by shifting our weight back onto the other leg, and the hip turns in parallel with the front. During this move, arms and hands turn outward in a spiral motion. We are back to standing in our initial position. Hand and elbow are on one level so that energy can flow through the shoulder and elbow into the hand and fingertips (4). Yang is completed, energy has passed from the centre to the extremities, namely, from the inside to the outside. During a Yin movement energy flows back to the centre; during a Yang movement it flows from the centre to the outside.

Figure 31

Figure 32

Figure 33

Figure 34

Figures 31–34 Single-handed Silk-exercise: Chen Ying jun

Therefore, the movements (1) and (2) have a Yin character, the movements (3) and (4) have a Yang character. Continue to grow until completion, after which follows the change – one is suspended within the other. It's as if we are embedded in a large Yin and Yang symbol and in continuous change. As one has reached the absolute, the other will occur, growing and reaching its own absolute to suspend again within the other. The point of artistry is not only to produce the flow of energy but also to perceive the moment of change and to follow it. Moving a bit too far or a bit too short, I'm blocked by myself; neither Yin nor Yang can be fully exploited. I must move just enough so that the thread will neither rip nor stick. Not too much, but neither too little; not too hard, neither too slack, so that the effects set in. I have to watch for the right moment, so that I allow the change instead of obstructing it.

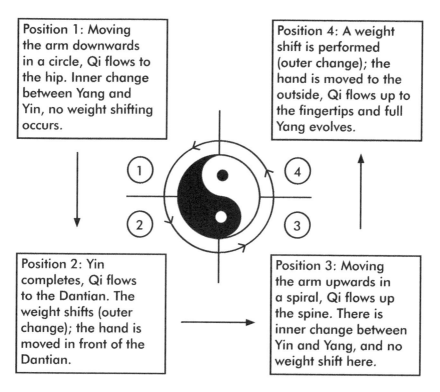

Position 1: Moving the arm downwards in a circle, Qi flows to the hip. Inner change between Yang and Yin, no weight shifting occurs.

Position 4: A weight shift is performed (outer change); the hand is moved to the outside, Qi flows up to the fingertips and full Yang evolves.

Position 2: Yin completes, Qi flows to the Dantian. The weight shifts (outer change); the hand is moved in front of the Dantian.

Position 3: Moving the arm upwards in a spiral, Qi flows up the spine. There is inner change between Yin and Yang, and no weight shift here.

Figure 35 Application of the Taiji Symbol to the Silk-exercises

As long as no change happens inside, that is, while Yin and Yang are still evolving towards their optimum, there will be change outside. This means that the weight gets shifted. If there is a change of Yin to Yang or vice versa inside my body, the outside will remain unchanged. This means that the weight is not being shifted. Hence, the weight is shifted during (2) and (4), as there is an outer change. Yin in accordance with Yang keeps growing inside. During (1) and (3) Yang changes into Yin and vice versa, and an inner change happens. In this case the situation remains constant on the outside, and no weight is being shifted. In this way a continuous flow of energy inside the body is generated. A circuit of energy is developed from the *Dantian* up the spine, across the shoulder, the elbow and then to the fingertips (Yang). From here it flows back to the hip and to the *Dantian* (Yin). At an advanced level this should be performed without interruption.

If this principle is properly understood, I'm not only capable of performing good Taijiquan, I also develop a deeper insight into the nature of things. I understand how they emerge, how they are, how they develop and how they will occur again. In other contexts, it is not considered unusual to foresee things. In the field of Taijiquan I have demonstrated this by being able to distinguish and predict moves, weight shifts, etc. about forms from other systems unknown to me. While in Sri Lanka I could even show someone the next stance – of a form I did not know myself. Viewing my demonstration, he remembered the stance and confirmed it was the right one. This example may help in understanding how it is possible in Taijiquan to counter attacks before they have happened, and how it is possible to recognise that in a given situation, what the only possible move to follow must be. This way in the course of time *Wuwei* evolves, the spontaneous acting, and the non-acting.

This first silk-exercise is performed with the right first and then the left or vice versa. The number of circuits being performed at a time depends on the practitioner's time and fitness. The arm is moved in a spiral way, tracing a circle not only externally but additionally turning within itself related to its movement. That makes energy flow through the body in spiralling tracks. Everything moves in spirals: *Dantian*, hips, legs and feet as well as upper body, arms and hands. Even the head follows this principle. This force is called *Cansijin*, 'the power of the silkworm'. An enormous potential is created with this. The whole body becomes enclosed in a web of spiralling energy. Single-handed, then double-handed during the Silk Exercises, the whole body is involved in the form, so that the body is energetically contained. It becomes more and more dense by energy, and turns into a compact whole. Energies of an assailant are taken into these spiral tracks, getting lost inside them or returned back to the opponent. The body grows strong and powerful through this inner build-up. Everything is flooded by energy. Hundreds of circular tracks enclose the body, which make it stable and healthy.

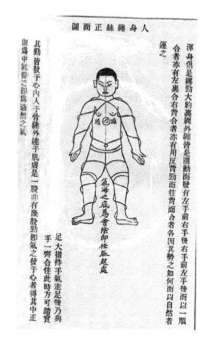

Figure 36 Theory of the silk-exercise after Chen Xin

After we've understood the single-hand exercise, we then practise it by adding steps. Each time during the movement (4) when energy passing the elbow we set one foot beside the other; similarly during (2) we make a step to the outside. The steps take the directions of the hand I'm using, i.e. during the exercise with the right arm they move to the right, during exercise with the left arm they move to the left.

However, if the 'thread be torn', never must we lose our centre. If the movement close to (4) is nearly completed and energy is flowing as far as the fingertips, we move the rear foot close again while the rest of the body remains, correcting itself along with the step being taken so that the flow of energy into the fingertips is further increased. With the movement of the hand being completed, the movement of the body is completed as well, and so is the step.

However, in reality it's the other way round: when the *Dantian* has reached the end of a movement, body and hand have followed. During (2), energy flows as far as the *Dantian*, and while it nears its end we move our foot out forwards, and the *Dantian's* energy increases. Considering our Standing Post and the silk-exercises in the context of learning to stand and move, it will indeed appear to us as if we are like children learning how to walk. We're learning all these things anew, this time however guided by our rationale of motion in its entirety.

These four exercises are to be practised as single exercises:

1. *Zheng mian can si (you)*   Front silk-exercise right

2. *Zheng mian can si (zuo)*   Front silk-exercise left

3. *Heng kai bu (you)*   Side step right

4. *Heng kai bu (zuo)*   Side step left

These will be followed by the four double-handed silk-exercises:

5. *Shuang shou can si (you)*   Double-handed silk-exercise right

6. *Shuang shou can si (zuo)*   Double-handed silk-exercise left

7. *Qian jin bu (you)*   Forward step right

8. *Qian jin bu (zuo)*   Forward step left

And by the backward steps:

9. *Hou tui bu (you)*   Backward step right

10. *Hou tui bu (zuo)*   Backward step left

These ten exercises are considered the first part of the silk-exercises. The remaining six exercises will not be described here in detail. They apply the same principle as the single-hand exercises while being complex insofar as two circuits of energy are being tracked simultaneously. Corresponding to the single-hand exercise, each hand follows a circuit from *Dantian* over *Ming men* from the spine to the shoulder, elbow, hand and fingertips. In the double-handed exercise, the two circuits move in tune with each other, however without being equal. While one side is specifying a Yin-phase, the related Yang-phase will prevail inside the other, and then again. During the single-hand phases, Yin and Yang alternate. Both sides together make the vision complete: Yin on one side, Yang on the other, each to come into being and continuously alternate with and inside the other. We are immersed in a symbol of Yin–Yang, that is of Taiji, fully enfolded around us. Even the legs during all silk-exercises follow this principle; it's the spiral mode here as well. Body and hip need to be open for this. It's the hip that links the upper body to the legs. If the hip is tensed up, energies from top and bottom can't combine, nor can a flow or wholeness develop. Similarly if the musculature around the hip area is tensed instead of being released, the *Dantian* can't relax and open. If the *Dantian* can't open up, it can't serve as the energy-collector. Instead the energy will rise high into the thorax, and the upper body will be blocked. No *Dantian* movement is possible in this case; movements aren't initiated from the centre, and the essential energy ('*zhenqi*') can't be developed.

This is why a released, opened and relaxed hip is of utter importance. If at this point we try to imagine all the circuits mentioned above – towards the hands, into the feet, Yin here, Yang there, and so on – we may conclude that it may well require a higher degree in maths to follow all these phenomena mentally or even try to initiate them by our mind's deliberation. Grandmaster Chen Xiaowang usually says at this point: 'Half thinking, half not thinking, half thinking, half feeling'. Our consciousness is suspended within the great and entire. We take care in performing our movements properly and with accuracy. The spirit takes command and control, keeping a clear view while being suspended itself within the entirety of motion.

The processing of energy in the legs is similar to the process in our arms. Following the movement, energy flows from *Dantian* across the hip down to the tips of the toes and back from there to the *Dantian*. While being able to practise this separately in isolated exercises, one should realise however that the whole body is completely involved if there is energy flowing, so it can't be perfect in the top half of the body and blocked in the bottom half. The circuits as described here are just a format for the possible circuits and courses of energy within our body. If one fits well they all fit well. If one is blocked, they are all affected. In short, it is enough for me to concentrate on the upper processes; I opt for one of the circuits and all the others will be accomplished accordingly.

Next is another set of nine silk-exercises:

1.	*Chuan zhang can si (you)*	Silk-exercises of the right hand drilling
2.	*Chuan zhang can si (zuo)*	Silk-exercises of the left hand drilling
3.	*Ce mian can si (you)*	Silk-exercise sideways right
4.	*Ce mian can si (zuo)*	Silk-exercise sideways left
5.	*Dan shou xiao can si (you)*	Small single-handed silk-exercise right
6.	*Dan shou xiao can si (zuo)*	Small single-handed silk-exercise left
7.	*Shuang shou xiao can si*	Small double-handed silk-exercise
8.	*Tui bu can si (you)*	Silk-exercise with the leg, right side
9.	*Tui bu can si (you)*	Silk-exercise with the leg, left side

These nine exercises are considered the second set of the silk-exercises. They focus on the front and back circuits of energy and on the leg spiral. The first four exercises are variations of the lateral circuits as described before in the first section.

In line with the *Dumai* and the *Renmai* meridians, the front and rear circuits run across the back, the head, chest, belly and abdomen and vice versa while the entire body is continually involved. The principle of these exercises is quite like that of the first set, but they will not be described here in great detail. Gaining exact knowledge of this is a matter of active teaching. The more intensely I've learnt to contain the energy inside the lateral, frontal and rear circuits, to combine them and bring them in tune, the better the network of energy inside my body will concentrate. A closely knit network of energy is spun along the eternally circulating spirals. This makes the body grow more and more compact, forceful and resilient. In this ideal condition it is healthy and gets a rich energy supply; energy itself is being nourished and we are vital and balanced. Alien energy, an attack for example, becomes accepted as well with ease, being neutralised and returned. For the opponent there is no chance of penetrating this tight web; instead we find easy access to his vulnerable areas and penetrate them. This is how we are able to overcome the opponent.

In summary, the principle of the silk-exercises can be divided into three parts:

1. the lateral energetic circuits (connections)

2. the front and back energetic circuits (connections)

3. the combination of all the circuits into a movement that determines the entire space needed for the exercise.

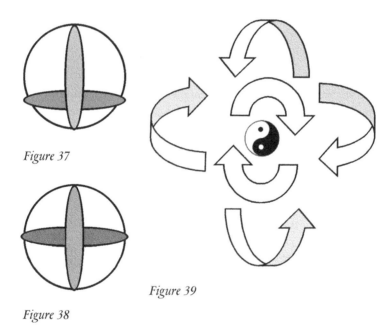

Figure 37

Figure 39

Figure 38

Figures 37–39 Levels and rotational directions of the three contexts of motion during the silk-exercises

Based on these energetic networks, what in Taijiquan is described as 'the ball' will in time be created. The term refers to a self-contained field covering the entire space around my body, inside and outside of which any point, being linked with the centre and triggered from there, can be addressed and controlled.

HAND FORMS

The hand forms, without exaggeration, do form the jewel of Taijiquan. Here is the place where we search to translate all the principles described above into movement sequences that are much more complex. The movements themselves are relatively easy to learn. You watch them a couple of times and right away you can imitate them approximately. Incorporating them with the essence of Taijiquan, however, requires a lot of practising. Therefore, we are well advised to develop the internal work during the pre-exercises, that is during standing exercise and the silk-exercises, in order to then transfer them into the form. The movements within the form are too complex to attempt this from the very beginning with the form exclusively. Advanced practitioners know how hard it is to achieve the Taiji-principle during the standing exercise or the single-handed silk-exercises. The forms do pose a considerable challenge in transposing Taiji into all kinds of movements.

The essential form of the Chen-style is the first traditional form, the *Laojia Yilu*. Out of this form all other known styles of Taijiquan have evolved. It consists of 75 movements and was composed by the Chen-style master Chen Changxing from the 14th generation (1771–1853).

He combined the five forms of Taijiquan known at that time, a form *Paochui* and the 108-form of Long Boxing (created by the founder of Taijiquan Chen Wangting) into the first and the second forms known today as *Laojia*, 'old frame'. The first form mainly consists of slow, harmonious and flowing movements which are occasionally interrupted by so-called *Fajin*-movements. During a *Fajin*-movement the entire energy of *Dantian* is concentrated in a certain part of the body out of which it then emits explosively. In contrast to the usual routine, energy will thus not flow softly and continuously, but instead, for the purpose of one tremendous explosive move, will focus on a distinct target. The fighter uses this energy, for example if the opponent has fallen off balance, in order to push him away or inflict injury on him. This way of moving energy is very valuable for our body as well, as it builds up an enormous moving potential and teaches the body to react instantly. Taijiquan has slow and soft movements as well as fast and explosive ones. As mentioned above, the first form mainly consists of slow movements, while the second form (*Laojia Erlu*, also called *Paochui* or *Paoquan*, 'cannon fist') is dedicated to the explosive ones. This explains why the second form by principle has not been adapted by other systems of Taiji with a lesser focus on the martial arts aspect. Whether this happened by intent or whether the second form for other reasons was not adopted is beyond my current knowledge. Not only the slow and soft (*Rou*) movements belong to the entire complex of Taiji, but the fast and hard ones (*Gang*) as well, otherwise the procedure would not be complete, and no complete exercise of the body or mind be achieved. I've noticed for example that people tending towards a Yin-mentality opt for a type of training that emphasises this trait as the exclusively soft styles in Taijiquan do, while the more robust, dynamic people turn instead to systems like Karate, Judo or boxing. This is absolutely OK, but it's not a balanced approach. The soft remain soft and the hard remain hard. Taijiquan however develops harmony between both, encouraging Yang in cases of too much Yin or Yin in cases of too much Yang. Quite often during my Chen-style classes I have seen how much physically or mentally hard structures loosen up, whereas more reserved and soft personalities have developed into being forceful. Since the Chen-style promotes both poles and evolves the union between them, everyone can compensate for his deficits.

As mentioned before, all other main styles of Taijiquan basically derive from the first form *Laojia Yilu*. Even more versions of the Chen-style refer to this form, for example the *Zhaobao*-style. While this system is considered an independent development, even the beginner can see that it has emanated from the Chen-style. The *Zhaobao*-style, by the way, is named after the small town Zhaobaozhen which is a neighbour to Chenjiagou. This is evidence against the idea of independent courses of evolution. *Zhaobao*-Taijiquan emerged from the *Xiaojia*-version, 'Small Frame', developed by Chen Youbeng (14th generation).

This also evolved from the *Laojia Yilu* and was called at that time *Xinjia*, 'New Frame'.

The forms known today mainly by the term *Xinjia* (1st and 2nd form) were created by Chen Fake during the 1940s. In contrast to the usual developments towards simplification, this version represents one that is more complicated. Additional spiral movements were added. Though the principle is the same, it is more difficult to master these complex movements. In terms of efficiency, however, Grandmaster Chen Xiaowang notes: '*Laojia* is like shooting with a rifle, *Xinjia* is like a machine gun.'

Therefore the New Frame should not be learnt until a good foundation in the Laojia forms has been achieved. Due to its seemingly higher appeal however modern *Wushu* athletes often learn this form exclusively. They often have hardly any relationship with internal energy work or none at all. To the layman their movements do look fascinating, yet they should be named *Kongjia*, 'Empty Frame', as they are indeed smooth, but without content and thus useless. Looking back, I have to confess that I won my first 20 tournaments in this section of forms, with European championships and international competitions in China among them, without really having a clue about it. Fortunately neither did the referees!

This may illustrate how hard it is to grasp the art we're trying for. It reminds me of my very first training experience with my Shifu, Grandmaster Chen Xiaowang. We had gone to the park, and it was the first lesson I received from him. I stood in front of him and was to present him my form. I did have some expertise already; I had, as mentioned before, successfully contested big tournaments and was no longer somebody unknown. Still my heart sank, just like during my very first public performance in a Chinese restaurant in the days under my first teacher Sui Qingbo. Anyway, I performed and pretended that I felt confident. When I concluded, my Shifu gave me lavish applause, saying: 'You have done the form very beautifully, Jan. The stances are deep, the body moves smoothly, and the *Fajin* does quite impress. I can well understand that you won the tournaments. It looks very good indeed, but for anything beyond that it has no use at all.' He slapped his hands on his knees and burst out laughing. The movements indeed were in some way impressive, yet they lacked something very essential:

content. They were empty, the principle of Taiji just being an outer phrase. What started then and continues till today was the correction and the serious development of the principle of Taiji. Vanity and elegance became less important, and reality set in. Now it was real skill that slowly substituted the wrestling techniques in *Tuishou*. This reality has nothing to do with a pleasant reading of the classical scripts and off you go. It involves hard work and real, intense correction. The form is only the tool. Not until I've learnt the form can I start dealing at all with Taijiquan. Learning the form is not the goal, but the pre-condition!

Beyond the developments of the hand forms named above, many various short forms have evolved through the years within the Chen-style, like the 38- or the 19-stances form after Grandmaster Chen Xiaowang. Within the 38-stances form he combined elements from the Old and the New Frame of the first form. The 19-stances form is a mixture of *Laojia*, *Xinjia* and *Xiaojia*. By design it's rather simple, which makes it quite suitable for a beginner or for people who want just to learn a little bit. There is also a simplified state-approved form with 36 movements, a standard form composed of *Xinjia*-moves from the first and the second form. This, once created for competition, became replaced during state-approved tournaments by the so-called 42-stances form, and by others. The 42-stances form bears the elements from all four mainstreams of Taijiquan (*Chen*, *Yang*, *Wu* and *Sun*-style), but just like the Beijing-form, however, it is no longer taken seriously in terms of a true form which may involve higher energy processes. Next come the 24- and the 48-stances forms after Master Feng Zhiqiang (not to be confused with the Beijing-form or the state-approved 48-stances mixed-form), an 18-stances short form by Master Chen Zhenglei, and many more recent developments.

As we see, there are also many various forms within the Chen-style. There are traditional forms and new ones, some following the traditional rules, others being entirely modern. The purely modern ones like the competitive forms or the state-approved short form are no longer attributed to the system itself, because they no longer abide by its principles. All in all, the most essential form is and will remain *Laojia Yilu*, the First Form of the Old Frame.

The first step towards mastering a form is of course to learn the outer movements. That's the most simple part of Taijiquan and just requires a good eye, copying skills and a good memory. After this, however, the real training of Taijiquan actually begins, namely, filling the moves with content.

All movements of the form follow the same principle as the silk-exercises do. This can be considered under three aspects:

- the energy circuits of the lateral guiding lanes as described for the first set of silk-exercises

- the energy circuits of the frontal and back circuits, as described for the second set of silk-exercises

- movements which are a combination of both processes.

So if we take to the lateral and the frontal circuits and the combination of both, we will obtain a globe – covering the entire space. There are movements promoting a particular aspect, others promoting another one, but every single movement has its own combination of these circuits. All the time something of all this is present, and primarily the entire body is continually being filled with energy. No matter what type of movement is being accentuated, the whole body is always involved in making this movement, so that all the paths of energy remain permanently involved.

There are different energy states during the form. The double-handed silk-exercises teach us that one hand is always Yin while the other in correspondence is Yang, and that they are an expression of these processes inside the body. This is the same during the form, but not in this sequence exclusively. If we look at the *Bagua*, we see all the various changing phases as symbols:

Starting from a complete Yang, the amount of Yin grows, then prevails, and complete Yin is generated in order then to transfer into the opposite again. So we have interim conditions within the form where one hand is Yin, while the other is Yang. There are states also where both hands show the same condition. I call this doubled Yin/doubled Yang. We must keep in mind that Taiji is not only soft but hard as well, and not only slow but also fast. Either giving way is only one side of Taijiquan. Normally there is always one part of the body that gives way, while another pushes forward. One side for example yields to an attack and swerves, while the other pushes forward at the same time,

Figure 40 Taiji symbol and the eight trigrams

i.e. attacks. In this way Yin and Yang are in harmony, and we have no problem in keeping our balance. However, an attack may be so forceful that an instant counter-attack would be ill-fated. In that case I just yield and let the opponent's enormous force veer off into the void. In this case it would be a bilateral or externally complete Yin. In another case the attacker's force may be so weak that I can defeat him on the straight path. Many people training in Taijiquan in an incorrect way are steadily worsening their defence capabilities, while their training enthusiasm increases. This is regrettable, but it has a very simple reason: they become softer and softer without building up any substance over time. Someone with years of such a training may be asked to give a push and may even try to do so, but you'll keep waiting for something to happen, because he doesn't actually know how to really apply force. Wolfe Lowenthal describes this in one of his books about Zhen Manzhing by the term 'spaghetti arms'. Yin and Yang must always match. Softness must bear substance, and hardness must have an elastic core.

Of course I can simply push away someone who, let's say, attacks me in the open street and whose power compared to mine is far inferior, and I don't need to reflect whether that's been Taijiquan or not. Of course it was Taijiquan. There is no technique which is either Taijiquan or not. What turns it into Taijiquan is the way I perform it. Many people complain about *Tuishou*-tournaments, claiming that this was not Taijiquan. Of course it is Taijiquan, only in most cases not a good version of it. However, if these people, knowing so precisely all about what Taijiquan is and what it's not, entered the ring themselves they would in most cases not last for more than three seconds. Can that be Taijiquan? Let's be brief: Taijiquan deals with nothing but the balance and the evolution of Yin and Yang; it deals with nothing but being able to react in the best possible way both mentally and physically. Some years ago during a seminar I was teaching how to perform a fist-stroke. After a short time I was instructed by an attendee, himself a teacher of this art, that in Taijiquan there were no fist-strokes as it was a defensive martial art. I had him demonstrate his form, and after three minutes he had arrived at the fist-stroke. What next?

Master Shen Xijing once asked me how people in Europe ever got the idea that Taijiquan consisted of one technique only, namely, pushing away. Don't these people practise any form? Inside the form, he said, so many techniques were contained. So the point is not which technique from the vast area of martial art belongs to Taijquan and which does not; the point is how this technique is being executed, and whether it abides with the principle or not. Thus there is only good Taijiquan or bad; there is no such thing as Taijiquan or no Taijiquan. Also while performing an externally complete Yang move, i.e. a plain attack, I wish to do it as well as possible, materialising my Taiji-principle in an optimal mode. My physical energies must be contained in the best possible way in order to enable me to apply the maximum force.

I can also combine full Yin with full Yang, for example by setting one after the other. The opponent approaches with such a high amount of force that first I let him run completely into the void and then add my own force. But I can either stop him by letting him run halfway into the void, countering already his approach (synchronous Yin and Yang). Or I can keep him from even starting his attack and act immediately (full outer Yang) or completely get out of his way (full outer Yin). I can mix all elements just as indicated by the situation. Any range is eligible, just as described by the eight trigrams in *Bagua*. Therefore the various energy states also occur during the form. Either of them is of course always supported by the other. Despite a full outer Yin I'm keeping my structure (inner Yang), and a frontal attack (full outer Yang) is always flexible within (inner Yin). This is the case for example during the stance 'The white Crane spreads its Wings'. The moment we spread our arms, energy flows across the shoulders and elbows into the hands and the fingertips. It's a Yang-movement, and in fact both right and left, in both arms at the same time. I don't find the related Yin inside my other arm at the time, but inside the inner continuity of my body. This is more like Yin, being rather flexible. Yang on both sides affecting the outside is supported inside by full Yin. This enables me to confront attacks directly, as this kind of flexibility works like a shock absorber while I remain in balance.

With the arms now being spread I sink a bit, during the final phase of the movement. Now the energy flows back from both arms, across the hips and back into the *Dantian*. It's a both-side Yin movement. The energy flowing back enriches the inner continuity and generates a complete inner Yang, so that the softness acting outside will remain stable inside.

Hence there are Yin and Yang continuities, not only on the right or the left side and on top and bottom, but also outside and inside, and into the smallest units of the body. Thus the mistake of the double weight shift or double weighting '*shuang zhong*' can be avoided during all kinds of situations (see also Chapter 11, 'The Mistake of Double Weighting').

Many martial artists fail because they think they have to apply their system to any condition. In a case of defence, they feel they must apply their practised Karate technique or whatever, instead of simply reacting in natural fluency. Perhaps this is why their style is incorrect. In Taijiquan we try to react spontaneously out of *Wuwei*, namely, naturally and consistent with the situation. By way of our training, however, we do this better and better and with more and more accuracy.

But how am I to realize the Taiji-principle during the form? The key to this question lies hidden inside the silk-exercises. Once I've learnt them precisely I can transfer the skills into the form and elaborate them here in a mode of higher sophistication and complexity. The silk-exercises therefore represent a training of eminent importance which is simple at the beginning, but attributed the most high value by advanced practitioners. I once watched my Shifu while doing his very early morning exercises. He was practising the single-handed silk-exercise. When

I asked him during breakfast why he had trained this exercise only, instead of higher forms, he replied: 'My basic exercises aren't really good yet.' He has trained for more than 40 years and is considered the greatest living Taijiquan-master of our times.

Alongside the descriptions of the silk-exercises, I'd like to decode in terms of energy the movement 'Buddha's Guardian Is Pounding the Mortar', to make the idea of internal movement comprehensible. This movement appears in the *Laojia* form after the preparational stance.

Body and mind are in the best possible preparation. Mental and physical posture are calm and released; we're going through the points (1) to (5) as described for the standing exercise. Only the hands remain down, placed on the left and the right side of the body. This is the preparational stance (Figure 41). Energy is released inside the entire body, centring however inside the *Dantian*.

We raise our arms as our hip opens and the *Dantian* makes a backward half rotation in the front, so that part of the energy can flow down to the feet and part of it up to the fingertips (Figure 42). We find exercises to prepare this within the second set of the silk-exercises.

Then we sink our arms again as the entire energy – again controlled by the *Dantian* – flows from top to bottom and into the extremities.

Energy eventually collects inside the *Dantian* again (Figure 43).

Now we slightly shift our weight to the right, the hip turns in a bit, and the hands rise sideways left in front of the body so that the right palm points upward, the left to the outside (Figure 44). With the positioning of our arms, we identify our single-handed silk-exercise. The left hand is completely Yang; Yang energy has flowed across the *Mingmen*-spot up along the spine and over the shoulders and elbows into the hand and fingertips. On the right side the energy is inside the *Dantian*.

We now move a little further, changing the position of the arms (left hand turns to the top, the right one to the outside), and shift the weight on the left leg and move our

Figure 41

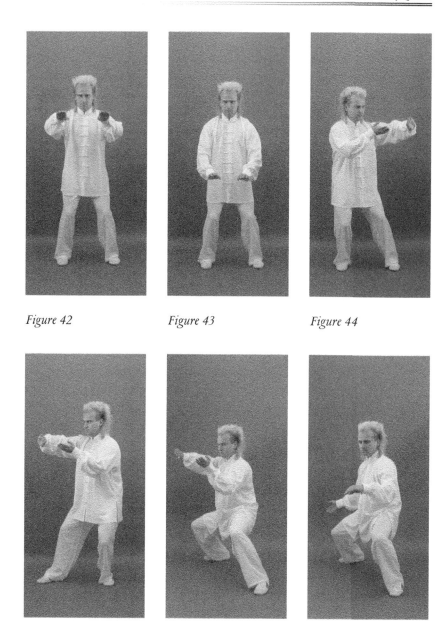

Figure 42   Figure 43   Figure 44

Figure 45   Figure 46   Figure 47

Figures 41–47 Buddha's Guardian Is Pounding the Mortar: Jan Silberstorff

arms forward to the right (Figure 45). At this change the energy on the left flows back from the fingertips to the hips and to the *Dantian* (Yin), while the energy that has resided in the *Dantian* flows across the *Mingmen*-spot up along the spine and over the shoulders and elbows into the fingertips of the right hand.

Thus we may have on one side Yin-energy and Yang on the other. The movements result from the related movements of the *Dantian*. The movement visible outside displays the movement inside. The *Dantian* movements must be explained in great detail by a careful teacher. To a certain extent it is possible to sense them by laying the hand on the teacher's lower belly.

The left hand thus describes the movements (3) and (4), then, after the change, it continues with movement (1) and (2) from the silk-exercise, the right hand concluding with (3) and (4). Next step is shifting weight to the right, and the left foot is set one step forward (Figure 46). Nothing changes during this phase in terms of energy; energy inside the *Dantian* and the fingertips becomes just a bit amplified, then again a change will follow. The left palm turns downward, the right one points upward. Only then the weight is shifted (Figure 47).

Why is that? It is quite simple. During the change of arms and hands, energy will again flow up across the spine, then across the shoulders and elbows into the hand and fingertips, (3) and (4); on the right side it flows from the fingertips back to the hip and to the *Dantian* (1) and (2). When, however, am I to shift the weight? Precisely when the energy has arrived at the hip. By way of shifting weight it arrives at the *Dantian* (see also for the silk-exercises). This corresponds with the other hand as well when energy has flowed up the spine. This internal work comprises the nuts and bolts of Taijiquan. Weight shift is thus achieved when energy has arrived at the hip, and when it has reached the top along the spine. Otherwise no shifting of weight would be possible, in case somebody intended to interrupt me during my transaction. If energy is still within the rising phases of Yin and Yang instead of being within those of completion, my inner silk thread will tear apart and the body separates internally. I lose my structure, and if someone steps in my way, I have no force to push him away. In contrast, my own force would turn against me. Later on, however, these processes take place within movements which are getting smaller and smaller, and in cases of advanced skill, without any external movement at all, so that I no longer depend on the necessity of outer moves. In all cases however the principle remains the same.

This is the difference between those who (properly) train Taijiquan and the untrained. Many don't know about it or cannot translate their knowledge, which is why they keep failing in Tuishou. Thus we may conclude that the essence of self-defence in Taijiquan is not within the technique but the principle I apply it with. I can detach from the tightest leverage or the strongest clinch if I have understood these inner processes, namely, not only that energy can flow without any blockage, but that I'm also able to apply it in a specific way. Not only do I learn to develop Qi and make it grow and flow throughout the entire body, I additionally learn how to control it and to physically release and apply it at will. I must learn how to 'ground' this energy and when to use it without losing the relationship with the whole, i.e. without the thread of silk being torn. This is the very making of training in its entirety. At the same time I learn to do the right thing in accordance with the (energetically) right moment, i.e. to adapt to the nature of things.

Without this understanding of motion, the movements may still appear with ease and grace. They may also enable the mind to relax to a certain extent, but they cannot cause any deeper effects on health. Without this knowledge, they cannot be used in self-defence. Since the principle of Taiji isn't really exerted, its philosophy remains without a spiritual dimension.

That's also why any attempt to place Taijiquan in the same category for example as dance or anything similar is ill-fated from the beginning. Due to the mindset itself, they take an all too different course, and practitioners can never experience true seriousness in the sense of Taijiquan.

It reminds me of a funny story from 1996: I was at a kind of village festival, and as often during such events, there was some friction around. The particular thing about that bout was that I was indirectly involved. A friend of mine had been drinking too much, and caused so much of a fracas that a couple of guys wanted to teach him a lesson. These situations by the way are a nightmare for any philosophically inspired martial artist, having spent successful years avoiding any standoff or even not letting one arise at all. Any fight that did not happen was a fight being won, and what next? Then it's time to realise that those around you, be it friend or girlfriend, do not quite abide by these rules, and you're right in the middle of it all.

Twelve guys had shown up meanwhile, wishing to beat up my friend. When I moved in between them, more or less by necessity, anticipating to really be on the receiving end, the dream of any martial artist came true: one out of the crowd yelled: 'Hey, we better not try it on with that one, I've seen his picture in the martial arts magazines!' He pointed at me. Another then told my exasperating friend, 'He's your friend, that's why we'll leave you alone. We don't want any trouble with him.' At that moment I really did feel great...

That didn't last long, because later of course we got into some talking, and when I answered the curious questions saying, 'I'm training Taijiquan,' there was some silence at first, then the girls were the first to giggle and say: 'But that's not a real martial art', and someone else sneered about 'Karate for retired people'. You could see how courage was returning into those who had been rather meek a moment ago. An unmistakeable meaningful glance from me was enough, however, and eventually we left the scene unharmed.

Still I asked myself: what in the world has happened to Taijiquan? Taijiquan that my Shifu's grandfather Chen Fake cultivated during the first half of the 20th century in Beijing? In those days everybody knew how to tell great stories of the Taiji-masters' heroism and their incredible power, but today they call it Karate for senior citizens!

While my personal ambition is to re-establish Taijiquan as a health system and as a martial art as well, this doesn't mean that anybody interested needs to be a confessed martial artist, but for one's own good one should not cut off the roots of an art and still expect it to bear fruit. Because I either comprehend Taijiquan in its entirety, with true benefit from it in all domains, or I don't and will accordingly achieve minor effects only or illusions.

However, let's return to the described movement. After I have successfully shifted my weight forward the energy flows back to the *Dantian* on the right; on the left it flows back into the fingertips. Now I can rise and set down the right leg with the tip of the foot. The right arm is shelved under the left hand (Figure 48). If we start to wobble while rising, this is a sign that our internal energy is in disorder. Either

THE SYSTEM OF CHEN-TAIJIQUAN

because we rose too early – energy hasn't arrived at the Dantian yet – and/or it is not contained within the body. In Taijiquan we must move very diligently and thus slowly in order to sense these imperfections at all. All the described phenomena are minute impulses. I must learn to listen to the whispering of my body. Everything inside body and mind must therefore be at rest, otherwise it is like trying to listen to the whispering words of a friend while turning up the stereo.

Paul is a private pupil who is 12 years old, and who comes to see me once or twice a week. Paul has been challenged since birth in his motion and in his sense of balance. Learning the form's movements is a bit more difficult for him. What actually seems to be a handicap is actually an advantage: the moment he moves just one centimetre off balance, he starts to sway, and a firm step is possible only if he concentrates and works very precisely. In this way, he feels even the slightest imbalance. Other people perhaps consider themselves gifted because they have had a firm stance since birth. But they may never reach a consciousness of this profound and sensitive tracing of a move necessary really to understand this sensation. This means that they do not have control of most issues the way they think they do, even if the deal is 'only' about their own movements. They really don't have a clue. In a seemingly different context, Jesus said how difficult it is for a rich man to enter heaven!

Because some people are doing fine they miss perhaps the very important things in life, and perhaps they are neither willing to work hard on themselves, or to surrender themselves. Those who are concerned, however, may take to searching. And the end of the story? 'He who seeks will find.'

History has shown all too often that the very masters of *Wushu* in many cases were challenged during childhood, so they were forced to confront themselves seriously regarding their lives and abilities. All in all, everything depends on my level of concern and the intensity I follow it with.

Back to the posture: after raising the circuits, change back again from the lateral to the frontal ones, respectively the rear and reverse circuits as in the beginning of the form. I lower the right arm, and energy flows down; together with the knee I raise it again with a fist, and the *Dantian* makes a vertical turn. Energy flows downwards as well as

Figure 48

Figure 49

Figure 50

Figure 51

Figures 48–51 Buddha's Guardian Is Pounding the Mortar (cont.)

upwards. In this way I obtain a balance that releases much force. At the end I set the foot back down again; the fist sinks into the left hand held open in front of the *Dantian*, while energy flows back into the *Dantian*, and the movement is concluded (Figures 49, 50, 51). Every single stance during the form energywise starts and ends within the *Dantian*, in a way constituting a small form within itself. During a sequence, the last movement of one stance is suspended within the first movement of the one that follows. One could say that 75 single forms by concentration generate one form, so the condition of one seamlessly transforms into the state of the other.

The processes of motion as described contain frontal circuits as well as rear and lateral ones; altogether the form of course always consists of combination steps during both processes. Through these, the body becomes rounded and contained. I will not give an in-depth description of the connection of both these circuits, as it would be too abstract for the reader to follow. This may be demonstrated more clearly during teaching. The following symbol illustrates the synergy of the energy circuits (Figure 52).

Figure 52 Taiji ball

Therefore I learn to master the form by the following subsequent steps:

- Learning the outer forms of motion.

- Correction of the outer forms of motion.

- Generating the inner flow of energy by movement according to the principle of the silk-exercises.

- The process now becomes inverted. It's the inner flow of energy that makes the outer movement. The *Dantian* controls motion.

- The body as a whole flows together.

The determining steps are the fourth and the fifth. While performing the first three steps requires a lot of study and work – only few can claim to have mastered that – the threshold from disciple to mastership is to be found in the fourth and the fifth step.

The descriptions given so far are all aimed at explaining how the outer movements have to be so that the energy can consequently flow through, along its channels. It is easy to see however how limited this condition is if I imagine a situation where I can no longer perform this movement, be it for example because I've broken my leg or someone stops my freedom to move by techniques of leverage. I can no longer do my movements then, inner energy cannot follow, and my Taijiquan has become suddenly inefficient. This is the reason why so many practitioners even after extended periods of training remain incapable of liberating themselves from simple leverage techniques. They have never learnt to 'switch', that is to move from inside to outside.

As in all cases, the same principle applies to health issues. Why do the Chinese put such high value on preventive healthcare? The best options are held by prevention, particularly for self-healing, and Taijiquan belongs to this. While we are doing fine, while we are free from pain in body and soul, training Taijiquan is a joy, and we can stabilise our condition. Once we've fallen ill, however, and suffer great pain, our incentive to train rapidly descends towards zero. I then have to overcome this reluctance with determination, because my mental power and my motivation are already weakened. Body and mind simply won't allow real exercising. When merely tired, we already become negligent in

THE SYSTEM OF CHEN-TAIJIQUAN

exercising. However, when we're in a bad condition, we particularly need training. It is sad that those who could well profit from Taijiquan don't have the time for it, people who are under stress, managers vulnerable to stroke, for example, while those who have time and leisure and are not in need of stress management.

My father suffered a stroke in 1980 so grave that though he survived, his body remained partially paralysed. He had to accept very strong restrictions. Maybe he still could have improved, but his motivation had sunk so much that he dedicated his life afterwards to television, and his condition slowly but steadily deteriorated. This was certainly also caused by the fact that at the time he fell ill he was holding a prominent position in terms of his work, which he would likely never have been able to regain. He may have lacked a true goal. Learning how to work on oneself in keeping or regaining health before having fallen into such a condition is of course much harder. However, even if he had learnt to move in a way that internal energy could have flowed, it would not have served him much, as he was hardly able to move his body at all.

Hence there must be something else, namely, the step of outer motion must result from the internal one, because even while being restricted externally, this does mean that I cannot be free to move inside. Out of this freedom, out of this mobility, I can then take to working on the external side. The path of the therapeutic approach is: developing inner mobility from the outside first, then correcting the external from the inside. This is to be understood in a comprehensive sense for all states of life.

This sounds easy, but it is quite hard to realise. The *Dantian* must be well established and free to move so that out of its movement all further consequences will result. By way of the standing exercise I learn to build up my *Dantian*. In the course of time I learn by way of the silk-exercises and the entire form to create movements inside the *Dantian* and make them flow through the entire body. Everything inside the body is connected to the *Dantian*. Just like a pebble cast into silent water will create circles growing wider and wider, the *Dantian* will spread out throughout the entire body. Then I no longer move my arm, with the energy flowing into the fingertips; instead it's the energy that flows up to the fingertips; that makes the arm follow and move. When the energy inside the body is contained within – and only then – such a movement can be performed and a very large force can evolve. Then it suddenly becomes easy as child's play to disengage from very tight locks or to rise while someone tries to keep us down. The motion of inner energy thus connects with outer moves. Speaking on a higher level: it's energy that creates external motion and is completely absorbed therein. Consciousness, energy, muscles, tendons, bones: all are connected and work in a contained and aligned mode entirely as one.

Another example: in 1993 I broke my left leg while training *Tuishou* in the PR China, and as usual in those times, it got put in plaster. The inability to walk the form with a plastered leg would have meant stopping for six weeks; the muscle tissue would have atrophied and a very gradual training to rebuild would have become necessary. I did not want that. So I learnt that by inner movement I could reach points that are externally immobilised. And so, due to six weeks of intense training while being seated, my muscular tissue had remained almost unchanged, supply with nourishment and energy took place throughout the whole period, with almost no obstacles. One week after the plaster was removed, I was completely restored and even allowed to prove it: exactly on the seventh day without plaster I gave a performance during the European Championships in Switzerland (I had been invited as a referee) under the patronage of Grandmaster Feng Zhiqiang – and just one week later I could, while being the first foreigner in Chenjiagou then, achieve the third place during an official tournament, right behind the nephew of Chen Xiaowang and the son of Grandmaster Zhu Tiancai. I took this as a convincing evidence for the deep effects of Taijiquan on rehabilitation, insofar as rehabilitation was hardly needed!

We may focus again now on a phenomenon described in a previous chapter. It is this:

Nei san he (The Three Inner Containments)

Xin yu yi he	'The heart joins with the awareness'
Qi yu li he	'The energy joins with the force'
Jin yu gu he	'The tendons join with the bones'

Xin yu yi he means: 'The heart (understood here as an area of the emotional, the sensible and intuitive consciousness) is one with the consciousness of mind.' There is no room for two opinions here; we need reasonable determination in order to bring something about.

Qi yu li he has already been explained before. Internal energy steps outside together with external force. That is, muscles no longer stand in opposition with each other. The inner energies of the body are contained within, outside and inside are one. They take combined effect as one force.

Jin yu gu he means that tendons and bones work as a unit, which on a larger scale applies also to connective tissue, organs and so on. Viewing all three issues, it means in brief: the entire mental and physical body acts as one unit. All distinguished areas, thoughts, emotions, muscles, tendons, bones – all go one direction and work as one. Nothing works against; unity makes the body work. The entire body is compared to an army; from the top brass to the last foot-soldier there is full consent. Everything is in tune. This requires a certain order. What's to be concluded from the Three Inner Containments then is also this: heart and awareness (mind) join with each other. It's the entire contained consciousness that controls energy and its moves. Out of this, the force will emerge, being followed by tendons and bones, namely, the whole body. This direct sequence of spirit and physique is expressed in Chinese terms of *nei san he* as: *xin yu yi yu qi lu yi yu jin yu gu he*, which translated means: 'Heart joins with awareness joins with energy joins with force joins with tendons join with bones.' All is combined in a direct sequence from the very first instant of 'inspiration' up into the most subtle move that is to emerge. Beyond mastering full control over the whole body's moves, the goal is to bring body and mind into union so that this sequence takes place at one and the same instant. No more time is lost then and therefore no gap is left between mind and body. To the opponent this leaves no option for countering, because in the very sense of the term no gap is left for him to enter.

In order to have everything combined in the described way, another principle is an indispensable requirement: 'The three external contexts *wai san he*'.

Both of them, the inner and the outer three contexts, form a union and cannot be separated from each other. When the internal motion renders an external one, a very dense network of energy and force inside the body will develop, and the body can become very powerful indeed.

Since Taijiquan is a very sensitive and subtle art and subject to imagination and 'presumption' in the beginning, one should care about results during training. It is here where one can really tell whether one is on the right path or not. This is a very narrow path. Bear in mind: One centimetre off the path will result in deviation of a thousand kilometres! This sentence is to be taken very seriously.

WEAPONS AND WEAPON FORMS

In Chen-style there are basically six weapon forms, called *qi xie tao lu*. Four of them use single weapons; two of them use double weapons.

These are the six weapon forms:

Sabre (*Dandao*) with 23 movements

Sword (*Danjian*) with 50 movements

Pole/Spear (*Lihuaqianjiabaiyuangun*) with 71 movements

Halberd (*Chunqiu Dandao*) with 30 movements

Double Sword (*Shuangjian*) with 39 movements

Double Sabre (*Shuangdao*) with 35 movements

Besides these six forms there are a number of others, for example the double maze form, and the one using iron rods. Not being part of the actual base repertoire, however, I shall not give further explanation on them at this point. The famous though not widespread *gan*, a very long and thick rod, will be mentioned elsewhere (see 'Training Forms with Equipment', p.159).

The sabre-form with its 23 movements is by far the shortest among the traditional weapon forms of the Chen-style. When I asked my Shifu why the form was so short he replied: 'Prior to my uncle Chen Zhaopi, the form was even shorter.' Chen Zhaopi extended the form by adding a jump that is performed twice.

As a weapon the sabre is robust and resilient. Its blade is slightly bent and sharp on one side. The sabre form includes strokes, cuts, stabs, dodging moves as well as many round actions of cutting in circles. It's quite tempestuous and dynamic. The viewer feels indeed as if attending real shadow fighting. Part of the stepwork may be performed by leaps.

Figure 53 Chinese sabre

The sword compared to the sabre represents a weapon of much higher sensitivity. The blade is sharp on either side; it is thinner and of lesser weight. Therefore the sword not only allows, but due to its less robust character, requires work with heightened sensibility. A straight fend-off with the sword is reserved for exceptional cases. One routinely gives way and, resembling the pushing

Figure 54 Chinese sword

hands, yields to the opponent's force. The sword-fighter will not position his force straight against the opponent's force, but rather direct it off into the void and attack by himself also. Here we find strokes, stabs and cuts and many circular slicing moves. With its tip, the short near-tip edges and the long edges, the sword has altogether five edges. It is considered the most aristocratic among all weapons. Like the hand form, the sword form is sensitive and fluent.

The pole and the spear form are one and the same form using two different weapons, the long pole and the spear. The weapons are quite alike in character. The pole surmounts the pole-fighter by length and is used for pushing, striking, diverting and so on. Quite similar is the spear, the only difference to the pole being a sharp peak at the front end so that instead of a push we speak of a sting. In terms of performing, however, these techniques remain almost identical so that it

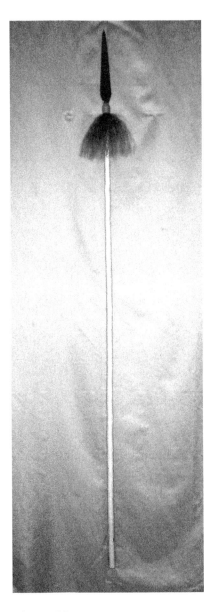

Figure 55 Spear

makes sense to train with both weapons within one form. While training the spear form one morning in the park near my home, the spear's point suddenly flew off. Unconcerned by this I continued to finish the form. OK, so this was the day for the pole form. In case you, dear reader, should ever be granted the opportunity to attend a *Wushu* demonstration of weapons, don't take your seat in the front row, or if you do, put on headgear! Chinese training weapons are often poorly manufactured, and I have witnessed more than once pieces breaking off and flying sharp as razors through the air.

The spear is called *Lihuaqiang*, 'Spear of the Pear Blossom'. The pole is the so-called *Baiyuangun*, 'The Pole of the White Ape'. Combined in one form, this bears the name *Lihuaqiang-baiyuangun*, 'Spear of the Pear Blossom Combined with the Pole of the White Ape'. The form is very combative and dynamic.

This is also true of the halberd form (combined spear and battle-axe). Some of its basic techniques and the steps are identical with the pole and the spear form; other techniques are entirely different due to the weapon characteristics. The halberd is the heaviest weapon. In the training version it weighs about three kilograms; the real appliance, however, sometimes exceeds ten kilograms. I had learnt my form with a genuine and very heavy halberd. Without much expertise with this weapon at this time, during training I felt reminded of the walks I had with our new dog when I was a five-year-old child. The dog was taller than me by about the length of a head, and instead of leading him by the leash I rather flew behind it...

The halberd is about as long as the spear, but its blade is very wide. The waved shape on the blunt side is not a decoration, but serves in disarming a sword- or sabre-fighter for example. Depending on the type of the halberd, a peak, a ring or a bolt is attached at its rear end, making it very dangerous in both directions. Due to its size and its weight it is the most sedate and ponderous weapon, while having a tremendous impact. As mentioned above, the halberd form is very dynamic, placing quite a challenge to both body and mind.

As for weapons, both Double Sword and Double Sabre are identical with their single piece version. The practitioner learns to handle two of these weapons simultaneously. Considering the enormous

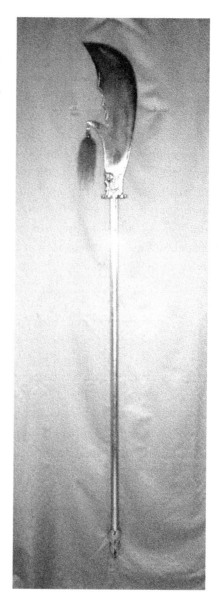

Figure 56 Halberd

supremacy of a weapon compared to a hand form, it is quite comforting to have two at hand, being able moreover also to handle them. Weapons, in particular the sword, have always caused deep fascination for their operators. Often they were treated as sanctuaries. Dealing conscientiously with the psychology and operating of a weapon, I became aware very soon of the power that I'm granted by having such a weapon. It is – in the case of skilled handling – eminently superior to any hand technique. The weapon not only helps me in determining the outcome of a combat in physical terms, it makes things easier in mental terms as well. I am no longer directly confronted by my opponent; something instead is standing between us, establishing a distance not only of space, but most of all one in the mind. Just imagine the extreme case of having to either shoot dead a person who is 100 metres away, or strangling them with your bare hands. What makes the prior alternative much easier, and wars of today so dreadful, is that by modernisation of arms, the spatial and mental distance from the enemy is enlarged, making action much more feasible. It is this anonymity that does not justify things but makes them easier. While a stabbing weapon or a stick is still quite an immediate device when dealing with an opponent, it does provide its owner with an extraordinary power. Warriors of former times were very aware of this and therefore had the highest esteem and respect for the weapon. All the more they (at least the 'good ones') put the highest value on taking care that the power granted by this weapon was never abused. That's why it is always of vital importance to practise martial art as a 'way' and not as a sport or a technique. Any human is subject to the danger of being capable of abusive conduct of power. The philosophy, the way of the martial arts – a term that gained high popularity by the Japanese word *do* – protects us not only from abuse but is rather the one thing to give training its very meaning: wisdom and peace.

Beyond its actual achievements weapon training represents a very interesting way of fitness training, as all weapon forms are highly active in physical terms. Weapon forms do give an opportunity for some real rampaging. Aspects like the so-called lung-training can be fully exploited by way of weapon training (as well of course by way of the *Paochui* hand forms). Many Taiji-laymen are not aware that the complete classical Taijiquan system not only includes soft and meditative exercises, but also those that are physically very challenging.

What all Taiji weapons have in common is the principle by which they are operated. As during the hand forms, the body is being moved in an entirely contained way in order to make the physical energies fully unfold, but in this case the body includes the weapon. It becomes part of us, and is suspended within in the entirety of our movements. Therefore we keep focusing our attention on making our energies flow throughout our body into the outmost and most significant points of our weapons. The goal of these forms is to make the weapons virtually become part of ourselves.

For each weapon the Chen-style offers an extensive concept of (formerly usual) martial usability. More detailed descriptions are a matter of teaching. We should not forget that the founder of Taijiquan, Chen Wangting, had been a battle-hardened warlord. This usability is an interesting issue still today for those who seriously wish to study the various scenarios of ancient battles. However, it is of fundamental importance for self-defence, because only by way of the weapon can one obtain a full and valid impression of the enormous mental and physical complexity of human conflict. The weapon can show us a path of seriousness, respect and humility that is, even in our own times, more than worth following.

TRAINING FORMS WITH EQUIPMENT

There is a whole range of exercises to be performed with various types of equipment other than weapons. These items of equipment serve in further strengthening of the body with distinct focuses varying with each type. As always the aim is to understand better and realize the Taiji-principle. There is for example a bent piece of wood that helps me to improve my techniques of seizing and levering, or a floating ball I try to push under water to heighten my sensitivity for power and my inner weight-scale. There are many such exercises; the ones most known are perhaps two training devices: the pole (*gan*), about three metres long, and the ball, nearing a basketball by size (*Qiu*). The purpose of the pole is among others to build up the strength of the hips. From out of the hip the pole is brought to swing and so to make all energy spread throughout (like a whip being lashed) into the peak. It's astonishing to witness how some senior masters from Chenjiagou of around 80 years are able to bring that weighty device into action. In ancient times this pole did indeed serve as a weapon. It was used in getting riders off their horses.

It does not belong generally among the weapons, though it would be wrong to say it was not a weapon.

Things are different with the ball. Training with this device pursues an interest quite different from tossing it at someone's head... The Taiji ball, made from wood or iron, is moved by the hip as well. Round, spiral movements, continuous control of the device, and an eternal flow of a never-ending motion turn this exercise into an extraordinary pleasure, the effects of which we sense not only during *Tuishou*. By visualizing the ball and and the spiralling moves, one becomes conscious again of the flow of nature as endless, round and spiralling. For various therapeutic purposes a ball of less weight may be used, such as a plastic ball or one made of sandalwood or similar.

During a travel to the Wudang mountains Master Shen Xijing gave me two round plastic bowls normally used for feet-washing. We were hosted by a police inspector at the Baihe, the White River, not far from a Daoist cult site. As there wasn't much time for individual teaching, I was instructed to fill the two bowls with water and balance them on both my hands without one drop of water being spilled, and without having to set them down because of their weight. With the back-up of a picturesque landscape, I felt like Jackie Chan in his early films. Training with equipment should in general be performed with caution and only at certain stages of one's personal development. If improperly performed it may cause muscular tension and stiffness.

PUSHING HANDS

Pushing Hands, *Tuishou*, is a training concept which, as mentioned in the previous chapters, was developed by Chen Wangting in the mid-17th century. In order to get a little closer to an understanding of Pushing Hands, one has to understand first that *Tuishou* training within the routines resembles that of the form. So it is Qigong also, but it's done with two people. While during the solo form I'm listening to my own energies exclusively, during partner exercises this is only one part of the story. The other part consists of 'hearing' the other's energies as well, namely, to learn to perceive and to understand them. This enables me to recognise my opponent's intention before he is conscious of it himself. I extend my control and energy all around my opponent's space. I learn to accept his force with intuition, re-direct it and add my own. During combat this has to happen by itself. I rarely have the time for situational analysis during a combat and deliberations on which action to take. My action and reaction must be spontaneous (*Wuwei*) and adapt, triggered by a reflex. That way my body learns to spontaneously handle energies properly. Psychologically it is not necessarily an advantage having

Figure 57 Pushing Hands: Ralf Anlauf and Frank Marquardt

enough time to analyse a situation while it happens. Such concerns often block a spontaneous reaction. One would have time, in a way, to start feeling fear.

I have mentioned previously the guy in the park who suddenly started beating me. We were both quite surprised. Me, because I didn't really know yet what had happened, and him because he had imagined the whole thing would take a different course. However, he is or was a follower of a martial art that advertises its supremacy in very aggressive terms. And there I stand with my 'pensioner's Karate'... Perhaps all would have turned out differently if he had given me a warning. I didn't know him; he was massive, boasting about his system. Pupils of mine were present. Perhaps I would have become nervous, afraid not to look good in front of my friends or something. Despite leading a spiritual life, these things may happen...under fear, the body will freeze and cannot move freely. The way it was, however, with me being warned of nothing, I could of course function in perfect naturalness and fluency.

The trick is that no matter whether the right moment has come, no use is made of it, just waiting for things to happen. Those who have read the story of the Japanese sword-fighter Musashi may remember the event shortly before his final fight. The chosen venue where it was to take place was an island. While his opponent used the previous days for closer inspection of the site in order to be prepared, Musashi himself did nothing like this. He would not be depending on certain images he had set up before; he would rather be free and spontaneous, during an instant that determined all. He won.

The method of *Wuwei* works that way in all situations. And the proper answer to the question 'What would you do if this or that type of attack occurred?' is not: 'Perhaps I would do this or that', but simply: 'I don't know. I'll decide when it happens.'

One thing however is to be said in general: in the case of previously knowing about an imminent challenge, only an idiot would allow himself to be engaged. The presence of one challenger is enough. A surprise attack is worthless for the challenger; if he loses he'll be sad; if he wins due to a situation of surprise – what does he prove and to whom? Even Tarzan is accessible by a push from behind while he thinks of Jane!

Let us therefore put the issue of forced competition aside and rather get back to the subject.

Tuishou is practised in five ways:

Dan shou tui shou	Single-handed Tuishou
Shuang shou tui shou	Double-handed Tuishou
Huo bu tui shou	Tuishou with steps
Da lu	'The great yield', Tuishou in a very low stance and steps
San shou	Freestyle Tuishou

All five sectors are built upon each other. Gradually the pupil learns, first by single hand, then by double hands, to accept force, to re-direct and pass the energy, then to do the related stepwork. He learns to deal with forces from various directions and various intensities, until he eventually comes to the ultimate level, the free *Tuishou*.

The movements must be calm and relaxed. If I wish to throw or push someone and fail to do so, it is normal behaviour to intensify the force. That way however my body will be more and more cramped. As I'm seemingly unable to move the opponent, the power remains stuck inside my body; it does not flow. If I continue to increase the force, things only get worse. My body blocks more and more. The more power I'm trying to apply the more I'll remain stuck inside my own body. I don't actually fail because of my opponent but because of my own blocks. By way of the form, I learn to stay permanently relaxed, re-ceptive and fluent. Never will the silk thread tear. This means my body is contained within itself, and force can be passed. I'm making use of that during the pushing hands. By way of my own softness I dissolve the opponent's rigidness; I'm flowing through him. That way nothing inside me will stagnate, and the opponent has no way to counter this force. Pressure causes counter-pressure. If instead I act with no pressure, being 'without intent', the opponent has nothing left to oppose. That way it is even possible to beat the opponent slowly and obviously, with-out leaving him any chance to defend. He'll be faced with an energy that leaves him powerless.

'Softness' and 'ease' must not be mistaken for being 'weak' or 'non-substantial'. It is very important to keep this in mind.

Tuishou is not the application itself, but is a large part of Gongfu and the understanding that lies behind it. It turns application into something applicable – and should not be mistaken for it. The issue of *Tuishou* is too complex to be explained here in its fullest sense. You are recommended to refer to Chapters 4, 'Taijiquan – a Martial Art' and Chapter 7, the section on 'Taijiquan and Its Martial Technique'. True and profound insight is again reserved of course to teaching. Just one more thing shall be mentioned here: a limit to the technique of *Tuishou* is not in sight – and things get really interesting when techniques no longer counts. This is just another tip...

APPLICATION

I have already written something in this book on the practicality of Taijiquan. What I'd just wish to point out briefly is that every single move during the form has many different applications. This goes for all hand and weapon forms. To laymen in Taijiquan, this may not be obvious in the beginning, yet with an advanced understanding the im-pression will grow that it just can't be any other way. Any leg and foot position makes sense. In traditional Taijiquan there is no decorative move designed to impress the public – since in those times there was no such thing. One doesn't have to keep training these applications over and over again in a mechanical way, yet one should know them, and most of all one should discover the common principle that links them all. All applications are based on the same principle. I wrote in previous chapters that applications resembled the waterdrops that make a river. One should focus on the river's entire being in order to know about water.

If my opponent plans a move, the first thing to occur is an idea. This changes into a command for the muscles to react. It's a long way from the head to the fingertips. Once a decision has been taken and the order is passed by the cerebrum, it is like a torpedo. It can no longer be retrieved, and there are very faint muscle tensions going ahead of the planned move. By training the form and *Tuishou* I can sense all these phenomena prior to their appearance by keeping physical or mental contact with the opponent. As I am controlling the opponent at any time – something he may be aware of, something yet which in most cases remains undiscovered – it becomes an easy affair for me to (re-)act upon his intentions, at least if I've learnt to keep my centre and follow the changes without any break in my body. As the opponent however is already committed to his movement, he will be rigid and easy to defeat. Should his perception of energy yet be better than mine he will be able to attack me, leaving me without any idea of how I shall defend myself. That's why even someone who is already quite experienced in Taijiquan appears a beginner when facing someone who is better.

These processes run across something even beyond feelings, and during an actual self-defence they can't be measured in intervals of time. During exercise everything happens slowly. In an emergency however it's faster even than my conscious perception.

The applications in Taijiquan are based on a principle, not on a collection of techniques. Techniques themselves are nothing in particular. I find them in all the other systems as well. There are techniques of how to strike or kick as well as on how to lift and throw. There is combat over various distances, wrestling and groundfighting. In the best of all cases however there is no combat at all, because it didn't even get to that stage, or is concluded early during the initial phase by victory.

The aspect of martial art in Taijiquan is not plain theory but a concrete experience, regardless of the fact that on the Taiji-scene this is often veiled, unknown, not mastered, or not wanted.

A very important teacher once told me: 'Only he who has dealt with the subject of violence and mastered it can do without.' Pure denial is a perilous ignorance of our own animal energies that most are unaware of until a real emergency. If then I lack control, training on the subject will be too late. Similarly a spiritual life remains speculation and plain theory as long as I avoid reality.

III

Taijiquan – At the Centre of Life

In recent years, Jan Silberstorff has published numerous articles in various magazines. They illustrate the context and the variety of phenomena that become comprehensible through Taijiquan. They also convey the extraordinary breadth and profoundness of authentic experience Jan Silberstorff is able to share with his students and readers today. For this book we have compiled a selection of texts that have appeared in *DAO Spezial*, *DAO Magazin*, *Kung Fu Magazin* and *Taijiquan & Qigong Journal*. This selection may give you a true sense of the author's mastership. This is mastership within reach – which is what Jan Silberstorff the teacher claims.

Chapter 9

Something about Yin and Yang

Published under the title 'Wo die Stille herrscht' (Where Silence Rules) in DAO Special Edition Taijiquan 2000

Yin is dark, it is the night, the deep, it is the valley, it is soft and yielding. It is the cold, the earth and the feeling. Yang is bright, it's the day, the evident, the light, the mountain, the continuous. It is warmth, heaven and reason.

So far so good. This explanation is correct, and we find it everywhere, but what does it really tell us? How am I to earnestly understand Yin and Yang? A plain listing of criteria won't help us. That only appeals to the mind. I know what Yin and Yang is. Knowledge is Yang; yet how am I to know something which is only Yang? The feeling is Yin. Here is the point where two phenomenona meet which are of utter importance for understanding: the mind and heart for awareness and emotion respectively. A classical statement in Taijiquan says: *xin he yi he qi he li he,* which means: 'From the liaison of heart and mind (awareness) Qi will grow, and out of this there will come strength.' It is impossible for me to learn about the nature of things just by way of my intellect; I have to constantly involve my emotional world. I must sense all the things I wish to understand, I must have a feeling deep inside of me. It is not until then that I have truly understood something, only then I can truly act in accordance with my understanding.

Laotse says: 'The soft will defeat the hard. Everybody knows this, yet nobody is able to abide by it.' This indeed sums up the issue.

Knowing about Yin and Yang just means being able to talk about it; it does not mean being able to act accordingly. Even to speak about it remains meaningless and has no expression. I often use the issue of smoking to give a clearer explanation. Everybody knows that smoking is neither healthy, nor does it make any sense. That's why many wish to quit, telling themselves every day: 'I should quit smoking.' In fact, however, hardly anybody is able to do so, and year by year the smouldering drags on. No knowledge about Traditional Chinese Medicine, no knowledge of the body, no severe doctor and not even one's own consciousness are able to change this. What is lacking is the feeling, the body. Let us make our body be our ally. Once the liaison between body and mind is back to functioning, once I'm in touch with the feeling my body wishes me to perceive, that is, once I sense that smoking is no good, I'll quit in the same instant. Then it will immediately start tasting nasty as if I had licked out an ashtray, because that's the way it felt when I smoked my first cigarette, and my body revolted against it, before I deliberately suppressed my repulsion.

So knowledge alone won't do; I must understand the feeling as well. An understanding in entirety must arise; that's what Yin and Yang means – creating a balanced condition with all of my heart. This is instead of granting rulership to just one area of the body. Intuition, spirit, soul, the unconscious and the conscious, the body, the emotions, hearing, tasting, touching, seeing, smelling – all of these are manifestations of Yin and Yang. All must join the game to make me capable of really feeling Yin and Yang.

The primal source however is in another place. It is where no Yin and Yang exist, where both are not yet born, a domain of silence, far away from movement. Yin and Yang are described through Taiji. Its mother is *Wuji*, the undivided condition, where there is no high and no low, no left and no right, no good and no bad, where there is nothing but the One. Where only the One exists, there is nothing that can be defined as there is nothing to define it by. Happiness can be defined by unhappiness. Rain by water or sunshine. Where there is nothing but the One, however, how can it be described at all? This One is the primal source of all being. Only by way of life, by way of movement, will energy start flowing. That's what causes separation. A part is generated together with its counterpart; thus the two energies Yin and Yang generate, they will merge with each other, and out of the infinite combinations we shall obtain all that is and all that is not. These are *Wuji* and Taiji. This is Dao and all that it creates and dissolves.

Zhuang Zi indicates this condition in relation to ourselves as the 'fasting of the heart': heart and mind must flow together, then the real force will occur. However, neither heart nor mind are the very primal source of myself, nor of my present manifestations, or my present life. Not until mind and heart have come to rest will this One rise which guides all and which is the source of all energies within our body. The heart also must be supplied with energy, and the mind is too being nourished, so there is a deeper level, the source of heart and mind.

On a small scale this could be defined as our internal *Wuji*; energetically and bodily it is our centre, our *Dantian*. All motion arises from here; all energies find recollection here, not eventually after a period of time, but within the here and now, in everyday life. With the *Dantian* being at rest, Yin and Yang will merge, and separation no longer exists. Only by way of motion, by way of action, of life, will the oneness become mobile and create the other so that there will be two, Yin and Yang. Their combinations will then create everything else. So says Laotse: 'Out of one there will come two, out of two there will come three, and out of three the 10,000 things.' Yin and Yang arise from this ultimate ground, and if we wish to understand we must search to get near to this ground. We must go back from the 10,000 things to the three, the two and the one. Now, having arrived at the source, we recognise the nature of things, and as if we were newly born we shall be able to understand afresh, this time however the natural relationship between Yin and Yang. From the very centre of life, from the very energy, no more blockages exist, life is following its natural flow, and we follow the Dao. However, this time it is neither by the mind, nor not by the mind; neither by heart, nor not by the heart; neither consciously nor unconsciously. Our understanding is instead within the whole of creation. This is what the term 'being a child again' means. God's realm can be entered only by becoming a child, the Bible says. No matter whether it's East or West, Yin and Yang is not a belief, but a condition that's vested in words which vary with cultures, while still naming one and the same. The truth, whichever way it is expressed, is always the same.

Yang is heaven, Yin is earth. Both emerge from the eternal Dao which is beyond capture. Yin and Yang together form a unity; one cannot exist without the other. How can there be a mother without a father? A day without night? Health without illness? And how can there be good without evil? Let's take a closer look at the latter issue: what do good and evil mean? In one country a certain behaviour is considered good and is thus allowed, in another country it is considered bad and is therefore illegal. During one era it is this way, and in another it's the other way. Robbing other people is acknowledged to be an evil deed; however, Robin Hood is revered everywhere. Where is good, where is evil? It's not the definition that rules upon these issues. It's the circumstance, the situation, the energy of a matter. This is *Wuwei*, spontaneous acting, or what is called non-acting. It is acting in accordance with Yin and Yang, according to the relativity between both, and the situation just the way it is. As given by nature and not by the way I wish it to be. The latter option would mean to go against the natural flow of Yin and Yang. I would fail, and suffering would follow. Good and bad are defined by the intention, by the situation and the action that derives from it. It is determined by the proportionality of Yin and Yang and is suspended in harmony which creates their balance. This will grant man healing, and a definition of good or evil is no longer necessary. The Apostle Paul says, he who believes in Christ shall receive the Holy Spirit. This will help him to obey the Ten Commandments, for through the Holy Spirit any commandment will automatically be followed. It's the source again that lifts the barrier, suspending the definitions. What can be named is not the eternal Dao; the eternal Dao cannot be named. All I can say of God is not God.

At a basic level I recognise things by their differences. This is not like that; that appears different from this. Good and bad, all poles exist. When my recognition matures, I realise that one cannot be without the other. Each Yin carries a Yang inside and vice versa. This part of the other harbours inside of itself a part of the diversity, and more and more I will recognise how deeply matters are interwoven. Within the Taiji-symbols this is outlined by the lines depicting Yin and Yang and the trigrams and hexagrams that arise from them. Yin and Yang merge, they form a unity, and more and more my surface limitations will fade. They disappear. A new worldview will emerge, a sense of how things are, where they come from and how they renew. With recognition increasing, the definitions will vanish, boundaries set by man will disappear. They reveal themselves to be illusions and are replaced by the natural flow of matter. One who recognises this will realise himself to be part of the stream, and being part of it he will no longer swim against it, as he is the stream itself. This will put an end to suffering; one who recognises this will be healed in every way. Illness will not exist any longer. He is far beyond the definition of illness and health. He turns into what in China is called *xianren*, or immortality.

So far, so good. This explanation is correct, and we find it everywhere. What does it really tell us? A plain listing of the criteria won't help us. This only appeals to the mind, which brings me back to the beginning.

I have to understand these things all by myself. 'He who speaks does not know, and he who knows does not speak', to quote Laotse once again.

Taijiquan is a good method for approaching this knowledge slowly, through life and in entirety. It appeals equally to body, mind and soul. Just to learn the sequence of a movement certainly won't take us there. As time goes on I have to learn about and work out the texture deeply woven inside Taijiquan. By way of a good instruction I will gradually understand the internal principle of this artistry of motion. I develop a sense of how the movements are connected with each other, where they have their origin, and I discover their actual energy. During the exercises I get back to the origin, I discover my *Wuji*. This happens in silence, during the standing meditation. Out of my centre, I'll then start moving. First during the silk-exercises, then during the forms. The energy itself becomes motion and changes into Yin and Yang. If I'm able to move on a high level, this energy can flow through the body without any blockage and within an internal context. This will enable me to experience the polarity of forces and make use of them in daily life. I sense the way everything is being controlled from out of this centre, how everything finds its very origin here, as does my heart, and my mind. Deeper and deeper will I immerse into the subtle texture of my body, my spirit, of the entire existence.

Yin and Yang are just theory for those who do not practise. For those who are training on the right path, they turn into knowledge. A knowledge that is living and can be felt, with a sense of eternity.

Chapter 10

Taijiquan, Tournaments and the Problem of Success

Published under the title 'Winning is Fun' in Taijiquan & Qigong Journal 2/2002

'Taijiquan and Tournaments' is a favourite topic in discussions within the non-Asian Taijiquan scene. I'd like to begin my own contribution to this issue simply by describing my own experiences in this domain. I think this may help in gaining various insights into this array of 'problems'. It may encourage the reader to make reflections of his own. I'll then take a personal position from the perspective I have today.

My first experiences with Taijiquan began with suggestions of a world of profound wisdom, deepest mysteries and skills beyond limits. Nothing there had anything to do with sports, nor anything to do with competitions either. When I then met my first teacher Sui Qingbo, it became clear from his stories that tournaments were common practice in China. There seemed to be no contradiction.

As for myself, I had no particular ambitions to attend tournaments, and I had never liked sport at school. While I had no philosophical problems in assessing myself, it still was laborious and stressful, and as I said, I didn't like the sporty atmosphere. Still, there was an aspect of the 'Karate-Kid' about it, and dreams of gaining honour and fame in a final tournament, and most of all, winning back my girlfriend. After all, these had been the themes of countless martial-art movies. I was not interested in fame and glory, however, and having no problem with my girlfriend, thoughts of attending a tournament were even less likely.

At that time I was teaching as an assistant with Sui Qingbo. Lessons took place in a Kungfu school, where so-called External Kungfu was mainly practised. When the students had finished their training of this system that is related to Shaolin, they sat at the bar with their drinks and talked shop: that the stuff we were doing there was just Karate for the retired, and that I should instead take up some real fighting, and that Taijiquan wasn't even proper gymnastics.

I must admit I felt annoyed at seeing my system being put down. One day I eventually made a decision and told the thirsty athletes that I would appear in one of their tournaments and we would then see who indeed was doing Karate for pensioners!

In short, I won that tournament. I was young, and I discovered that winning is pleasant. So I continued. I won all of the 20 tournaments that were to follow. Among these were the first European Championships (carried out in Switzerland), several national championships in Europe, as well as championships in China and particularly in Chenjiagou. Certainly the greatest success on one hand was the top placement as a foreigner in Chenjiagou and on the other hand becoming the Grand Champion in a very renowned tournament. Here the award of Grand Champion (all 'Black Belts' who had won opposed each other again) was something special insofar as it had been the most important among all 'open' tournaments – most of the various systems were represented there, not only Taijiquan.

My primary goal for attending championships had been realised: nobody in my presence spoke of Karate for pensioners any more. Quite to the contrary; much to my pleasure and gratitude, these successes during the open tournaments in Europe resulted in recognition and re-spect from all the renowned masters of the various martial arts. My success in China on the other hand made me known among all the great Taiji-masters of the land, and getting into contact with them had a very positive effect on my further development.

During the tournaments, among the real fighters, one kept meeting the same faces again and again; many friendships were soon established, friendships that resulted in frequent exchanges on issues of martial arts and Taijiquan. One talked shop with people who had something to share; not only was this a pleasure, it was very fruitful as well. If you wished to attend all the tournaments current at that time, this involved a lot of travelling.

After those 20 tournaments, however, I had basically achieved all that was to be achieved by that time. At this point I realised that I wasn't really interested in tournaments. The pleasure of meeting 'famous' martial artists, the success, the victories and the novelty of travelling in 'jet set' mode had caused me to lose sight of that for a while. So I decided not to repeat the experience and finished my tournament career after about four years.

However, I was by then already too integrated into that scene to be able simply to stay away. I was asked to be a referee, and the whole thing started all over again: National championships, European and, yes, later even the so-called World Championships.

This time I was sitting on the other side, and this was an interesting experience too. Again I met with many like-minded, this time even more famous people, because usually they were the trainers of the champions, and they were there to evaluate the candidates together with myself. As for me, I had already successfully introduced some pupils of mine to tournaments. They later achieved victories the way I had before. The only difference was that Taijiquan was by now no longer a new feature for open tournaments: we held a position now and started founding our own sections for Taijiquan. Again it took me about four years to withdraw, and take on the last remaining role at such events: the presentation of the masters during the evening shows.

This wasn't really different from participating in a tournament. After all, one wishes to be brilliant, and brilliance is apparently confirmed by the degree of the public's applause. Not that one would hope to get more applause than the others! Still, it was quite reassuring.

The presentations were not limited to tournaments. There were specially organised show presentations worldwide with an audience of sometimes more than 15,000 people. There were Eurosport broadcasts and also TV appearances. The point was always to show something and invite approval or disapproval, indicated by scores or applause, or to gain a ranking from letters arriving later. Despite TV appearances in the East and West, including live appearances on ZDF,[3] the greatest event for me was, beside appearances in Chenjiagou and Shaolin, certainly a show presentation in Singapore. Officially approved as the first Westerner, I was allowed to show my skills in a large-scale state-approved martial arts show. Representatives of the local German embassy had been invited. For more than a week, the show was broadcast on Asian TV channels. Afterwards, while shopping or at the airport, I was asked to sign autographs. That's how a football star must feel, I thought!

Wushu is a national sport in Singapore; that's why comparing it to football isn't too far-fetched. And now there is some Westerner starting, and moreover it's that guy with the 'freakish hairstyle'. By then I had a nickname after a famous Asian novel protagonist with a lion's mane. Great applause, lots of interviews, recognition, turbulence, being a star – when all of a sudden I found myself back in my hotel room, and there was that feeling that seemingly causes so many stars to take to drug abuse: the deep fall. Suddenly it was all silent around me. No more admiration, no cameras, no nothing. A gigantic black hole opened in front of me, and I felt I was about to be engulfed. An experience, I thought, which must be even worse once somebody is a real big-scale celebrity. Here again, Taijiquan was a big help: I came back to my senses, feeling deep into myself, and started again to move from out of my centre and not to depend on being admired by others. The hole would disappear.

And I became clear about one thing at that point: the knowledge and the certainty of having decided to do Taijiquan was not for reasons of fame and glory. I found myself back with the goals that had brought me to my very first training session: the cultivation of life, wisdom, self-defence, philosophy, spirituality, health – in brief: Taijiquan.

Yes, I wanted to learn Taijiquan. Not for shows! I withdrew and put my central focus back on Taijiquan.

Perhaps the descriptions I've given here are going a bit too far for a contribution on the issue of Taijiquan tournaments, but to a certain

---

3   *Second nationwide TV channel in Germany; translator's note.*

extent they may depict a trait of the shady side that Taijiquan may have: the admiration.

Taijiquan is an art that only a few know how to master. More important, however, is making an effort. Taijiquan means to deal with oneself. All qualities, yes even the ones of *Tuishou*, in the end have to do with myself exclusively. My own physical and mental skills and the third entity that will derive from them, the unity within myself; they are the measure for anything that is to follow. It is often discomforting having to deal with oneself; not being allowed to blame others; honestly being subject to a thorough examination, of oneself and within oneself; willing to personally change, to release, to open oneself to what is new. In fact what type of pleasure is it to gain praise and recognition from the outside instead? This type of encouragement, however, carries with it something perilous: the belief of having achieved something already, attributing levels to oneself that are beyond the existing level, or even worse: to stop with explorations and research, surrendering to the idea of 'having made it'. That's the fate of so many, for those who remain on the surface of Taijiquan, either because they imagine they have already understood, or either because they, be it consciously or subconsciously, content themselves with what they have already achieved. I call this the Shifu-trap. Once you are considered a master by others and even feel pleased about it, even claiming to be a master: how hard things will become if one has a serious desire to continue and move forward. Suddenly one may no longer feel able to ask a question, or no longer, thanks to public surveillance, be allowed to make a mistake. And what's more: having the serious belief of having arrived at mastership.

Tournaments deal with recognition. I go there in order to measure myself against others. If I lose there are two options: I resign and quit, or I grow a lion's heart and tell myself: and now I must do even more; there is a lot to do, and next year I'm going to win.

If I win there are two options as well: I become complacent and consider myself good, or I don't feel worth the honour, and out of shame of not deserving the medal, I bounce back into my training.

The claim of going there for an exchange of ideas, just because I enjoy it, or just to venture out a bit, is threadbare; no tournament is required for that. Some joint presentation or an informal meeting for discussion would do. Yet it's the tournament that attracts people; it's the competition. It is as if somehow I know better afterwards what Taijiquan is and what it is not. So many factors are involved: are the referees qualified, and if yes, in which subjects? What do they wish to see? Can they be seduced by their eyes, or do they have real knowledge about inner processes? It's like some game of strategy: they get to see what they want to see, and so you win. The idealist is left behind. I remember my first *Tuishou* tournament and the first contest I had there: sweeping away the opponent's legs was forbidden in that tournament. It was billed with a penalty point, but was not sanctioned by getting disqualified. From China, however, I was used to being allowed the use of the legs, too. The first thing I did out of habit after the starting signal was to sweep my opponent off his legs. He fell. Big alarm. Penalty point, 0:1 in favour of my opponent. During the rest of the encounter, I strictly followed the rules. My opponent however was deeply insecure by now and in permanent fear I might sweep him off his legs again. This clearly weakened him, and I won by 16:1. During the finale, in the second round, I was ahead of a Chinese man with a small gap of three points. Due to an uncertainty about the rules, we became entangled in discussions with the referees, and, presto! the time was over. And the winner was: me. When the tournament was over I asked myself: is deliberately provoking such a situation an unfair action or is it just exploiting chances? Doesn't self-defence mean to make use of all options within reach out of necessity? And shouldn't a *Tuishou* tournament imply preparation for a real situation? There are rules and broken rules. Both are subject to regulations and thus can be understood as rules of the game. It was like in school days, when I won tournaments in Blitz Chess. I didn't win just because I might have been playing brilliantly, but sometimes just because my opponent had forgotten to reset the clock after he had done his move, and I hadn't notified him.

Despite this insight I have always tried to be 'fair' and 'idealistic' during tournaments, but this experience taught me that to win requires more than plain skill.

Fifty per cent was skill, 50 per cent was just being savvy and clever, I felt at that time. Nothing else is being told in his world about Musashi, the Japanese sword fighter. In self-defence this phenomenon appears again and again: the person to hold his ground during a serious emergency is not the one with the best technique or the fastest kick or whatever else, but in plain and simple terms the one who pushes through. The reader is invited to believe me when I say that the alleged skill (that is, a beautiful technique or something similar) isn't even half the job.

Things are different if I define 'skill' in a comprehensive way, that is to deal precisely with what I'm facing, and to distance myself from any type of ideal of how things ought to be. In that case my 'skill' covers the entire process. The technique of martial art in the way we know it will then turn into an important ingredient, yet just one among many. Martial art in general turns into a discipline which encompasses everything.

And then again a tournament may become a comprehensive challenge, reaching far beyond the plain demonstration of a form or some 'pushing around'. Now I can hear the critic saying: 'Yes, but this is not the code of honour of Taijiquan, not the love, the soft mind, the indifference to victory.' That has always been the most peculiar thing: Taijiquan experts lining up at a tournament while 'not wishing to win'. Usually they were the most irate when in the end they lost, and that they had lost was inevitable by any measure.

This whole issue is a misunderstood philosophy: in order to fight well, I have to be 'empty' in my mind, because otherwise I cannot be spontaneous. I've got to be calm, because otherwise I'm not fast and not direct enough. If my will for victory, i.e. my ambition, is too strong, I'm too inhibited.

But of course, the goal of any martial art is to win, or in more acceptable terms: not to lose, be it on a battlefield now or during a duel or a social conflict. The same goes for the idea of wishing to provide the world with harmony or at least to do so inside myself: there is a goal, and I want to realise it. Here as well there is the will to win. I want to achieve something, even if it's the 'nothingness'.

The point is not to hold ground by way of putting others down; it's the opposite. The point is to pursue the goals that I've set myself, and to take care not to stray off the path. Once I have indeed achieved the power of being able to win, I can admit to being good in an amicable way. Since I have nothing left to fear, I don't need to protect myself, and I don't need to attack others. Only after I have gained the power, will I be able to do without. Now I can be a philosopher; because now I *can*.

In context of *Tuishou*, I often describe this during my lessons using the image of being able 'to stand' someone, which means to like somebody. It means that the person is not a danger to me, he cannot push me over, he cannot defeat me, I remain standing, I can 'stand' him. Therefore I can be trustful, opening myself, I can be generous. I can be good. Let's remind ourselves here of something from ancient times or from the beloved spaghetti-Western: the stranger is considered an enemy until we learn he is not a danger to us. Once that has become clear, there can be friendship.

So the problem is not 'to win' but rather what I will do about it. If success turns me into a balanced and compassionate, a humble yet intuitive person, it is an evolution towards the positive. If the result is an ill-designed structure of power, however, an egocentrism that's addicted to fame and success, this is certainly negative. Again the point is not about what it is; instead it's about how.

Attending tournaments made me learn about very many positive qualities. I was able to help Taijiquan regain a better understanding, acceptance and respect within the martial arts scene. As for myself, the tournament victories provided me with a degree of being well-known which in turn made me get into contact with truly interesting people. This is also to a large degree the reason for the rapid growth of our association, which in turn is crucial for the propagation of Taijiquan. Thanks to the victories, I was granted self-confidence.

The *Tuishou* tournaments were the means to show me where (and how) I stand. Building Taijiquan-castles in the sky is easy. A *Tuishou* competition instead offers a very good option for learning about the level one has reached. No matter that the critics may say, 'This is not Taijiquan at all, it's just force!' – OK: 1000 kilograms are subdued by four ounces. Critics to the front, please! Could they defeat a ruffian? They would surely use force. Or maybe they couldn't? That's OK. But what skills do they have at all?

Of course you never get to see the actual masters lining up for a tournament. You may see their disciples, and they just aren't that advanced. Moreover, a tournament is the venue for people whose levels aren't necessarily so different from each other, which is why things initially don't always work well. Of course things may at that point degrade into something short of a beauty contest. However, no masters should be at work there: I recommend to any mocker to give it a try himself and step into the ring. He'll find out very soon what it's like in reality once it's not just one's own students doing a bit of pushing, but a real pounding, using enormous pressure. I feel that one should definitely have successfully endured such an experience before adopting an attitude of supremacy. Training can quite easily miss the essentials as long as it doesn't undergo a thorough examination. *Tuishou* tournaments can serve well for this purpose. Tournaments on forms are a bit more difficult, as they require referees who do understand, and who won't be charmed by the aesthetics of motion. They should have reliable knowledge themselves and be able to clearly recognise skill; in this case a test on forms can make sense. Here is the place where I can check on myself: do I really not care whether I lose or win? Can I remain as calm and relaxed during a presentation as I am during my training sessions? What we are taught here is that the proper attitude can initiate an enormous learning process.

Even so, tournaments in my view make sense only during a certain phase. After a period of experience one should put the 'sport' aspects aside and devote oneself to the very depth of Taijiquan. In my case the examinations didn't stop after my tournament career; they were replaced by so-called challenges. Being well-known means that you meet with others who wish to find out whether there's a basis for it. This can be very pleasant sometimes, but sometimes it's not nice at all, since the challengers aren't always polite. However, as I said: you do get a view on where (and how) you stand.

Someone who believes that my reasoning lacks philosophy or isn't spiritual enough misjudges the fact that Taijiquan is a martial art. Someone not considering Taijiquan a martial art may confuse it with Qigong, an essential aspect of Taijiquan. Martial art itself is highly philosophical and spiritual; by way of contest and by growth it is to be realised by deeds. What else have the grand masters exemplified for us with the lives they lived? Why do we know Yang Luchan? Because of his great ambition right from the very beginning, followed by his persistence and eventually his enormous fighting strength. Martial art, however, is not about building castles in the sky; it is to be experienced by practice. It is a spirituality that flows throughout the body, one therefore that deals with life.

We live in different times today. Within a small range, however, tournaments can serve to find out about our skills by way of contest, be it by way of a duel or by way of competing in forms.

Even so, the real fight takes place inside ourselves, and not only for our spiritual evolution. If I wish to get beyond average as a martial artist, I have to fundamentally pass through myself. Tournaments should represent one part only of the process of living with Taijiquan. For a while they may indeed be helpful. Then however the practitioner should return to the goal which he, as it is clear by now, has never lost from sight: the cultivation of his own perfection.

Chapter 11

The Mistake of Double Weighting

Published under the title 'When Yin and Yang Stagnate', Taijiquan & Qigong Journal 3/2000

The mistake of 'double weighting' is an important topic in many books and articles written about Taijiquan. It's usually described as the problem that occurs when the body weight is equally distributed on both legs. They say that if this occurs during *Tuishou*, one lacks balance. In most cases this indicates a misconcept or a rather superficial view of the issue.

Wishing to pass energy from inside out while performing a push or a blow, it can make sense to have the weight more on one leg or on the other. Even better is shifting the weight from one leg to the other.

This, however, is a raw and superficial concept of Taijiquan and of limited interest but for beginners. Because what if the opponent doesn't allow me to have more weight on one or the other of my legs? What if he wishes to grab me right in the middle of my weight shift? During free 'Push Hands' I have to shift weight or take a step once in a while. Even if I have determined a contest in my favour, should I step or shift weight? What if the opponent breaks in right at that point?

If the so-called mistake of the double weight shift is to be understood in such a superficial way, does this mean I have a weak spot? Is it the *Siegfried*-spot? Does Taijiquan thus have a weak spot?

My opinion is: the form is approved to be the essential part of Taijiquan training, and essentially the form is responsible for the high levels in *Tuishou*. Within the form however I have a shift of weight every few seconds, which means that every few seconds the critical point of a double shift of weight occurs. It is a short moment only, but it's there. During every Taijiquan form, this 'mistake' should consequently occur.

This is like a game we played when we were small: 'Musical Chairs'. Everyone walks around a line of chairs, and when the music stops, everybody has to find one. However, there is one chair lacking – the one who remains without a chair is out of the game. The point of the game had a handicap: at the very end, while turning to the other side, a small area had to be passed without a chair being in reach. Everybody walked by the chairs cautiously, and only during the turn-around did everybody make a quick move in order not to be caught without a chair, in case the music stopped right at this point.

Things are similar during the form: knowing about the mistake of the double weight shift which continuously appears during the form, I consequently ought to hurry and flit across that point. Just the same then during free application.

This simply can't be the case, and in fact it isn't. The real and deeper meaning of the double weight-shift is concealed deep inside the body. Taiji means Yin and Yang. Taijiquan is the martial art that abides by this principle. Taijiquan is a so-called internal martial art.

During lessons you often hear: 'Now the Yin hand…', 'Now the Yang hand…', or 'The attacking hand is Yang, the one that yields is Yin…'. And often that's the whole explanation given. What a superficial concept. No wonder that people talk about secrets, because somehow there must be more to it. That's right: in fact there is much more to it, but it's far from being a secret. It is a question of the level and the depth of the concept that is being trained. As the mentality of training in the world today is rather poor, it's not surprising that this 'more' is known to a few only and so keeps circulating in terms of mystery. Those however capable of understanding it do know how much training and expertise are required, and they speak about it in an unpretentious manner.

In order to resolve this 'secret' we'll have to deal with the matter of Taijiquan in a very profound way: moving our body in a Taiji-adapt way optimises the internal flow of energy. Not only does it improve, we become capable of consciously perceiving it, and of controling and applying it.

With existence being at rest, Yin and Yang will merge, and *Wuji* is created, the mother of Taiji. Within rest there is only the one and only energy, only one single part and not its counterpart, and thus not even the part. That is the nothing and the whole, it cannot be named as there is nothing I could distinguish it from. When this primal energy takes to motion, when life is created, this energy during motion appears to fall apart, and Yin and Yang will generate. When a human is born the energy that he incorporates will spread within, and Yin and Yang will begin to circulate. However, in the course of time and with the conditions of life, disharmonies gain influence upon that process. The art of Taijiquan is to bring those two forces back into their pristine and balanced flow, initially perhaps not back to their primal condition; they still are to be harmonised to make them work together and unite. That will prevent the blockages that inevitably arise with ageing and injuries of any kind. The last and final step would be to lead both energies back to their common root, so that they dissolve and find their way back to the very source that we all come from. This would be the so-called immortality, being beyond dependence on birth, life and death. We abide therefore by the existence of Yin and Yang, and it's here we find our problems.

With training and growing insight, I discover the streams of Yin and Yang inside my body. I am not speaking superficially in terms of intentions of wishing how to apply a part of my body; but in terms of energetic conditions that the single body parts are tuned into. Within Chen style we learn about this phenomenon by way of the silk-exercises. We consciously animate the natural ways of energy. Energy going from the centre to the outside is Yang. Energy flowing back from outside to inside, that is from the extremities to the *Dantian*, is Yin. In the beginning this is trained in an explicit way by large, simple movements.

With increased training, I become sensitive to my energies. I learn to recognise my flow of Yin and Yang, and about their counterparts. Within a Yang movement I sense an element of Yin energy and vice versa. Within this seemingly marginal part, I recognise with increasingly deep perception of my movement the counterpart again of a counterpart that has already begun to exist, and so on. The image of two mirrors facing each other may serve as a simple example. Looking into one of them makes you get lost in an endless depth of mirrors getting smaller and smaller. It's the same with our movements. As our training gets more and more profound, our movements 'vanish' within spirals that gain more and more depth and density, despite the fact that the outer movement remains the same, so that the opponent can no longer follow or understand this process. In this way his energy gets lost in contact with a martial artist of a master's level. He no longer has any chance of defeating him. In terms of Taijiquan, this can be depicted by the symbols of Yin and Yang: the beginner will recognise Yin and Yang within himself, namely, the line that's parted and the line that's continuous (see Figure 58).

Figure 58

The advanced practitioner will recognise the trigrams within himself, and a much greater variation of combinations of Yin and Yang (see Figure 59).

Figure 59

The master will sense the hexagrams inside himself, the 64 combinations of Yin and Yang made up of six coherent lines. He has the deep insight that there are no edges set, so the Taiji practitioner can with growing age become stronger and stronger and more and more 'un-earthly'. In this way, he will himself recognise everything else that exists, and all secrets will disappear. Nobody from outside will be able to follow him any more or to defeat him.

At advanced levels the body evolves energetic spirals of a continuously increasing subtlety and density, a more and more complex interlacing, so to speak, of Yin and Yang. This enables the artist to absorb and to emit energy upon and from smaller and smaller surfaces of his body. The result is the 'master' who no longer allows any visible movement to be perceived, because in fact he hardly needs to move any longer or to move at all. That's why we call it an internal martial art. This is a long road of course, but the better we understand the principle, the faster we will advance.

And so we come back to the mistake of the double weight shift: the non-practitioner does not recognise Yin and Yang inside his body and thus remains alike both on top and in the lower half of his body. Internally his upper body is equal to his lower body; therefore his stability and his balance are rather weak, similar to a tuna fish without a point of balance. Only by way of the balance point being low and its counterweight at the top, does it keep returning to its position. The weight is no longer double-shifted; it is more in the bottom than at the top. It is just the same with the Taiji practitioner: the centre of balance is shifted towards the bottom, and the upper body becomes released and light-weighted. Again we have here our continuous and our separated line of Yin. Following this description, things become more and more refined. The body is no longer simply subdivided into bottom and top. To provide an image: the legs are again subdivided in two parts which aren't double-shifted in the sense of being energetically equal, but bear different Yin and Yang values. The same goes for the upper body, the arms and the head. Any of the limbs mentioned previously are subdivided again and again. Even the hands now consist of very many small units which aren't double-shifted but differentiated in terms of Yin and Yang.

With continued training, this ramification will continue, just as with our image of the mirrors, until from outside it can no longer be seen where the practitioner's Yin and Yang energy is located. The body is being sensitised into numerous single parts, with each of them having a distinct potential of Yin and/or Yang. The double weighting becomes energetic and dissolves into into smaller and smaller subdivisions and refinements. Every single subdivision however stands in full relationship with the others. With increasing progress, the practitioner's external way of acting becomes less and less important; it does not matter any more whether his weight is more to the right or to the left or centred, or whether the elbow is high or low, or whether the opponent pushes from the bottom to the top or the other way round. For the inner condition is never double-weighted; it is in continuous change and adaptation. In this way, the moves of a 'master' can never be identified from the outside, and any contact with him results in a sensation of fading away. He can no longer be identified, but he identifies you, because in contrast to him you've got the flaw of the double weighting. He realises in an instant: here you are this way, there you are that way, that accounts for your rigidness, and that makes it easy for him to defeat you. Only by way of a very extended training and understanding the proper concept will you be able to slowly overcome the 'disease' (as it is often translated) of double weighting. In this way you will be a mystery for others, because you are able to perceive Yin and Yang, to understand and to sense them.

There are no secrets, there is only ignorance, and that's something we can reduce day by day.

Chapter 12

Taijiquan and Sexuality – Does Art of Life Need Art of Love?

Unabbreviated version of an article published in Dao-Magazin 3/1996

Taijiquan is nowadays everywhere and omnipresent. In most cases it is as simple gymnastics, as meditation in motion, sometimes as a sport, and much less frequently as a traditional martial art and art of health care. Always, however, it is as a concept of cultivating life.

The far-Eastern art of love is not universal. Making the art of love acceptable is a much more difficult issue. Claiming brilliance as a teacher of Taiji and movement while presenting a business card is much easier and has much more style than introducing oneself as an artist of love.

Yet both have similar goals, which are about vital, inner energies, to enrich them and thus make use of them, to collect them and not to waste them. In brief: to empower the body, by way of martial and amorous art. That way it can't but be healthy.

Within the arts of love they say that any ejaculation essentially weakens the male within his inner (*jing-*) power. Does this mean every male Taiji practitioner has to reach mastership also in this rather intimate art? Is he doomed otherwise to enrich his Qi during morning exercises in the park and deplete it at night? Women can also ejaculate. Some do, some don't, some may wish to. Does this mean they lose the same amount of energy as well? Taijiquan training does increase desire. Sexual potency grows. Am I trapped therefore in a cycle of up and down? A never ending increase and decrease of energy budgeting?

Asking the old masters, we often hear: 'regulate your love life. During winter a total of once or twice, during summer perhaps three or four times.' So then, that would finish the problem, and quite likely my relationship as well. Not wishing of course to sacrifice my joy of life nor my relationship, I'll search for answers. The far-Eastern art of love will provide them. Do I have to learn about them now in order to cash in the power accumulated by my Taijiquan training?

For the major part of the Taiji community, Taijiquan is a hobby to indulge in once or twice a week, like some sort of soft gymnastics. For them and for those who don't find anything valuable about the statements of the old masters anyway, it might not be essential at all, because where little exists there isn't much to lose. For those however who are compelled to practise Taijiquan even at the bus stop or in the cinema queue, or for those who seem to have turned love into a kind of vocation, the combination of a traditional love life with Taijiquan and health may be a contradiction. Whatever the situation, I'd like to recommend to all a combination of both, of the far-Eastern art of love and of Taijiquan.

Sexuality is one of the basic needs of human life. Anyone not feeling a vocation towards living as a monk or a nun (and even he or she), during the course of life has to deal a lot with matters of love. There may be issues of adolescent confusion, exuberance or helplessness, barriers of education, relationships that flame up or wane, sexual problems or wishful images, a decline of libido during old age or just the attempt of finding release from sexual desire. There is much that may stimulate the traditionally 'Western' human to a closer consideration of his or her sexuality.

How much more relevant then, for those who deal with matters of energetic arts like Taijiquan and/or Qigong, because it's here we can sense what goes on inside our body, and how it has an effect on us. All matters of life must be learnt, they say, with the exception of love, because love, people say, is a natural thing. But for us the goal is beyond this anyway. A baby learns to speak in order to improve its communicational skills. Screaming and crying seemingly won't make it in the long term. Neither do we need to train any martial art in order to defend ourselves, but real Taijiquan training of course will raise our capability of doing so. Being a martial artist, I ask myself after any lost fight how I might improve my skills and adapt my training.

And what about love? What are the 'lost battles' of love? Why does my initially so promising relationship slowly lose its fire? Why do bodies once so attracted to each other start losing their mutual energy, yes sometimes even to rejecting each other? Why is my sexuality so completely different from my partner's? Why do I come too early or sometimes not at all? And there we are right in the middle of the gender war, only I don't feel interested in going to war. Just ignoring the matter will not help, however.

During Taijiquan I sensitise myself to my energies and learn to harmonise them. It's just the same with the art of love. I begin empathising deeper and deeper into the matter, gaining knowledge and sensitivity in order eventually to reach harmony between the genders, that is between my partner and myself. Instead of a relationship with a curve that rises in the beginning and then declines more and more, I can (we can) keep reaching new heights. Sexuality with the partner will not fade, instead fascination and excitement keep growing. Body, spirit and soul belong deeply to each other. Love becomes an evolution that will last.

The Chinese art of love, its origins coming from the legend of 'polygamy' of the Emperor in ancient China, is today offering us a true alternative, in particular within a monogamist faithful relationship. Energy will not fade, it will rather grow. This happens not by way of a constant (and in the long term senseless) change of partners, but instead by energy and refinement which steadily increase within the relationship itself. The fascination of the new, day by day within the same relationship. This is possible.

Taijiquan offers a marvellous foundation for this: the body becomes smooth and rich with energy which has natural consequences for sexuality. The body becomes sensitised, it evolves empathy, it gets stronger in condition, and what is most important: we learn to perceive and apply energy consciously, both mentally and physically. Both things play a central role within a relationship. A fulfilling love life is essential for a happy relationship. Just as important however is the ability to act with empathy, recognition and harmony, not being helplessly entangled in the whirls of emotions.

Taijiquan grants a clear spirit and a purified body, the consequence of which creates a balance of the energies within oneself and those of the world around, be it mental conflict, the physical stand-off or be it love. All abides in the same principle, the Taiji-principle.

The art of love in turn can help me to improve my Taijiquan. I can recognise and learn how not to waste my energies in matters of love, but instead to make them grow continuously.

It's a peculiar thing indeed. During the course of my Taiji practice and in parallel to my energies gained directly from training, I begin to take care of not wasting them too much in other domains. I begin to stay away more and more from toxins like nicotine and alcohol, I care about nutrition, I live at a natural pace. Only in matters of love I keep wasting as I did before. Let's turn the problem into something positive, with the proficiency of the far-Eastern art of love.

The 'Yellow Emperor' made use of it in order to preserve energy – besides his concubines – for his state affairs. We use it in order to – besides evolving our relationship or our love life in general – be able to perform excellent Taijiquan.

In the Daoist view male ejaculation indicates a loss of (*jing-*) energy. But how are males and females supposed to handle this information? Is one supposed to feel remorse every time, just like a teenager after masturbation? What about our Taiji professionals? Are they to annihilate their relationships in order to perform the best possible slow movements in the morning hours in the park? Of course not. This doesn't fit with Taijiquan, in the very meaning of the word. The goal of Taijiquan is most of all to enrich life and to improve it, and that's exactly what it does. It achieves this even more in combination with the art of love, as in philosophical terms both deal with the same thing.

Technically both systems can complement each other quite well. An important step in learning about the far-Eastern art of love is for example the strengthening of the pelvic floor muscle. If it is too weak, it's like the case of a car with a worn out fan-belt. A major part of the male and female orgasm is closely related to these muscles. Moreover, they are the emergency brake in holding back ejaculation. It's the interchange between tension and distension that enables me on a physical level to strengthen my erection, to have orgasms or to control ejaculation. Traditional books describe training cycles of many contractions for reinforcing the pelvic floor muscle. The better books at the same time point out the importance of relaxation phases after exertion, because during this phase the blood that has just flowed into the area is being re-absorbed. Blood and energy always flow jointly, so that blood and Qi-circulation are increased in this (sexual) region. This increases the feeling of desire, orgasmic capacity and erection. With the help of Taijiquan and Qigong I learn to go much deeper into phases of relaxation, and so further increase the flow of energy. This turns the superficial technique of tension and distension into inner Qigong which considerably improves the outcome.

During a male ejaculation (*jing-*) energy is being lost directly, but this is seemingly not the case for the woman. Here energy is not held directly within the ejaculate. During female orgasm blood and Qi-circulation are allegedly increased (excuse me for saying 'allegedly', but I do happen to be a non-female). Orgasm and ejaculation, as mentioned before, don't have to occur synchronously, so that males can achieve this.

On a mental level, orgasm may be focused on too strongly. Can it be that I'm concentrating too much on something that is perhaps not even that important? The more I insist on something, the harder its realisation becomes, they say in Taiji. The message is: to let go. Perhaps the case is this: the less he is fixated on orgasm, the longer he can go, and correspondingly: the easier will she come to orgasm.

The way leads to the goal, and during practice over a long time, we learn that the goal is no longer that important. The one (ejaculative) orgasm becomes a minor matter; it's replaced by unending waves of desire going further and further. But what do I do with this energy that no longer depends on being discharged? At this point I find my Taijiquan and my Qigong as a way of controlling energy and passing it on. I no longer have to complete any process and neither am I disappointed if a state that was wished for does not arrive. On the contrary: I'm free of wishes and forceful images and thus more able than ever before to enjoy what I'm doing. Many problems will then disappear by themselves. Or I may learn about the art of love in order to improve my orgasmic potential, and after a time, while looking back, I see those goals by and large achieved, yet they no longer seem to be of such importance to me.

Honestly: who after all trains Taijiquan intensively day by day and keeps doing so mainly because of the original goals of health and self-defence? Certainly I've advanced in these matters, yet a long time ago they became an end in itself. Taijiquan advertising might promise us many advantages and the benefits we might gain. Taiiquan took its triumphant trail of victory all over the world, in simple terms because of one thing: a good feeling. Training simply provides us with a good feeling. We begin to feel our body, and we open our mind. It is this that makes a human rich: a good feeling. Because of this, love and sexuality are of such interest. Because what do they provide us with? A good feeling. Positive stimulation of body, mind and soul. On the basis of a good feeling we can reach faith, blissfulness, security, spirituality, health; briefly, all that's worth striving for in life, yes, including even success, can be achieved. In order not to spoil our good feeling with negative emotions, but instead to establish a harmony between the matters of life, we need to evolve a deeper understanding, a deeper empathy, via Taijiquan and the art of love. The novice finds himself at the beginning of a long path towards joy, desire, and, most of all: a good feeling.

Chapter 13

Taijiquan in the World – A Resumé

Published in Kung Fu Magazin 1998

It's just 100 years ago that Taijiquan became popular in Beijing. Prior to this, Taijiquan the way we know it today actually had its home exclusively in Chenjiagou. This however is such a small village that we may say with confidence that Taijiquan was previously unknown. Today it's performed in numerous countries. In earlier times there were just a handful of people who achieved Taijiquan at mastership level, and indeed there aren't really many more of them today. Of practitioners there were perhaps several hundred; today however there are several hundred millions. How can it be that nowadays so many more people practise Taijiquan while there aren't many more masters than there were in former times? And why is Taijiquan so much in vogue?

The Eastern culture is almost unknown to the Western world, in spite of the fact that many exist now and lots of exchanges have taken place. A culture can't be understood in depth unless it has really been lived, otherwise misunderstanding or misinterpretations will frequently occur. In particular, a culture so strange to us as is the case with the Chinese, makes it difficult to understand. Hence, very often highly mystical ideas are attributed to Taijiquan, not only because it is material that is difficult to scan through, moreover it comes from a land that's far away and derives from a time which we'd rather file under

'Thousand and One Nights'. So it becomes hard for the Westerner to find the proper approach to Taijiquan. Many fail because they don't manage to look beyond the metaphysical haze, unable to recognise the real Taijiquan. Others in turn have difficulties in leaving behind their Western attitude of trying to understand things in an exclusively rational mode. They expect to be able to explain Taijiquan in terms of a purely mechanical structure.

That the structure of Taijiquan often gets misjudged is in my view mainly based on a wrong concept of softness. Taijiquan refers to the teachings of Yin and Yang. In overall terms it means hard and soft, fast and slow, top and bottom. It does not mean either of the two. It does not mean: we are soft, the others are hard. Or: we are slow, the others are fast. Neither does it mean the others are on top and we are underneath, does it? Yin and Yang belong together. The reason for training is to be able to combine all these aspects within myself, in order to have a wholesome effect on everything internal and external. People very often only regard the aspect of softness; they became too Yin-focused. Often they are that way by disposition which makes things worse, just as people who are physically very active tend towards Karate or kickboxing. Everybody looks for something like himself. In this way he will basically only enforce what he's already got. True balance is found only if we unite all aspects within ourselves.

That's why the traditional forms of Taijiquan aren't only soft but explosive as well, showing not only softness but also hardness. One is always born within the other. So then, have no fear: hardness of course is permeated by softness. That way I avoid anything that's just partial and remain able to react spontaneously in any situation. I don't need to pursue a dogma, all I follow is nature herself, so that *Wuwei*, so-called non-acting, spontaneous, effective and free action may arise.

As often in life, real understanding lies in between. In order to experience and understand Taijiquan I must have not only a knowledgeable teacher, be it a man or a woman, I have to come to terms as well with the Chinese culture and the Chinese way of thinking, otherwise I will not recognise its true character and run the risk of surrendering to wrongful concepts.

It is certainly a positive thing to state that Taijiquan has rapidly spread across the world, but due to poor understanding and training periods being too short or too superficial, Taijiquan has taken a course far away from its roots. This development still keeps growing. Nonetheless, it's a fact that by now real masters of Taijiquan do teach in Western countries. Grandmaster Chen Xiaowang for example is committed to the life-task of providing a remedy for the confused ideas on Taijiquan. For 90 per cent of the year he travels the world, also with the intention of passing on the Taijiquan of his family, the Chen-style. His main intent, however, is not to enforce a certain style. He is committed to exposing the Taiji-principle in all its entirety and transparency to the people outside China. 'This is the very secret of Taijiquan,' he says. 'The secret is not that it remains unspoken, but that so many indeed don't know about it and so very few are able to really understand it. That is why I travel so much, doing so in order to provide people with explanations and help them understand.'

I have joined my Shifu Chen Xiaowang for many years on many of his travels, and I must say that this work is beginning to bear fruit. The influence of the West also adds to Taijiquan, and in quite a positive way. In our part of the world it's rational to raise many questions, and Grandmaster Chen Xiaowang has realised that spiritual evolution is of high importance for the West. 'In China the greater role was always on physical development. Here in the West it's the other way round. Taijiquan is very effective in developing both components to an equally high level.'

In the West there is much more scrutinising; people want to know much more, and they love to discuss and talk about it. Unfortunately this may be at the expense of time dedicated to the actual training. In China there is much less scrutinising; people train much more. Without real knowledge about the very essentials of training, however, the form will remain forever empty. People then train a lot, yet without any significant progress.

Knowing about the inner essentials of Taijiquan, but not realising how much training is required in order to make them work, then not only my form will remain empty, even my phrases will. 'Both must merge and unite. Just as I need a roadmap to get from A to B, I need a precise plan on how to do my training, otherwise I can't reach the destination. If I don't follow the road, then even with employing effort and endurance, I will not advance. Mentalities of both East and West must complement one another, then the highest results can be achieved,' says Grandmaster Chen Xiaowang. Like no other he has succeeded in demonstrating the Taiji-principle in full. He is willing as well to lead his students by way of corrections precise to the nearest millimetre towards real success.

Now it is possible to learn Taijiquan in the West like it is in the East. This was not the case when I began. I had to make frequent and extended journeys to China in order to study Taijiquan seriously, with dedication and from scratch. Whether Taijiquan is going to be implemented the same way in the West mainly depends on understanding its principle, and of course on the immense diligence of training that's required. The first steps have been taken. Let us stay the course.

Taijiquan is a science of life. It is a philosophy to be lived and experienced. It's a flow through ourselves, and we are part of it. We are fulfilled by it. Country borders have no influence on that. The essence of truth is always the same. *Wan fa gui yi* – 'Ten thousand roads, one principle.' These are the words of many of Grandmaster Chen Xiaowang's calligraphies. No matter what my studies might focus on, if I pursue them with diligence and work on them unceasingly, I will advance. The Chinese call this *Gongfu*. Diligent work, however, requires the right background of course, conditions that allow truly effective work. Inner and outer components must fit. The outer component means I need a teacher who is proficient in his craft. I need the free space and time in order to deal with the matter. The inner component means I need to be intelligent, in order not only to hear and listen, but to personally understand, transcend and realize what I am hearing. With all these conditions in place nothing will block the way for real development. It does not matter whether it's East or West: with the conditions being the same everywhere it's up to the individual to make an effort to gain a result. Meanwhile we do have an opportunity to create these elementary conditions in our own environments too. We should refrain, however, from attempting to exert an influence before these conditions are established. All too many teachers in the West make use of Taijiquan for this and that. Hardly any one among them, however, has understood Taijiquan at all. Taijiquan is of umlimited range and therefore it is neither in need of modification nor add-ons. The further I travel towards the core of a matter, the more liberated and experienced I will be.

In this way the essence of Taijiquan will not only be preserved, it will advance. Then, with Taijiquan being spread further and further in the East and the West, there will not only be more and more practitioners of Taijiquan, there will be more and more real Taiji-masters, too. A beautiful vision.

IV

Taijiquan in the Mirror of Medicine

Chapter 14

The Medical Point of View within the Chinese Tradition

Gerhard Milbrat

TAIJIQUAN AND TRADITIONAL CHINESE MEDICINE

Taijiquan has gained real popularity as a training method serving both for purposes of health and cultivation of life, enabling us to create the conditions for a healthy and vital existence. All over the world millions of people currently dedicate themselves to Taijiquan for a variety of health-related reasons. The various ailments and disorders which Taijiquan can help with ranges from illnesses of the skeletal system and the supporting anatomy, the respiratory organs, the digestive system, as well as cardiological and circulatory diseases to immune deficiency and stress-related disturbances. Taijiquan is applied with successful results in rehabilitation clinics. Entire books full of case studies and first-hand reports could be written as evidence. Taijiquan and its medical effects are increasingly scrutinised by science – which is a good thing. The practitioner of Taijiquan is in turn invited to take a closer look at the traditional medicine of the Chinese.

Traditional Chinese Medicine (TCM)

The most eminent and distinct theory of Taijiquan is the one of Yin and Yang. Together with the concept of Qi the idea of Yin and Yang permeates Chinese philosophy, and it's also the basis of Traditional Chinese Medicine (TCM). As we know, Yin and Yang stand in permanent interchange while showing four main aspects:

1. the antagonism between Yin and Yang

2. the interdependence of Yin and Yang

3. the interactive consumtion of Yin and Yang

4. the interactive transformation of Yin and Yang.

The application of Yin and Yang within TCM pursues the use of four strategies:

1. enforcing Yin

2. enforcing Yang

3. removing Yin-abundance

4. removing Yang-abundance.

An attribution of the organs to Yin and Yang is shown by the concept of the five organs of accumulation and the six organs of the palace, *Wu Zang Liu Fu*. The five organs of accumulation (*Zang*) are Yin: Liver, heart (pericardium), spleen, lungs and kidneys. Assigned to them are among others the production, storage, guidance and control of the elementary substances Qi, blood and body fluids. The six palace or concave organs (*Fu*) are the colon, small intestine, stomach, gallbladder, bladder and Triple Warmer (*San Jiao*). The *San Jiao* consists of the thoracic cavity, and the upper and lower dorsal cavities, and includes the heart and lungs. Their main functions are the absorption, separation, distribution and excretion of nutrition and body substances and also the production of Qi.

One Yin organ and one Yang organ establish a functional entity upon which a phase of transformation, meridians, sense organs, certain tissues and more can be attributed. They form a circle of functions with certain assignments. If a part of the functional circuit is conspicuous or pathologically altered, the TCM doctor will identify the related functional circuit and so adapt his therapy.

Wu Xing

Just like the theory of Yin and Yang, the concept of the five phases of transformation is the basis of the Chinese theory of medicine. Each of the five phases of transformation represents among others a certain meridian, an organ, an emotion, or a season of the year. Moreover, the five phases of transformation, or five elements, also symbolise five different directions of movement.

- Wood corresponds with outward expansion, a movement in all directions.

- Metal in contrast stands for a contracting movement.

- Water is associated with a downward movement.

- Fire is associated with an upward movement.

- Earth is associated with stability or neutrality.

The *Wu Xing* (like Yin and Yang) are interrelated. The interactions between the five phases of transformation are of significant importance for the entire concept. Different interactions and sequences are distinguished: namely, reproduction, control, overcoming and contempt (see Figure 60). The first two circles deal with the normal balance of the elements among themselves. The others describe a disturbed relationship of the elements among themselves.

Vital substances

TCM defines the functioning of body and mind as the result of interacting vital substances. Following the sequence of substantiality, *Qi* is named as energy; *Qu*, blood; *Jing*, essence; *Jinye*, body fluids. However, all is eventually Qi in its various scales of substantiality. TCM distinguishes among Qi the *Yuan Qi* (primal Qi), *Gu Qi* (Qi of nutrition), *Zong*

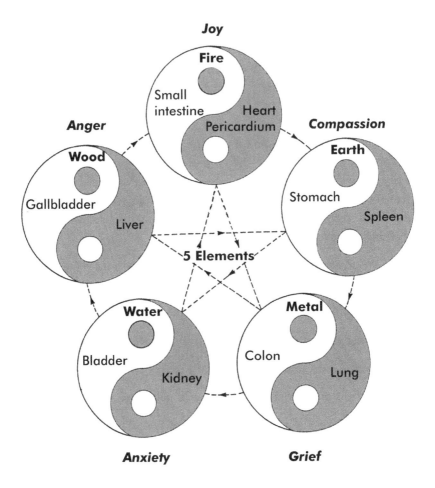

Figure 60

Qi (collecting Qi), *Zheng Qi* (true Qi), *Ying Qi* (nourishing Qi) and *Wei Qi* (defensive Qi). Independent from the various kinds of Qi the elementary functions of Qi are: transformation, transportation, retention, raising, protection and warming.

Pathological disturbances of the Qi-family show four types: Qi-insufficiency, pathological decline of Qi, stagnation of Qi and rebelling Qi if its flow takes the wrong direction.

Jing Luo

Qi is distributed across a system of carrier lines inside the entire body (Figure 61). Fourteen main and six special meridians are distinguished, forming a network and maintaining a large variety of functions. Twelve of the main meridians are coupled in bilateral settings. Six correspond with Yin, six correspond with Yang. They begin and end at the fingers and toes respectively. Yin and Yang of the arms is distinguished as well as Yin and Yang of the legs (Figure 62).

The Yin of the arms flows through the carrier lines of the lung, heart and pericardium; the Yang of the arms flows inside the meridians of the colon, small intestine and Triple Warmer. The latter has been described as the upper, middle and lower part of the body. The Yin of the legs flows through the meridians of the spleen, kidney and liver; the Yang of the legs flows through the meridians of the stomach, gallbladder and bladder. Two

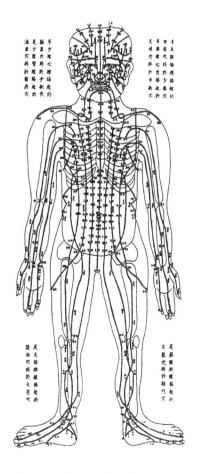

Figure 61 The meridian lines

of the 14 main meridians continue along the middle of the torso from the perineum to the head, whereby the back of the body is related to Yang, and the front of the body is related to Yin.

In the ideal situation, the meridians are continuously and harmoniously filled with Qi. Similar to the pulse wave in the arterial blood vessels, a wave of energy passes through the system of meridians in the course of 24 hours (see Figure 63). The meridians are functional circuits and have a close relationship with the main organs.

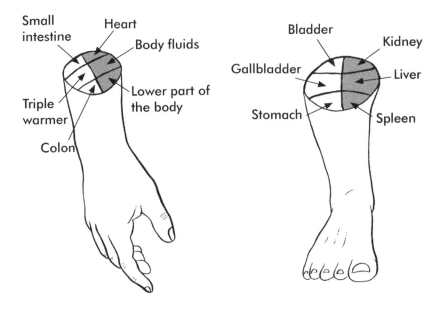

Figure 62 Yin and Yang of the arm and leg

Diagnosis and therapy

On the basis of the concepts mentioned above and the interactions and functions, the TCM-therapist will form his diagnosis. He will use sight, hearing, smell, questioning and sensing. He will form a comprehensive picture that considers all the symptoms and signs of the illness. He does not primarily look for causes, but for patterns instead. These can be identified on the basis of eight principles. These principles are a summary of all the other methods of identification and apply to all diseases:

- Inside – Outside.

- Emptiness – Fullness.

- Heat – Cold.

- Yin – Yang.

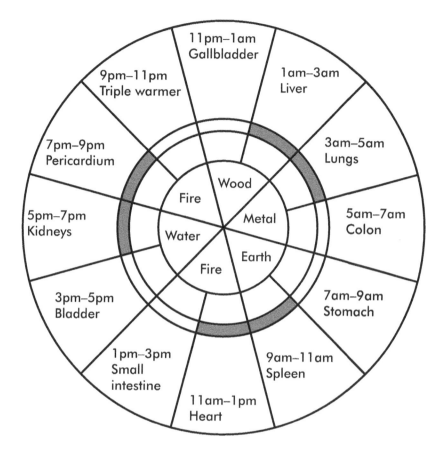

Figure 63

Further patterns can be identified by their relationship with the Qi, the blood and the body fluids, the internal organs, the five elements, the meridians and pathogenic factors. When the pattern of a disturbance or a disease is identified, the methods of treatment are applied.

TCM makes use of acupuncture, moxibustion (therapy using *moxa* or mugwort herb), diet, herbal medicine, chiropractic, massage, cupping glass therapy, Qigong and Taijiquan as well as special forms of these methods. Diagnosis and therapy should be the preserve of professionals. In order to do something for oneself, Taijiquan is a choice which may be made.

Taijiquan (practice and effects)

Practising Taijiquan helps us in finding an internal as well as an external structure of healing which enables all the joints and meridians to open and the vital substances to flow freely. Corrections on a scale of millimetres provided by a Taijiquan teacher help us in gaining sensitivity for our body and our energy. Though we may not know their functional mechanisms, we do sense whether or not we are on the right path. Taijiquan means the nurturing of one's own life and health, and if taught by a skilled teacher, it can effectively complement the work of a therapist.

By way of our daily Taijiquan training we purge our body and refill our store of energy. Probably everybody has been able to sense the protective Qi-coating (*Wei Qi*) that builds up after the exercise of the Standing Post. In most people who start Taijiquan, Yin and Yang are not in harmony which is the result of postural deficits and the given constitution. The ideal case would be: solid in the lower body and soft at the top. Often, however, our centre, instead of being in the lower *Dantian,* is rather seated in the head or the heart. This means that our body's centre of gravity is too high, we have no roots, and like a ping-pong ball we are subject to the impulses of mind and emotions. I call that a Yang-biased constitution (see Figure 64). Adapting the Taijiquan-specific position allows the head and the body to become empty and the belly to gain fullness. We start rooting ourselves to the ground. Being open in the lower body and keeping the pelvis and hip in an exact position is of extreme importance (see Figure 65). The formerly Yang-biased constitution may then harmonise itself.

Opposed to this is the Yang-biased constitution with energy focused too much in the lower body which results in a descending, a collapse of the supportive structure. There is a lack of Yang. In TCM we attempt to harmonise Yin and Yang on an increasingly fine scale. This does not work, however, by pushing a button. If we wish to use Taijiquan as a medicine we have to take it day by day, and of course this medicine sometimes tastes bitter. This means at the start of our daily training practice, we'll be going through various pain barriers and sensations.

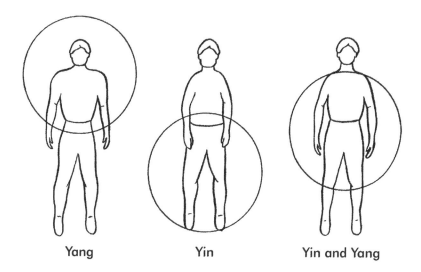

Yang   Yin   Yin and Yang

Figure 64

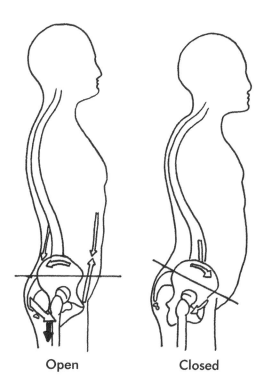

Open   Closed

Figure 65

During Standing Post for example we will, besides the pain caused by tension, be introduced to a whole palette of sensations. During the first weeks of training almost everyone will feel numbness, rigidity, prickling, pain, warmth and uncertainty. After some six weeks of daily training, however, well-being and relaxation will set in. In the case of lasting discomfort or pain, the reason for this may be a misadjustment of ribs, vertebrae or pelvis which requires professional inspection. Along with the training intervals we deepen our sense of energy, and eventually positive mental effects will become evident. A good correction of the stance during exercising will remove deep-seated blockages which often appear on a mental level.

By way of the standing meditation, we develop a deeper perception for the best posture; we begin by re-programming our traditional posture. This correction causes a widespread release of muscles and tendons, and in the course of time a true inner calm is reached. Very often the pains in the back that have plagued us so much will disappear. During the silk and the form exercises with their spiral movements, we activate the flow of energies with Qi and blood circulating freely, the cerebrum is harmonised, and we take in more oxygen. By using the abdomen, a kind of soft intestinal massage, a cleansing and immune stimulation takes place. Interesting information on the application of the abdomen are found within the controversial discussion on the so-called intestinal brain. This topic deals with nerve cells enclosing the intestinal walls like a network, and which have unimagined functions within our body.

Taijiquan in the view of TCM

Considering the possible health effects of Taijiquan as a balance of Yin and Yang, of harmonisation of Qi and *Xue* (energy and blood), the receptiveness of the meridians and the cultivation of of *Zhen Qi* (the real Qi), we recognise the place of Taijiquan within TCM. The central aspects of the common ground of all inner exercises of TCM can be summarised by six principles:

- Expansion, restfulness and naturalness.

- Imagination and Qi follow each other.

- Movement and rest belong together.

- Relaxed at the top, firm in the lower body.

- The proper measure.

- Step by step.

The rationale of Taijiquan as given by TCM is the primal attempt of the human body to balance the never-ending antagonism between itself and its environment. In order to keep the biological processes going, the human body by way of exchanging matter stands in close relationship with its environment; at the same time functional circuits and metabolic processes are working inside all the body's organs. In the view of TCM, such biological processes are caused by the inner transformation of Qi (*Qi Hua*). The effect of Taijiquan is to enforce this transformation of Qi by enabling man to control his Qi through proper body posture, effective breathing and the use of imagination. The enforced transformation of Qi can enable the balance of Yin and Yang, the harmonisation of Qi and blood, the perviousness of the meridians and the cultivation of the real Qi.

Chapter 15

Medical Examinations of Taijiquan

Frank Marquardt[4]

In order to analyse the effects of regular Taijiquan training on health and well-being, I carried out a scientific study in the year 2000. The basic results are presented here.

EMPIRICAL RESEARCH

The practical part of the study is based on various empirical research projects. The first three will be presented and discussed here.

Obtaining data was performed by various means:

- A questionnaire-based investigation on health effects in the view of the Taijiquan practitioner.

---

4   Frank Marquardt is a certified sports academic. His scientific work is focused in particular on Taijiquan in relation to movement, training and health. His large-scale empirical studies are given here in summary. The original script contains detailed information including the full listing of the results and is available from WCTAG's office.

- Measuring the heart rate during the 19-form after Chen Xiaowang, with focus on various degrees of intensity.

- EMG (electromyography)-studies during the single-hand silk-exercise (right arm).

- Measuring of fitness according to a 'fitness scale' directly following a training session.

THE HEALTH EFFECTS OF TAIJIQUAN AS SEEN BY THE PRACTITIONER

Rationale and purpose of the study

The empirical study presented here concentrates on the Taijiquan practitioner's concept of health and illness, focusing on the personal perception of Taijiquan's health effects. Perception refers to the personal state of health, and is to be related to the general health-promoting effects of Taijiquan.

The content of the study is explained in its theoretical part and will not be repeated here. The various philosophical, theoretical and practical explanations share a holistic approach. The holistic concept of man, environment and motion is considered to be the foundation for physical and mental health.

Taijiquan practitioners' health consciousness enables conclusions to be drawn about the expected or already realised positive health effects. Since the tested persons had been experienced in Taijiquan over several years, we may presume that they were convinced of their discipline and therefore needed to relate all their results by means of interpretation and bias: a test person's recording of his own rating of Taijiquan's health effects is bound to document belief and conviction in relation to the high value attributed to Taijiquan. This doesn't necessarily result in a contradiction if we consider that people believing in the advantages of a certain system of movement have intensified their training to such a degree that they have indeed been able to gain positive and significant results in terms of health-related improvements.

Expected health effects can form a large part of the motivation for beginning or continuing training of Taijiquan. Besides the many health references of Taijiquan appearing at various stages, the questioning brings out certain personally favoured health criteria attributed to this art of movement.

The current state of research is largely based on experimental studies. Personal opinions on Taijiquan-related effects as perceived have had only marginal consideration in research. This is the case in particular with the meditative aspect and the various perceptive levels of Taijiquan. As the aspect of meditation is a necessary part of its many references to the topic of health, its relevance within this study is self-explanatory. All results gained in this field can be viewed here with limitations. Gathering systematic results on meditative experience is a difficult task. Verbalization is not easy, due to the very personal and intuitive nature of the experience.

This study aims to provide a contribution on the health-relatedness of Taijiquan as given by the personal experience of Taijiquan practitioners. In its own way it can complement the findings gained by physiological and functional gymnastic studies.

Test persons

During this questionnaire-based study, subjects from three different styles of Taijiquan were interviewed. They were not subject to any special requirements except for having done regular Taijiquan training.

The group of subjects was composed of practitioners from the Taijiquan styles *Chen*, *Yang* and *Wu*. These have the highest level of dissemination and popularity in Germany. A closer attribution of the various styles can be obtained by way of various memberships. Subjects of Chen-Taijiquan are members of WCTAG (World Chen Taijiquan Association Germany) under the guidance of Jan Silberstorff. Subjects from the Yang-style are in most cases members of ITCCA (International Tai Chi Chuan Association) with its European guidance being in the hands of Chu King Hung, resident in London. The Wu-Taijiquan subjects are connected within an association under the leadership of Ma Jingbao (Netherlands) and Martin Bödicker (Germany). Twenty-one female and 19 male test persons were interviewed.

Questionnaire and method of approach

The study was performed by way of written questioning. The questionnaire especially designed for this study was arranged largely in accordance and with the pattern of a study performed by Klaus Moegling.[5] Compared with an interview, the questionnaire ensures an economic evaluation. Moreover it leaves necessary time and rest for the interviewee to deal with the questions, some of which are open-answer questions (on philosophical or health-related issues).

Besides an introductory part for dealing with socio-demographic factors, the questionnaire concentrates on issues of subjective meaning and rating concerning the health-related values of Taijiquan. By including open-ended questions as well as closed ones, the questionnaire combines an efficient statistical evaluation with the open answering of single questions.

Implementation of the survey

Data were gathered during a four-week period from mid-August through mid-September 2000. Distribution of questionnaires was organised regionally as well as beyond (greater Dortmund area and catchment area of Münsterland and greater Düsseldorf). Distribution and return of questionnaires was partly organised through related persons or by way of personal contact. Questionnaires were then answered by the recipients at home.

Results

THE GENERAL HEALTH EFFECTS OF TAIJIQUAN

The many health effects of Taijiquan were surveyed by means of the practitioners' personal experience. The various statements in question no. 18 refer to the most frequent improvements supposed to be

---

5   Moegling, K.: Untersuchungen zur Gesundheitswirkung des Tai Chi Chuan, Prolog Verlag, Kassel 1998, p. 341 ff.
6   See *De Marees, H.*: Sportphysiologie. Sport und Buch, Strauß, Köln 1996, p. 119.

attributed to Taijiquan. These include: improvement of back-related disturbances, problems with the joints, heart and blood circulation ailments and mental disorders. With the requirement that Taijiquan was being regularly practised, the subjects were to give a rating on the corresponding modes of effectiveness. Figure 66 shows the median of all the results.

Significant about the median analysis in Figure 66 is that a large part of the results are above level 4. The majority of answers thus attribute a positive effect to Taijiquan. The highest rates (each at 4.8) were given on the statements: 'Taijiquan can reinforce the back; it strengthens the muscles of the legs and improves coordinations.' Besides these physically defined advantages of Taijiquan, the subjects also rated the mental levels of Taijiquan's efficiency. According to these ratings, regular training promotes mental stress control (4.6) and eases an overreactive nervous system (4.6).

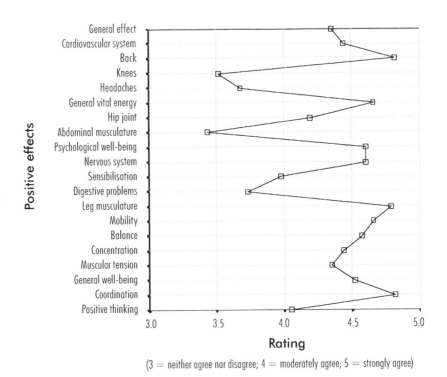

(3 = neither agree nor disagree; 4 = moderately agree; 5 = strongly agree)

Figure 66 Positive health effects of regular Taijiquan training

The health effects of Taijiquan by self-perception

The following results deal with the subjects' self-perception. General well-being has improved from a mid-level rating (M = 3.22) which indicates a neutral position towards the next higher level. Test persons rate their momentary well-being as 'quite good' to 'good' (M = 4.38). Aspects of health in psychological terms appear greatly increased. Ratings here show a rise from M = 2.84 resp. 2.84 to M = 4.09 resp. 4.34.

Compare your personal health before and after a period when Taijiquan exercises have been regularly performed. (Question 19)

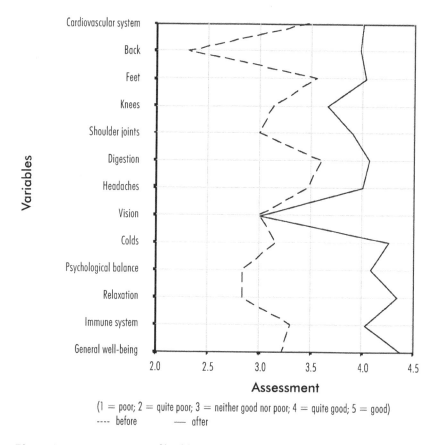

(1 = poor; 2 = quite poor; 3 = neither good nor poor; 4 = quite good; 5 = good)
---- before   —— after

Figure 67 Comparing states of health prior to Taijiquan training and today

The clearest improvement in physical terms is seen with the back-related variable. By median value the test persons showed an improvement from a rating as 'quite poor' (M = 2.31) to 'quite good' (M = 3.97).

According to the subjects' statements, Taijiquan has no significant effect on vision. A constant result however over a longer period may indicate improved vision. This is in spite of the fact that human vision usually reduces over the course of time.

It must be remembered at this point that this research does not produce evidence of causality, i.e. a relation between improved health and the training of Taijiquan. On the basis of the data as evaluated so far, it can be assumed however that subjects consider their own improved health a result of exercising Taijiquan. This assumption is also consistent with the results of questions 15 and 16. Both were open questions to give subjects an opportunity for longer answers. Question 15 targets the general effects of regular training on health. Question 16 asks subjects to relate this question to their personal health. Evaluation of the answers proved that the subjects had named no practical differences between the general effects on health and their own health improvement. Both questions received identical answers from the majority. The subjects related their statements on the general health effects of Taijiquan to themselves, and apparently they can confirm them in relation to their own health condition.

Based on this fact the results of questions 15 and 16 were summarised in a table. The structure of the statements reflects the findings gained by now on the health effects of Taijiquan.

The answers provide a summary of the general effects of Taijiquan and the physical and psychological improvements. Increased well-being and a generally improved condition of health were noted by 21 subjects. Improvement of back problems were reported by 13 subjects, with the majority relating the improvements to corrections of body posture. Inner balance and understanding inner relations were highlighted in particular by 13 test persons. One test person would not state any connection between general health effects and his own condition.

To accomplish and illustrate the statements as given in Table 1 some of them are given here in the original wording.

Which effects did Taijiquan have on your own health? (Question 16)

Table 1 Personal rating of the health effects of Taijiquan

Perceived change	Number noting the change	Percentage (N = 40)*
1. Improved well-being (ease and balance)	21	52.5%
2. Improving back problems (correction of posture)	13	32.5%
3. Positive effect on cardiovascular system, respiration	12	30%
4. Understanding inner balance, inner relations	9	22.5%
5. Motional improvements (mobility, coordination)	7	17.5%
6. No correlation	1	2.5%

*Sum of statements beyond 100% due to multiple answering options.

TYPICAL SELF-RELATED STATEMENTS OF TEST PERSONS ON TAIJIQUAN-CAUSED HEALTH EFFECTS (SEE TABLE 1)

Clearing energy within, greater flexibility and a heightened awareness for pathological factors, able to deal better with disturbances. I feel Taijiquan as a protective coating, I feel healthy all over and have got rid of my back problems.

Maintains mobility, less back disturbances, relaxation and balance.

One is more relaxed both in physical and mental terms; external damaging factors don't even get close. My allergy has almost vanished, problems with my back have been improved a large amount due to correction of posture.

One feels more relaxed afterwards and is no longer thrown off balance so easily. I feel fit after training and not so tired any more.

It makes body and mind stronger, and more than before it helps me to stay calm in many situations.

General improvement of health, as well as with individual health problems. Better ability to relax, improved body structure, in particular body posture. More calm and at ease in situations of stress.

Improved immune system, better circulation, improved body posture.

MOBILITY AND MOTORIC QUALITIES IN A TIME-RELATION WITH THE PRACTICE OF TAIJIQUAN TRAINING

The results as shown in Figure 68 clearly prove a strong improvement of mobility and motor qualities. According to this study, the main effects

The following section of questions deals with mobility and mobility issues before and after a period of regular training in Taijiquan. Please choose numbers from 1 to 5. (Question 20)

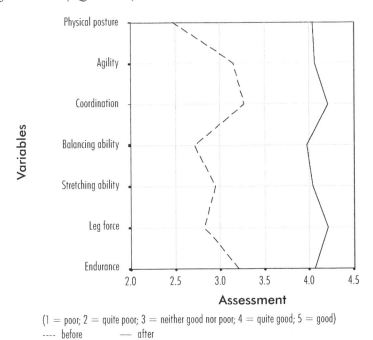

(1 = poor; 2 = quite poor; 3 = neither good nor poor; 4 = quite good; 5 = good)
---- before   — after

Figure 68 Median value of mobility and mobility related issues prior to taking up Taijiquan training compared with present condition

to be attributed to Taijiquan are body posture (Md = median value difference from M-after and M-prior = 1.56), leg strength (Md =1.39) and balancing capacity (Md = 1.26).

Improvement of endurance shows the smallest median value difference, though even here an improvement from 3.21 towards 4.06 appears. This result should also be viewed in relation to the empirical study on heart-frequency measuring during Taijiquan, and will get closer review in a further section.

The significance of meditation

Figure 69 shows the importance of meditation in Taijiquan. On a scale going from 'totally unimportant' to 'very important' the most negative rating was not named by any subject. More than half of them rated meditation in Taijiquan as 'very important'. Another 14 subjects (35%)

The aspect of meditation in Taijiquan to me is... (Question 22):

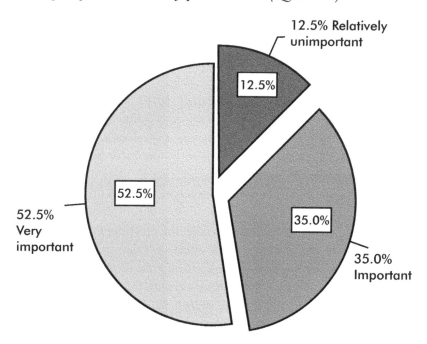

Figure 69 The importance of meditation in Taijiquan

chose the scale position 'quite important'; the remaining 12.5 per cent considered meditation in Taijiquan 'relatively unimportant'.

Other questions of interest in this context could ask about the importance of martial art aspects and the single subjects' changing life attitude and philosophy. An evaluation of these results would allow a weighting between the significant three major elements of Taijiquan.

Discussion

The evaluation of this study focuses on the subjective health-oriented rating of Taijiquan as a system of movement. The study is of descriptive character and therefore must be strictly distinguished from approaches targeting the analysis of causality which might exist between the single results and Taijiquan. The questionnaire-based analysis here deals with views and self-perception of a target group (Taijiquan practitioners of various styles) in relation to certain health-related factors that may be connected with Taijiquan.

A certain representative character of this study can be assumed by considering the number of the participating test persons ($n = 40$). While viewing the single results, however, a possible idealisation of Taijiquan by the subjects should be considered.

The results presented here do largely agree with the health effects of Taijiquan as published in many instruction books. Whether the real level of personal health experience is given or whether the test persons have adopted views as presented by books or by their teachers is not clear. We can assume, however, that in particular practitioners with a longer and more intense expertise do report their personal experience.

As clearly proven by results as a whole, the practitioners of Taijiquan are convinced of the positive health effect of Taijiquan. This knowledge, combined with an inner philosophical attitude and regular practice of movement, can turn into a health reality for the practitioner of Taijiquan. Taijiquan in this way combines an idealised feeling of life with physical and mental health. It becomes an educational factor serving as a guide towards a healthier and more conscious life. Personal theories and feelings turn into an aspect of influence on the health condition. This feeling of health offers a basis for interaction on many social and personal levels. This also includes the deliberate separation of the sports-competition aspect, from the meditational aspects. Taijiquan serves as an alternative art of movement without any pressure in terms of achievement or competition. Subjects described the benefit experienced in terms of ease and balance. A state of meditation can be helpful in particular when dealing with stressful conditions of life. Meditation eases both the mind and body, which in turn may help in easing the stress-related symptoms of illness.

This wide variety of positive influences makes Taijiquan a valuable preventive method of treatment. The results equally apply to remedial gymnastics and/or a psychosomatic approach. TCM emphasises the preventative significance of Taijiquan. This trend finds increasing acceptance and application in Europe. Health insurance companies and doctors have in most cases heard of preventative effects and are showing more interest in far-eastern systems of movement (such as Taijiquan, Qigong, Yoga, Aikido, oriental dance and others). Besides the many positive effects, a few negative aspects of Taijiquan were named. This indicates a critical and objective study of Taijiquan.

Within the entire review it is important not to lose sight of Taijiquan's range of efficiency. In a case inflammation of the appendix, the effects of Taijiquan are limited. This review deals instead with the minor everyday ailments which eventually can lead to serious illnesses. It's here Taijiquan offers an option to put mind and body into a balanced condition. Self-healing potentials are optimised. Awareness is improved on various levels, which is considered a necessary condition for changing reality. People become sensitive to toxic environmental factors and behavioural patterns. While Taijiquan has often been applied successfully in fighting disease, its primary focus, however, is prevention.

The methodical evaluation of the results has not been fully exploited yet in the form presented here. Based on detailed questioning in the socio-demographic section of this study, further statements from certain target groups (male, female, Chen-style, years of training expertise) and their correlations could be derived.

HEART RATE ANALYSIS DURING THE 19-STEP FORM REGARDING VARIOUS DEGREES OF EXPOSURE

Heart rate

Our heart supplies our entire body with blood. Rhythmic contraction of the heart sustains blood circulation. Blood circulates through the entire body and provides it with oxygen and nutrients. As well as this the heart controls the circulation for the discharge of carbon dioxide and degradation products of metabolism. The heart beats per minute are called heart rate or heart frequency (Hf). The average heart frequency of a body at rest is 60–90 beats per minute. Hf is just like other physical functions in that it is subject to adaptation by increased training efforts. Increased training of endurance will make the resting body's Hf sink. Compared to an untrained body, the Hf of someone trained to endure can reduce to half the rate.[6]

Increased physical impact raises the musculature's demand for energy. In reaction to increased muscular challenge, the blood circulation is increased. The same is the case with the heart-volume per minute correlating with an increased Hf and volume per beat. During higher challenges the increase of volume per beat is of minor importance, therefore an increased heart-volume per minute is mainly based on an increased Hf.

As a rule-of-thumb, the maximum Hf under average conditions can be said to be '220 per minute minus years of age'. The maximum impact of a person who is 60 years old is thus around 160 beats per minute.[7]

The effects of physical work on the human body are manifold. They range from an adaptation of bones and joints to changes of blood count. The Hf can be used as a parameter for determining the performance of endurance. In cases of identical physical performance, diagnostics of Hf can be an indicator related to the training level. These statements refer only to intra-individual comparison; inter-individual comparisons are

---

6   See *De Marees, H.:* Sportphysiologie. Sport und Buch, Strauß, Köln 1996, p. 119.

7   See *Neumann,G., Pfützner,A., Hottenrott, K.:* Alles unter Kontrolle – Ausdauertraining. Meyer & Meyer, Aachen 1993, p. 50.

not possible, as the initial values of heart rates may greatly differ within identical training levels depending on whether the person is at rest or under impact. The heart rate also depends on the nervous system. Factors of central influence in this respect are the medullar and hypo-thalamic centres. Among the peripheral factors are the various types of receptor and the constitution of the working musculature. Factors also to be taken into consideration are age, gender, physical posture, tem-perature, nutrition, daily rhythm, emotional setting as well as psycho-vegetative cardiovascular disturbances.

Rationale and target of the study

The study presented here deals with the physiological aspects of chang-ing heart rates during a Taijiquan-form, in relation to various levels of impact. Its subject is the question of training control by way of deliber-ate choice of varying intensities of impact. Moreover a contribution is given on the training options of general aerobic endurance and per-formance of Taijiquan. Promoting general endurance capabilities is of preventive character. It supports the health-promoting processes inside the body and thus contributes to physical and mental well-being. The empirical research thus integrates into the structure of the study pre-sented here and supports previous findings.

Test group

The test group is composed of persons practising the system of Chen Taijiquan. This restriction was necessary insofar as the topic of the study, the 19-step form, is peculiar to Chen Taijiquan and therefore cannot be directly compared with forms from other styles. This restric-tion thus was made only for reasons of comparability.

Fifteen subjects took part in the study, three female, 12 male, their age ranging from 31 to 40 years.

Carrying out the study

The study was carried out with the Chen Taijiquan group in Dortmund (in western Germany). The group formed as a section of WCTAG and is coached by the author. The test phase covered four weeks (August 2000).

Following a general warm-up, the practitioners performed the 19-step form by themselves. Each person was asked to keep the given sequence of high, medium and low stance. The recording function of the pulse-clock was stopped during the pauses between the single forms. Test persons paused for about five minutes to set the pulse frequency back to the rate of a resting condition. Transmitter belts were put on during the warm-up phase to enable a certain acclimatising to the rather tight-fitting belt.

Results

EVALUATION OF TRACKING HEART RATES

Table 2 shows the average pulse rate (bpm = pulse per minute) and the duration of the single exercises.

1. **High stance**: While performing the Taijiquan-form in a high stance (with knees only slightly bent) pulse rates are expected to be lower compared to other degrees of knee bending. The total median value of all 14 test persons was 103 bpm. The duration of exposure here is 6.07 minutes. Test person No. 14 is the author with the longest training expertise, followed by No. 7.

2. **Medium-high stance**: Test persons routinely practise the form in a medium-high stance. They are most familiar with this angle of knee-bending and the movements while practising at this height. The total median value of heart rates is 106 bpm. Medium duration has increased by 21 seconds to 6.28 minutes.

3. **Low stance**: Muscular impact is the highest in this stance. This can be tracked by way of pulse rates as well as by the duration of the exercise. During the low stance the average heart rate had

the highest score with 116 bpm. Duration of the exercise in this case was 5.51 minutes and thus the shortest.

Table 2 gives a summary of all the results. It allows tracking the progression of heart rate values and the time-related dimension of the single exercises within an intra-personal comparison. Values of a high stance compared to a low one show a progression of heart rate with all subjects. For a better illustration of Table 2, Figures 70 and 71 show the test persons' average *Hf* and duration of their exercises. A closer examination of the results given in the table should – beside absolute values of the single test persons – be regarded in relation with other test persons. Here an approach would be either an intra-personal comparison between high, medium and low stance related to *Hf* and duration as well as an inter-personal consideration of the parameters.

Table 2 Summary results

No.	High stance		Medium stance		Low stance	
	bpm	Duration	bpm	Duration	bpm	Duration
1	115	5.39	112	6.12	113	4.46
2	94	5.50	98	5.12	106	4.56
3	122	6.07	124	6.30	141	6.00
4	92	5.15	94	5.22	108	5.32
5	97	6.44	105	6.17	127	4.24
6	95	5.56	105	5.10	116	5.01
7	98	6.30	100	6.19	115	5.20
8	113	6.00	118	5.40	125	5.21
9	97	8.03	100	8.30	108	7.36
10	91	6.50	94	6.53	104	6.00
11	139	6.04	139	7.09	145	5.45
12	102	6.09	107	6.02	109	5.29
13	109	7.25	107	6.17	117	7.16
14	72	9.02	79	9.01	88	8.26
Ø	103	6.07	106	6.28	116	5.51

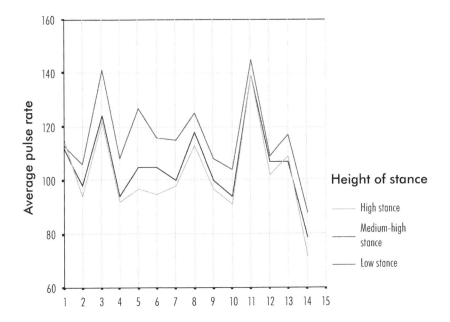

Figure 70 Graphic presentation of average heart rate

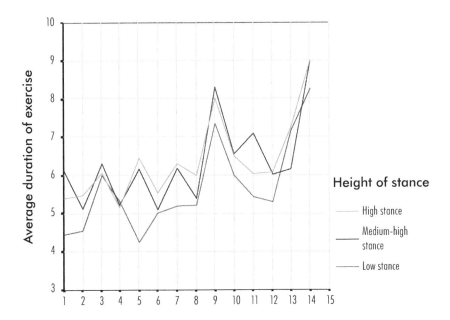

Figure 71 Graphic presentation of average duration of exercise

Assuming that a deeper understanding of Taijiquan movements (the 19-step form in this case) can be proved by the parameters of *Hf* and the duration of a fixed sequence of movements, the results gained here can be interpreted.

Hf in this case would indicate inner rest, calm and a state of relaxation during the exercise. The time-related component sheds light on the quality of motion and the ability to reproduce the inner processes consciously during motion. A higher quality of motion in this case means a more exact understanding of the single movements and their elements. Many refined movements adjusted to each other result in the fluency of movement. The more refined and precise the way in which each part of the movements is executed, the more clearly the principles of inner calm and optimal posture can be realised. All information on the duration of the exercises must take into consideration, however, that the fluency of movement must not be interrupted. Hence one may speak in terms of optimised duration of exercise with a moderate *Hf*. A definite conclusion from this would be: 'An optimised duration of exercise with a moderate *Hf* is an indicator for inner calm and a high quality of movement.'

As by now only median values have been presented by way of diagrams and graphics, Figure 72 is to illustrate the entire course of the heart rate during the exercise. A clear distinction among the different stances according to height becomes evident. Characteristic peaks of impact can be distinguished, and they appear within all three different heights. Hereby a minor shift in time between the curves may be seen.

Discussion

Reviewing the study presented here reveals that impact on the cardiovascular system can be controlled and scaled. Taijiquan therefore offers individual options for everyone to check out personal limits of impact. Variations of intensity result from age and actual physical condition. Taijiquan as a whole has a positive effect on the motor system. All muscles, bones and joints are involved and get equally stimulated. Though a decreased angle of knee-bending results in a lower heart rate, the positive effects on the motor system are proportional.

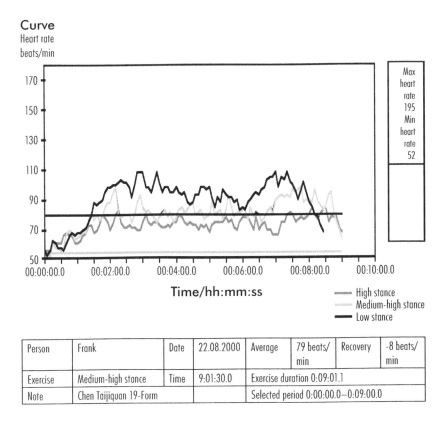

Curve
Heart rate
beats/min

Time/hh:mm:ss

High stance
Medium-high stance
Low stance

Person	Frank	Date	22.08.2000	Average	79 beats/ min	Recovery	-8 beats/ min
Exercise	Medium-high stance	Time	9:01:30.0	Exercise duration 0:09:01.1			
Note	Chen Taijiquan 19-Form			Selected period 0:00:00.0–0:09:00.0			

Figure 72 Graphic view of heart rate of test

The significance of Taijiquan regarding the improvement of general aerobic endurance can also be indicated on the evidence of this study. Indeed the heart rates as diagnosed here are too low compared with measures taken in strictly sport-scientific endurance training, because during a Taijiquan-form no rates usually occur that reach beyond 70 per cent of the maximum circulation-related capacity.[8] These high rates, however, are not desirable within Taijiquan, as the principle of inner ease can hardly be achieved with a pulse rate of 160 bpm.

A daily training instead with an average heart rate of 100 bpm does contribute to improved general physical capacity. A training with such

8   See *De Marees, H.*: Sportphysiologie. Sport und Buch, Strauss, Köln 1996, p. 166.

a rate of impact is a good fitness programme for people whose work is performed mostly sitting down, and it can be used by seasoned athletes for balancing, recovery or as an alternative. In terms of general prevention the point is to help people move from a level of lower capacity to the next higher one. The risk of overstraining is minimised by the principles to be applied while practising Taijiquan. As the central aspect of Taijiquan is the principle of conscious slowness, excessive and thus dangerous pulse rates can hardly occur. Exaggerated ambitions, often seen among joggers and easily resulting in excessive strain don't exist within Taijiquan; the goals we strive for are different. Conscious slowness, harmonising every single movement of the body and the feeling of ease during motion are the goals to be pursued and are thus of central importance.

Based on this view, a certain value regarding a training effect for aerobic endurance must be attributed to Taijiquan. The results of the heart rate analysis in this case are consistent with the self-perception reported by the subjects in relation to the improvement of their endurance due to training Taijiquan.

It can be assumed that the data raised here are representative. While the limited number of subjects may mitigate against generalising the results of the data obtained, quite similar heart rates have been monitored during other comparable studies on Taijiquan.

The time-span for the 19-step form as performed here is, however, too short for an efficient training of endurance, even on a lower level. The 19-step form was originally designed as an entry-level form of Taijiquan, and this is the purpose it meets. With advancing practice in Taijiquan, longer forms are performed which may endure 30 minutes and beyond. This is a span that meets with the requirements of an adequate endurance training.

More detailed findings of the effects of Taijiquan on cardiovascular functions would require a more homogenised group of subjects. Parameters such as age, gender and duration of exercise would have to be given more consideration.

EMG-EXAMINATION OF THE SINGLE-HAND REELING SILK-EXERCISE

Rationale and objective of the examination

The measuring technique EMG (electromyography) allows monitoring and recording of the degree of muscular tension. EMG analysis enables measurement and comparison of muscular tension during a Taijiquan sequence. The study presented here is of exemplary character as it has been done with only two test persons. As Taijiquan largely deals with relaxation, i.e. with no muscular tension, the question is whether the EMG-based study is a proper tool. The study thus aimed at comparing the muscular tension of beginners vs advanced practitioners of Taijiquan.

Due to the motion-related concept of Taijiquan, the movements should be performed in a more and more economic mode as the level of expertise grows. Inner calm, relaxation and the fluency of motion are criteria visible from the outside. The physiological and psychological have been covered by heart rate analysis and measurement of condition. Within this framework, the EMG-study gives information about muscular activity. (A precise description of the setting and instrumentation is given by Freiwald and Konrad[9] and by Laurig[10].)

Subject and implementation of the study

For reasons of comparability and technical realisation, the exercise of *Cansigong* (single-handed, right-hand side) was chosen. Cansigong is considered the essence of all Taijiquan movements and therefore meets all criteria of this kind of motional conduct. Each time after five cycles, one was measured and recorded. One circle includes the sequence of lowering, closing, raising and opening.

---

9   See *Konrad, P., Freiwald, J.:* Einführung in das kinesiologische EMG, lecture script, 1997 (unpublished).

10 See *Laurig, P.:* Elektromyographie. In *Willimczik, K.* (Ed.): Forschungsmethoden in der Sportwissenschaft. Grundkurs Datenerhebung 1, Bad Homburg 1983, pp. 63–89.

Training expertise of both subjects covered a range of one year (subject No. 1) to about nine years (subject No. 2). The research was performed at the Kinesiological Laboratory of the University of Dortmund.

Results

Of each of the eight muscles that were tested, the average value both of the mean value and the peak value were examined and are illustrated in Figures 73 and 74. Mean value indicates the average activity of a muscle during the entire recording interval.

The average values both of mean and peak show clear differences between both subjects. The less advanced (subject No. 1) shows a higher muscle tension than the one with higher training expertise (subject No. 2) with the only exception being the M. erector spinae lumbalis. By general tendency however both curves show a similar course.

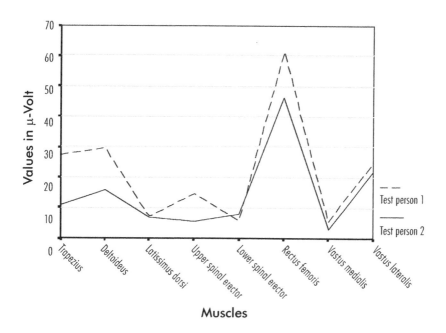

Figure 73 Average of peak values during Cansigong

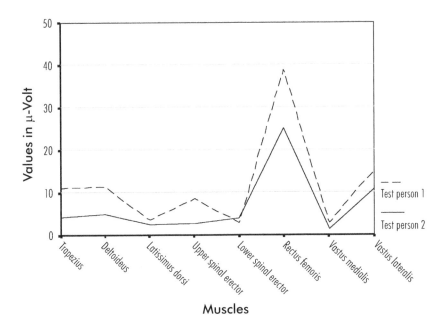

Figure 74 Average of mean values during Cansigong

The highest values in each case were measured at the femoral muscu-lature. The main exposure was on the M. vastus lateralis. The other muscle activity remains relatively low. A more specific view is given from the evaluation of the single muscles (see Figures 75–82).

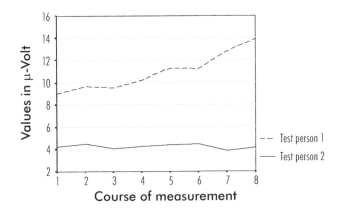

Figure 75 Musculus trapezius

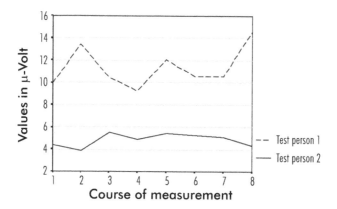

Figure 76 Musculus deltoideus

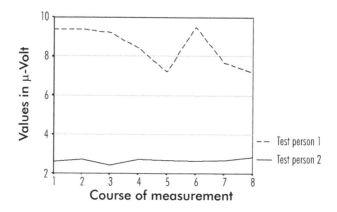

Figure 77 M. erector spinae thoracalis

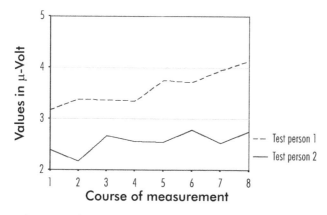

Figure 78 M. latissimus dorsi

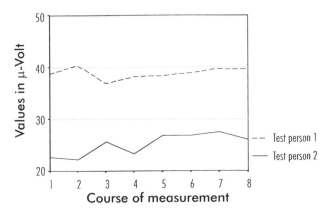

Figure 79 M. vastus lateralis

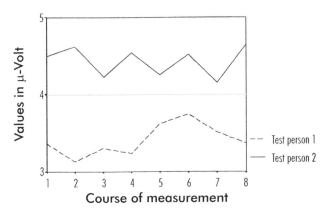

Figure 80 M. erector spinae lumbalis

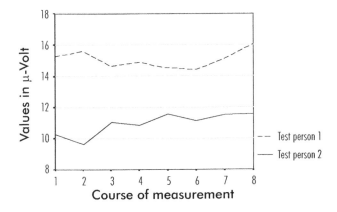

Figure 81 M. vastus medialis

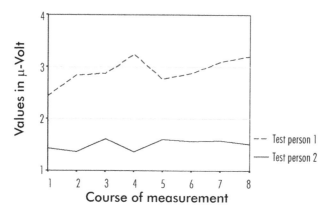

Figure 82 M. rectus femoris

Discussion

The results in comparing single muscles allow a closer inspection of muscular tension as well as tendencies of fatigue. Due to the lack of standardised basic conditions, a comparison of the subjects in terms of fatigue could not be performed. The more advanced of both subjects performed the exercise in over 20 minutes, a time-span caused by the very slow and even course of the single transits. The other test person performed the transits within a much shorter time, thus cutting down the entire span of exercises by more than half. Both subjects can be compared only within the limits mentioned above. A strengthening of leg musculature which the subjects had pointed out as positive in answering the questionnaire can be evidenced by the EMG-study.

By way of conclusion it should be noted again that this EMG study can be seen as an example only. Therefore, the results described here can be rated only as a first attempt in giving deeper explanations of certain muscular effects of Taijiquan.

Words by the Patriarchs of the Chen Clan

Prior to publication of the German edition of this book, some of the texts presented here had never been published before in a European language. They are a small selection of writings since the early 17th century and are attributed to the most important masters of the Chen clan. This selection spans works by the founder of Taijiquan, Chen Wangting, to the great reformer Chen Changxing, to the man of letters Chen Xin, to the famous fighter Chen Fake and to today's Grandmaster Chen Xiaowang. It thus offers insight into the thoughts of this system's masters from all epochs.

Chapter 16

Verses and Dicta

Translated into German by Jan Silberstorff; English version by Jarek Szymanski.

WORDS OF CHEN WANGTING, NINTH GENERATION OF THE FAMILY TRADITION

Contemplating the years that have passed, how bravely I fought the enemy forces, and how much I have risked; all the honours no longer serve me in any way. Now that I am old and weak I submit to the guidance of the book of the *Huang Ting*. Life for me consists of creating boxing forms when I feel depressed, working in the field when the season has come, and during the remaining time in teaching the young, so they shall grow to be worthy members of society.

Actions are varied and are performed in a way completely unpredictable for the opponent. I trust in spiral movements and a whole number of actions by hand contact.

Nobody knows me, while I alone know all.

WORDS OF CHEN XIN, 16TH GENERATION OF THE FAMILY TRADITION, TO HIS NEPHEW CHEN CHUNYUAN ABOUT HIS BOOK *CHEN SHI TAIJIQUAN TU SHUO*

This is the harvest of my entire life. Publish it and pass it to those who may esteem it. Otherwise burn it. Be sure not to pass it to ignorant or arrogant persons.

More from Chen Xin

Having studied the circular illustrations of the Taiji symbolisms of the ancient classics I recognised that in order to train Taijiquan it is essential to understand the essence of spinning the silk thread. The silk exercises are a method of mastering central Qi. As long as this remains misunderstood, the art of boxing will remain misunderstood as well.

Only someone capable of moving his Qi will be able to protect his life: when someone is capable of protecting his own life, this shall be an essential support in rebuilding his very own nature. In this way the Qi may unfold. Taijiquan will benefit the evolution of the spirit, the consciousness, of one's own personal nature and life. The sage would say that cultivation of an immaculate character is to be found within rebuilding one's very own way of being. This means that protecting life and moving the Qi is the essence of cultivating an immaculate character or its rebuilding.

Taijiquan is a method of 'spinning the silk thread'. There is spinning forward, backward, to the left, to the right, upward and downward, to the inside and to the outside. There is large and small spinning; there is conforming and there is opposite spinning. The important issue is to apply it either while yielding or pushing ahead. The issue is not to utilise a certain application of a certain figure.

The hands are like a pair of scales. Weigh something, and you will know its weight. The path of martial art practice is to have a pair of scales within your awareness. By way of these invisible scales you may approach your opponent in all his moves forward or backward and adapt to his speed. Make use of the consciousness which is to be mastered by way of daily practice. Measuring visible signs by means of invisible scales and regulating what both hands perceive, with adding or taking away if necessary. One who masters this is called an Excellent Hand (Master).

The Qi (...) enters the bones, outwards it reaches the skin. It is one power, it is not various powers (...). Being conducted centrally and properly, it is central Qi (*zhong qi*). Being nourished, it is noble spirit (*haoran zhi qi*).

If someone is like the nature of heaven, he shall by way of his training of how to box follow the secret of nature (*tianji*). Alive and natural. So the real condition of Qi shall be revealed all by itself within his body.

Verses by Chen Xin

Yang is born within motion, the stillness is Yin. Stillness and motion in union is the source. Without doubt you will find joyousness within all that is round, and you will see the truth of heaven in turns and spiral motion performed by the spirit.

Yin and Yang have no beginning and no end. Creation has residence in coming and going, in contracting and expanding. Note this carefully. Execute the vital principle in round turns, do so without reserve.

At times it is clear, at times it is not. To open and to close, to rest, raise or move downward: all is conjoined. Many moves must be overcome before the principle is revealed, but with sudden inspiration it shall become clear as glass.

- The principle has no limits, yet it is contained within the ants.

- Do not make the faintest noise inside the garden for three years. Have a will and a determined mind.

- It is important to have good teachers and to go and see wise friends.

- Follow the rules with all respect, and a narrow beam of recognition will appear.

- The stage following next is deeper than the one before. The meaning of the single stages is unlimited.

- Opening is combined with closing. Opening and closing evolve in good order from one to the other.

- Sometimes one is taken to victory and unable to stop exercising, even though one would wish to do so.

- Time, study and endeavour must be driven to the utmost, and your mastery will grow day by day.

- Only once there is no obstacle, will you in an instant understand the 'great emptiness'.

A QUESTION TO OLD GRAND MASTER CHEN FAKE, 17TH GENERATION FAMILY TRADITION

Should the movements in Taijiquan be fast or slow?

Beginners should train slowly so that their movements are correct. It is practising that results in mastership, so the practitioner, after a long time of practising, can be fast and stable in a natural way. During combat, one's own tempo must be regarded as dependent on the opponent's tempo. However, this is not the goal. By way of slow exercising, the legs become trained during an intensive period, which is of further benefit.

Chapter 17

Ten Essential Statements on Taijiquan

By Chen Changxing, 14th Generation of the Chen Family, Founder of the Old Frame Lao Jia and Teacher of Yang Luchan.
(Translated into German by Wang Ning)

LI – THE THEORY

All things flow apart, yet they will be brought together again (reassemble themselves) too; they separate and they shall be brought together again (they reunite again) too. All things between heaven and earth have their own sources and roots. Therefore the saying goes that out of one root thousands of characters will emerge, and vice versa – thousands of characters have the same root in common. The same principle applies to the teachings of the fist. Taijiquan involves thousands of movements; all depend on force (jin). While the intensity of the movements may vary, force can be traced back to the Oneness. This is the union from top to bottom of the body of internal organs, muscles and bones through to the outer skin, between all four extremities and throughout the hundreds of bones. It is not divided by 'po', that is by breaking, nor driven apart by 'zhuang', that is by pushing. When 'top' starts moving, 'bottom' will follow in the same instant. When 'bottom' starts moving, 'top' will instantaneously do so. When 'top' and 'bottom' start moving, the 'middle' will reply immediately. When 'middle' starts moving, 'top' and 'bottom' will instantly join in. 'Inside' and 'outside' will unite, 'front' and 'rear' require each other, and unity will so be created. All this must never happen unintentionally and must continuously keep evolving. 'Dong', the move, must be like a dragon or a tiger shooting forward, fast as lightning. 'Jing', the silence, must be quiet and clear like a mountain at rest.

'Jing' means quiet all over from 'inside to outside', from 'top to bottom'; 'dong' means action from 'front and behind', from 'left and right', without the slightest hesitation – like a waterfall whose energy no one can withstand, and like a fire inside, the explosive energy of which will not be suppressed. There is no time for considerations or planning ahead. All happens in a fully natural way. As we know, force builds up day after day, and 'gong', success, is achieved by endurance in training. By reading the holy books one learns that things are brought towards mastery by persistence only, and that opinions may be formed not until one has reached mastery. There are no simple things in the world; nor are there any difficult ones. In order to achieve success, 'gong', one must exercise continuously without exaggerating or rushing things but rather proceeding continually step by step. Then the hundreds of muscles and bones and joints (the connecting members) shall be connected with each other. 'Top and bottom' just as 'outside and inside' communicate between themselves.

That means that all things flow apart, yet they will be brought together again (reassemble themselves) too; they separate and they shall be brought together again (they reunite again) too. Eventually all extremities and hundreds of bones are part of one entire unity.

QI (AIR, BREATHING, ENERGY)

Nothing exists between heaven and earth that would vanish without returning in a different form.

Nor is there anything straight if there is nothing that is crooked. Therefore the saying goes that all things have their counterparts and move in circles. This truth has existed since the beginning of time and shall continue into eternity. When we speak about 'chui', i.e. to strike with the fist, we speak about Qi as well. One matter divides from one into two. Two in this respect means to breathe in and to breathe out. To breathe in and out means Yin and Yang.

'Chui', to strike with the fist, cannot exist without 'dong' and 'jing', to move and to be at rest. Qi cannot exist without breathing in and breathing out. To breathe out is yang. To breathe in is yin. Rising to the top is yang, sinking to the bot-tom is yin. Rising yang qi is yang, sinking yang qi is yin. Ris-ing yin qi is yang, sinking yin qi is yin. This is the distinction between yin and yang. What is then the meaning of 'qing' and 'zhuo', the clear and the dim? Rising to the top is 'qing', clear, sinking to the bottom is 'zhuo', dim. 'Qing' is yang, 'zhuo' is yin. When we speak about the contrasts of a matter, we speak of yin and yang. When we assemble them in a unit we call them Qi. Qi cannot exist without Yin and Yang, just as a human cannot be without 'dong' and 'jing', moving and being at rest, a nose cannot be without breath-ing in and out, a mouth cannot be without eating and spitting out. This is the essence of the 'circulation'. So Qi consists of two elements which are connected yet are one. Anybody approaching this issue must give particular regards to this aspect.

SAN JIE – THREE SECTIONS

Qi penetrates the entire body. The body is made of numerous parts. Within martial art there is no sense in mentioning every single body part. It is true, however, that we subdivide the body into 'Three Sections'. These 'Three Sections' are called top, middle and bottom or root, middle and tree top. In rela-tion to the entire body, the head is the top, the chest (upper body) the middle, and the legs are the bottom. In relation to the head the forehead is the top, the nose the middle, and the mouth the bottom. In relation to the middle of the body the chest is the top, the belly the middle, and dantian the bottom. In relation to the leg, the hip is the root, the knee the middle and the foot the bottom. In relation to the arm the upper arm is the root, the elbow the middle and the hand the tree top. In relation to the hand the wrist is the root, the palm the middle and the fingers the tree top.

We can clearly imagine the distinction in relation with the foot. From the top of our head down to the sole there are 'Three Sections' in every part. It must be carefully considered which the section one's mental energy is focused upon. If one does not know precisely where the upper section is one will not know its origin; if one does not know the mid-section pre-cisely, one will have nothing but emptiness in one's belly; if one does not know the bottom section precisely, confusion will occur. This is why the 'Three Sections' of the body must not remain unnoticed. When the Qi starts moving it will begin at the tree top, fol-lowed by the mid-section, which drives the root section. This is the analysis of the single sections which, however, can be considered as one entity. From the head down to the sole, between all four extremities and hundreds of bones, the body is one single section. Hence there are no 'Three Sections' any more and nor any sub-divisions.

SI SHAO – FOUR TREE TOPS (TIPS OF LEAVES)

Now that we have spoken about the body we can take a step forward and talk about the Four Tree Tops. What we intend with this term is the 'remaining loose ends' (yu xu). While we are talking about the body they are not mentioned. While talk-ing about the Qi they are rarely being thought of either. 'Chui', however, striking with the fist, comes from inside to outside, while Qi is pervading the entire body and is dis-charged through the fist. If Qi is being used without having it permeated the whole body, then this is called 'xu' (empty, void or pre-tence) and not 'Shi' (solid, massive or in being); if the Qi does not move through the tree tops it is called 'shi' (solid, massive or in being) as well as 'xu' (empty, void or pretence). Should one not mention the tree tops? Besides the fingers and feet which count among the body's tree tops, there are parts named tree tops beyond the tree tops. What is Si Shao, that is, the Four Tree Tops?

The hair counts among them. Hair is not one of the Wu Xing (Five Elements), nor does it have anything to do with the Four Extremities. Indeed it seems to be of no importance. The hair, however, appears as the tips of the leaves in relation to the blood, while the blood itself is the ocean of Qi. Leaving the hair aside and speaking about the Qi only,

Qi still remains directly connected with the blood and created out of it. So we cannot treat hair as being separate from blood.

The hair rise high because the very ends of the blood's leaves are filled with Qi. Comparable to the very end of a branch, the tongue is an extension of the flesh. The flesh itself is an adaptable vessel of Qi. When Qi is not able to proceed to the very end of the flesh this means that there is a shortfall of Qi. When the tongue is touching the teeth the extension of flesh is filled with Qi. The extension related to the bones is the teeth, and the extension of the muscles is the nails. The Qi derives from the bones and is connected with the muscles. If the Qi does not reach the teeth this means that Qi does not reach the extensions of the muscles. And in order to fill both, the teeth must permeate the muscles, and the nails must permeate the bones. If all this happens exactly so, Si Shao, i.e. the Four Extended Branches, are filled. When Si Shao are filled, Qi is at fullness. Then there will be no weakness such as 'xu' only (empty, void or pretence) or 'shi' (solid, massive or in being) or either 'shi' (solid, massive or in being) or 'xu' (empty, void or pretence).

WU ZANG – FIVE ORGANS

When the issue is 'chui', striking with the fist, strength is be-ing measured. Man gains his build by way of the five organs; these five organs generate the Qi. Therefore the Five Organs are the source of life, the root of vital energy (sheng qi). They are: heart, liver, spleen, lung and kidneys. The heart belongs to the element of fire, thus it appears like heat. The liver be-longs to the element of wood, thus it has a twisting or straight character. The spleen belongs to the element of earth, so has real strength. The lung belongs to the element of metal, with the implication of the talent of transforming. The kidneys be-longs to the element of water and thus it have the ability to moisten. The purpose of the Five Organs is that they shall adapt the Qi and communicate among each other. People who practice martial arts must pay particular attention to this. The channels of the lung are in the chest, while the lung for its part is the elite (hua) of the five organs. That is why, once the channels of the lung go into motion, all the other organs begin their work. The heart has its place within the sides of the chest with the lung around it. Beneath the lungs the heart-channels have their place. The heart is the ruler. When the 'Xin Huo', the fire of the heart, is moving, the 'Xiang Huo', the Opposite Fire, will join immediately. Below the diaphragm on the right side is the liver, the spleen on the left, and beside the 14th ver-tebrae are the kidneys.

The waist is the traditional home of the kidneys. They are described as the very first of the former Heaven organs and the origin of all other organs. When the kidneys are properly filled there is enough energy for metal, wood, water, fire and earth. Every organ has its own place. Since they are many of them they shall not be named here individually. They have their special places within the body. By and large, the heart belongs to the middle. The lung belongs to 'wo', the armpit. Where the bones show themselves there are also the kidneys. The liver is seated between the muscles. Where much flesh is accumulated the spleen will be found. Considering their im-portance we may depict the heart as a predator and the liver as an arrow. The spleen is described as over-forceful. The lung-channels are the swiftest, and kidney Qi is fast like the wind. Every practitioner must check this in his own body, since there is too much detail to go into here.

SAN HE – THE THREE INTEGRATIONS

The Five Organs having been explained, now we may discuss San He, the Three Integrations. San He means that heart and mind, Qi and power, muscles and bones are in harmony. These are the Three Internal Integrations. Hand and foot, el-bow and knee, shoulder and hip are called the Three External Integrations. When there is harmony between left hand and right foot, between left elbow and right knee, left shoul-der and right hip or the other way round, as well as harmony be-tween head and hands, hands and body, and the body and the steps – can we not describe that as 'External Harmonies'? Everything is subject to a process of change. Basically this means that when one is moving one does not remain standing still, nor when one is at harmony with one-self, one will not remain standing and separate.

LIU JIN – SIX WAYS OF MOVING FORWARD

Once we have grasped the Three Integrations we still need to explore the Liu Jin, the Six Ways of Moving Forward. What actually are the Liu Jin? The head is called the integration of the 'Six Yang Channels' and the ruler of the entire body, with all organs and bones being subordinate to it; thus the head is not allowed 'not to proceed'. The hands are the advance guard while the feet are the root, and if the feet do not go forward the hands will not be able to do so either. Qi is gathered in the wrist, the motor is at the waist, and if the waist does not move forward the Qi is not saturated, i.e. it is not 'Shi' (solid, mas-sive or in being). Therefore the waist is not enabled to move forward. This idea pervades the entire body; movement de-pends on the steps, and if the steps aren't able to move for-ward, just the idea won't be of any help. Thus the steps must be set to move forward. In order to move left forward, right must move the same way, and in order to get right to move forward, left must move forward as well. Altogether there are six ways of 'Moving forward'. They must be thoroughly held in the intention. For example it must be carefully held in mind that the entire body does not show the faintest movement in case 'not to move forward' is required. As soon as 'moving forward' is required, the body moves into action without the faintest hesitance. This is the essence of the 'Six Ways of Moving Forward'.

SHEN FA – BODY MOVEMENT

The fist stroke completely depends on the movement. What may this movement's exact appearance be like? There are only eight different movements: Zong, heng, gao, di, jin, tui, fan, ce. Zong means: releasing force and moving forward with no respect. Heng means: to organise force and toss everything aside. Gao means: to stretch the body upwards and so grow tall. Di means: to duck and thus get small. Jin means: to move ahead with full force. Tui means: walking backwards while carefully gathering qi. Fan means: turning the body to the back, so that back becomes front. Ce means: watching right and left so that no one may attack from the sides. During these moves one must not rigidly adhere to only one movement but rather apply skilful variations.

Learning the opponent's strong and weak points, developing one's own strategy, one may act with zong as well as with heng, all depending on the situation. There can be nothing fixed or preset in advance. Gao may be the proper way in one case, di in another.

Gao and di may take turns any time. Every situation is differ-ent. Sometimes the situation calls for jin, moving forward, since otherwise to retreat in such a moment may reduce cour-age. Sometimes tui, retreat, is the right thing to do in order to start moving ahead anew. That is why Jin means truly moving forward, and tui, retreat, means moving ahead as well. When we turn around, the back will come into full view and thus no longer will appear as the back. Once we watch the right side as well as the left there can no longer be any danger from ei-ther of these sides. In brief: observing with the eyes, analyz-ing with the heart, finding the center of gravity is part of the principle of movement. If the body moves forward, all Four Extremities will do the same. If the body gets scared, all the hundreds of bones will hide away. This is why Shen Fa, the ways of how to move the body, must be thoroughly under-stood.

BU FA – THE TECHNIQUE OF PLACING STEPS

All Four Extremities and the hundreds of bones determine the motion, yet motion is realized by steps exclusively. The step is the root and the junction of the body in motion. While mov-ing the body in order to resist or to strike back the steps are the very pillars of support. In rela-tion to the changing situa-tions one may deceive the opponent with the hands which is possible only by applying steps. During jin tui and fan ce, forward and backward, turning round, moving right and left, the steps are the driving force. During dodge and stretch it´s the steps which deliver perfect deception. Observation is done with the eyes, analysis is provided by the heart, and by way of changing steps one provides innumerable ways of deception. None of this must happen without the will. The action must be based on 'non-reflection' (wu xin), the courage come from out of the 'unconscious' (bu jue). The steps are to deceive the enemy while the body takes action, so one pushes forward making steps while the hands lift out for a strike (dong). Camouflage is perfect when neither being or pretence or movement or standing still can be distinguished any more. This is the true meaning of the term: when 'top' begins to move, 'bottom' will do the same immediately. Steps are dis-tinguished as early steps and later steps (qian bu and he bu). The steps are placed on distinct and non-distinct places. An early step moving forward is followed immediately by the later step. Either of the two are put on a place of their own.

When the early step acts as a later step and the later step as an early step, then the early one shall be the later one prior to the early one and the later step will be the early step prior to the later one. All steps have their distinct place. In brief: when the strike (chui) depends on force the center of gravity depends on the steps. Whether flexible or not flexible is up to the na-ture of the steps. Efficient or inefficient is also up to the steps. Thus the technique of stepping is of importance.

GANG ROU – HARD AND SOFT

Nothing counts but qi and the power. There is strong qi as well as weak qi. There is strong power and soft power. Someone who has strong qi may use hard power, too. Some-one with weak qi will of course make use of soft power. With a thousand kilograms of force the stronger one will crush the weaker one with only a hundred kilograms of force, but the weaker one with a hundred kilograms of force will break the thou-sand kilograms in two. Force or skill make the difference between gang and rou, hard and soft.

Knowing about this distinction we must act in various ways. Four extremities start moving, so qi will then spread far into the extensions while calm prevails inside. This is the power of hardness. With qi rest-ing inside it will appear light-weighted and soft to the outside; this is the power of softness. The hard cannot be applied without the soft. Without the soft one lacks swiftness inside. The soft cannot be applied without the hard.

Cornering the enemy without applying hardness will not be pos-sible. But as long as the hard and the soft are supporting each other, one will master with great ease nian, you, lian, sui, teng, shan, zhe, kong, peng, lue, ji, na. The hard and the soft must not be used in isolation from each other. Whoever takes to fighting must not disregard this aspect.

Chapter 18

The Five Levels of Evolution (Gongfu) in Taijiquan

Grandmaster Chen Xiaowang

Translated into German by Jan Silberstorff

Learning Taijiquan means to educate oneself. It is like slowly advancing from primary school to university. As time passes, more and more knowledge is gained. Without the foundations of primary school and secondary school, one will not be able to follow the seminars at university. Studying Taijiquan requires starting from the very bottom, working one's way systematically and step by step towards the more advanced levels. Someone who does not accept this, thinking that he may take a shortcut, will not be successful. The entire process of learning Taijiquan, from the beginning to success, consists of stages or five levels of martial skills (*Gongfu*) built upon each other. Each level of *Gongfu* has its own particular and very distinct specifications. The highest goal is achieved with the fifth level. During the following five sections every single stage with its own requirements and purposes will be described in detail. This is done with the hope of offering a chance to Taijiquan enthusiasts worldwide to gain a realistic assessment of their own current level. From this point they may then realize what they should learn next and which steps they have to take in order to reach the stages that follow.

THE FIRST LEVEL OF GONGFU IN TAIJIQUAN

When we practise Taijiquan the principles for the various parts of the body are:

- the vertical alignment of the body

- adjusting head and neck as if the body was suspended from a thread from above

- relaxing the shoulders and sinking the elbows

- relaxing hip and chest, allowing them to sink

- slightly bending the knee and relaxing the lower belly.

With these conditions provided, internal energy will sink to the *Dantian* in a wholly natural way. Beginners will not be capable of mastering all these points immediately. During the exercise attention must be paid therefore that the body's positions have the proper alignment, that the angle is correct, and that arms and legs are properly coordinated. During this phase the practitioner should not focus too much on the requirements of the single body parts in relation to the movements. Relative simplifications are acceptable.

An example: For head and upper body it is important that neck and head are erect while chest and hip are sunk. Within the first level it is sufficient to ensure that head and body are held upright in a natural way, that they neither lean too far to the front or to the back, or too far right or left. It's like learning calligraphy: in the beginning it's important just to ensure that the lines are properly drawn. Therefore in the beginning the movements may feel taut, or solid from the outside, but empty within. Or one may find oneself rigid while doing strikes or punches. Or one may take a sudden uplift or feel the entire body or the torso collapsing. The force we apply will be broken within or over-exerted. These mistakes are normal in the beginning.

Those who are devoted enough and train every day can usually learn the form within about a year. Internal energy, *Qi*, may eventually cause a refinement of the movements within the body and all its joints. One will then be able to reach the stage of channelling the internal flow of energy by external movements.

Hence the first level of *Gongfu* begins with mastering the single stances, so that step by step we may discover and understand the internal and external forces of the body. The martial skills to be reached within the first level are still very limited. That is because at this stage the single actions are neither yet very coordinated nor systematic. The single stances are not yet correct, so that the energy or the force being evolved remains stiff and broken, weak or alternatively too strong. While we practise the form it appears to us as too empty or too square. While being able to perceive the internal energy, we are not able yet to channel it into each section of our body by way of a movement. Consequently we are still not able to conduct energy straight from the heels into the legs in order to then discharge it while maintaining control over the hips. The beginner remains limited to transferring only partial force from one section of the body to another. In this way the first level of *Gongfu* cannot be used for purposes of self-defence.

If one should wish, however, to try a test on a person who has no expertise in martial art, up to a certain degree an effect may be achieved. Perhaps that other person has not learnt yet the applications of Taijiquan, and the disciple by way of deception might succeed and throw him to the ground, but even then he will usually be unable to maintain his own balance. This stage is described as: 10 per cent Yin and 90 per cent Yang.

But what are Yin and Yang in fact?

In the context of Taijiquan, Yin is the emptiness, while Yang embodies the solid. Softness and gentleness are Yin, the forceful and the hard are Yang. Yin and Yang are the union of the contrasts. Just as neither of the two can be left aside, both are able to substitute each other, capable of changing into each other and to transfer. If someone is capable of holding Yin and Yang at balance within himself, we call this 50 per cent, so that the person can make use of his potential by 100 per cent. This would be the highest level and indicate success in practising Taijiquan.

During the first levels in Taiji-*Gongfu*, it is quite normal being limited to 10 per cent Yin and 90 per cent Yang. This means that the martial skills are hard rather than gentle, and an imbalance prevails between Yin and Yang. The student is not able yet to replace the hard with the soft, or to perform the applications with simplicity and ease. At this point, when the student is still at the first level, he should not be too zealous in the pursuit of the adaptability of the single stance.

THE SECOND LEVEL OF GONGFU IN TAIJIQUAN

The second level begins with the last stage of the first level, when the student is able to perceive the flow of internal energy, Qi, and it concludes within the first stage of the third level. This second level still deals with resolving imperfections, for example:

- rigid force becoming evident during Taijiquan training

- too much or insufficient exertion of force

- uncoordinated movements.

Resolving imperfections provides an organic flow of internal energy through the body in a way that is consistent with the requirements of each movement. In the end these efforts should result in a gentle flow of Qi throughout the body. This will create a good coordination between internal energy and external movement.

When the student has mastered the first level, he should be able to easily perform the initial requirements that each posture or movement requires. The student is able to perceive the flow of internal energy, even though he is not able to control it yet. There are two reasons for this:

First: The student has not yet sufficiently mastered the distinct requirements necessary for each body section and their coordination. If for example the chest is sunk too much, neither the hip nor the back will be straight. Or, if hip and waist are too relaxed, the chest and bottom may protrude. Therefore, there is an absolute necessity for precision in order to be consistent with the distinct requirements of all body sections, so that they may move in union.

This allows the entire body to integrate and accordingly to be in full and coordinated unity. The latter means coordination between both internal and external unity and integration. Inner closure implies the co-ordinated incorporation of heart (*xin*) and mind (*yi*), of internal energy (*qi*) and force (*li*), of tendons (*jin*) and bones (*gu*). External integration of the movements implies the coordinated union of the hands with the feet, of the elbows with the knees and the shoulders with the hips. At the same time the body should be open in other sections, so that opening and closing movements unite and complete each other.

Second: The student finds it hard to control and synchronise the various sections of the body. This may, for example, cause one part of

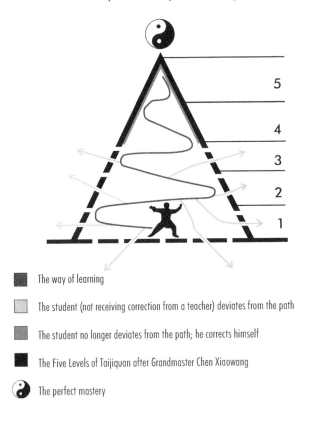

The way of learning

The student (not receiving correction from a teacher) deviates from the path

The student no longer deviates from the path; he corrects himself

The Five Levels of Taijiquan after Grandmaster Chen Xiaowang

The perfect mastery

Figure 83 The Five Levels of Chen Taijiquan

the body to move faster than the rest, which may result in too much force. Or one part of the body moves too slowly compared with the whole, or it moves without enough force. In this way the entire amount of force would be undeveloped.

Both phenomena contradict the principle of Taijiquan. Every single movement in Chen Taijiquan must conform to the principle of the Reeling Silk exercise (*cansigong*). In terms of Taijiquan the *can si jin*, 'the power of spinning the silk thread', arises from the kidneys and is always found in all sections of the body. This enables the entire body to be integrated in a coordinated way, and includes the union of internal and external movement.

Internal integration implies the fusion of heart and mind, of internal energy and force, and of tendons and bones. External integration implies the fusion of hands and feet, of elbows and knees, and of shoulders and hips. Each movement finds a correspondent within. During the process of learning Taijiquan, the method of the reeling silk and the force arising from it can be performed not until:

- shoulders, elbows, chest and hips are as relaxed and permeable as the lower belly and the knees

- the hip is the turning point of all movements of the body.

When we start rotating our hands counter-clockwise, the hands should move the elbows, and these should move the shoulders. The shoulders should move the hips on the corresponding side. In reality, however, it's always at the hip where movement begins. When the hands are rotating clockwise, the hip should guide the shoulder, which should guide the elbow, which should guide the hand.

Within the upper body, the wrists and the arms should be gyrating, that is doing circular moves, while the lower body, the ankles and the upper legs should rotate. In the same way the torso, the hip and the back move by rotation.

While building up the movements across the three sections of the body, we should be careful about the spiralling connection within this space. The spiral connection begins in the legs, is centred in the hips and ends in the fingertips. If the practitioner feels uncomfortable during the single stances of the form, he is advised to correct the position of the legs and hips according to the movement for coordinating all sections of the body, so that the energy flow of the spinning silk (*can si jin*) can be created. In this way every mistake can be corrected. If we now pay attention to all requirements of each part of the body for reaching a full coordination of the entire body, then mastering the rhythm of every Reeling Silk exercise and the force resulting from it and its transfer into the form, is a way of resolving all conflicts that may occur therein. This method of self-correction of any mistake is used during the exercises of Taijiquan once we have mastered the second level of Taiji-*Gongfu*.

During the first level of Taiji-*Gongfu*, the student learns the various forms. After he has become familiar with them he can perceive the flow of internal energy inside the body. During this phase he may feel fascinated and motivated; each training session yields new impressions. After entering the second level of Taiji-*Gongfu* he may feel that by and large he is no longer learning anything new. At the same time, he will misunderstand several very crucial aspects. The student will not have mastered sufficiently these important points, and he will feel unskilled in his movements. Conversely, the student may execute the form in a very smooth and gentle way. He may also feel able to emanate quite an amount of force. However, he is not yet able to verify this during pushing hands. Some students then lose interest or lose confidence, so that they may give up their training.

The only way of reaching a level where enough force can be evolved, not too hard and not too soft, where matters can be consciously changed and applied, allowing one to move effectively yet with simplicity and ease, is the way of endurance and keeping strictly with the principle. The student must train the form in a very determined way so that the movements of the entire body align and coordinate. The result will be activity that can be released by one single small movement inside any part of the body. This way a complete and inherent system of movement is created.

There is a saying that goes:

If the principle is not clearly understood, consult a teacher. If the path is not clearly in sight, search for the help of a friend. When both the principle and the method have been understood and training is done with persistence, success will in the end prevail.

It is said in the classical texts that everyone can achieve the highest goal if only he keeps working hard enough on it, and that if the student only persistents, the highest success will all of a sudden materialise.

Generally we can say that most people are able to reach the second level of Taiji-*Gongfu* within four years. Someone who has reached a state of perceiving a gentle flow of Qi inside his body will suddenly begin to understand. The student at this point will be full of confidence and enthusiasm and will train with sheer joy. In some cases a strong desire may develop of wishing to train more and more, and not to stop at all!

At the beginning of the second level the martial abilities are limited similarly to the first level of Taiji-*Gongfu*. The skill isn't sufficient yet for real application. At the end of the second and at the beginning of the third level, martial ability will be achieved to a certain extent.

The next sequence deals with martial art abilities which should be established mid-way during the second level. This is to be described separately for the following levels.

Training of the Pushing Hands (*tui shou*) and practising Taijiquan (the forms) cannot be separated from each other. Whatever shortcuts or simplifications we might have allowed ourselves during form training will emerge as a weak point during the Pushing Hands. This will in turn allow the opponent to take advantage over us. Therefore it must be borne in mind again and again that during training every single part of the body is interwoven and coordinated with the other. No unnecessary movements should be performed.

During the Pushing Hands *peng* (ward off), *lu* (give way), *ji* (press) and *an* (push) should be executed with such a degree of precision that the upper and lower halves of the body work in harmony. That will make it very difficult for our opponent to attack. The proverb says: 'Regardless of how much force is exerted, I mobilise four ounces in order to deflect 1000 pounds.'

The second level of Taiji-Gongfu aims by way of correction of the single stances at achieving a gentle and continuous flow of Qi inside the body. Furthermore it aims at reaching a stage where the Qi inside the body permeates every single joint, as required by every single sequence. This process of adjusting each movement necessarily involves the temporary use of unimportant or uncoordinated movements. Therefore it is not possible yet in this phase to apply martial skills during Pushing Hands in a controlled way. The opponent will focus on these weak points. He may either attempt to defeat the learner by exploiting the error or over-exertion, collapsing, falling down or by the direct confrontation of force with force. During Pushing Hands the advancing opponent will leave no time for the learner to correct his movement fully. The opponent will exploit the weaknesses of the learner to attack and bring him off balance, or he will force him to retreat in order to avoid the force continuing head on. Should however the opponent attack with less and more gentle force and altogether move more slowly the learner may have time to re-adjust his body. This way he may perhaps be able to ward off the attack in a more satisfactory way. In terms of the discussion given before, it is not possible within the second level of Taiji-*Gongfu* to perform either an attack or a defence without greater effort. On this level it is often an advantage to be the first to start an attack. The person forced to react will be in a less favourable situation. On this level one is not able yet to 'forget about oneself' or to match the opponent's moves. No gain can be drawn from the opponent's moves, as one is not able to adapt to the changes and to follow them. While being able to dodge or to ward off an attack, one will still easily commit mistakes, such as falling down for instance or collapsing, overstraining or standing up straight against the force.

For all these reasons, the student is not capable yet of acting during the Pushing Hands in accordance with the principle of *peng, lu, ji* and *an*. A person who has entered this level is characterised as 20 per cent Yin and 80 per cent Yang. This is described as 'a new and undisciplined hand'.

THE THIRD LEVEL OF GONGFU IN TAIJIQUAN

If your boxing skills are to gain quality, you must learn to make the circles smaller!

The single steps in practising Taijiquan include progressing from mastering large circles to medium circles and from there to small circles. The term circle in this respect does not describe the path of the single body parts movements, but the gentle flow of internal energy, Qi. In this sense at the third level one should begin with large circles, and conclude with medium circles (the circulation of energy).

The classical texts of Taijiquan say that *Yi*, the awareness, and Qi deserve higher regard than the forms. This means that while practising the forms one should pay great attention to the awareness. Within the first level, awareness is focused on learning and mastering the outer form sequences of Taijiquan.

During the second level the awareness is focused on revealing blockages and inconsistent internal and external movements and sequences of the single body sections. One should adjust the body and the form sequences to each other in order to create a free internal flow of energy.

By the time we enter the third level of Taiji-*Gongfu*, we should be able to create this flow of energy. The goal is true awareness and not brute force. The movements should be easy without being 'spongy', heavy without being ponderous.

This means that the movements should appear gentle, but with their internal energy being strong. A strong force has been created within the gentle movements. The entire body should be very coordinated within, and there should be no more incorrect movements.

One should not dedicate one's attention exclusively to the flow of internal energy while neglecting external movements, otherwise one may end up in confusion, and the flow of internal energy is not only retracted and disturbed, it may even dissolve. That's why the classical texts state: 'Awareness should be focused on the spirit and not only upon the Qi.' If we concentrate too much on the Qi, stagnation will be the result. Within the first and the second level of Taiji-*Gongfu*, one will have mastered the external sequences of the form, but not the coordination between internal and external movement. Sometimes rigidity or stagnation in our movements will make it impossible for us to inhale fully. In the same way it may not be possible to exhale the breath completely without a proper coordination between internal and external movements. While practising the form one should therefore breathe in an entirely natural way. By the beginning of the third level we have achieved a better coordination, however, between the internal and the external movements. Generally we are able to synchronise movement very precisely with respiration.

Conscious synchronisation of movement with breathing is important for performing several more refined, more complicated and faster movements properly. This is necessary in order to achieve naturalness gradually by synchronising respiration and movement while further progressing. The third level of Taiji-*Gongfu* mainly deals with mastering the internal and external requirements of Chen Taijiquan as well as with the rhythm of the single exercises. Moreover, the student here attains the option of correcting himself. He learns to perform the movements with even more simplicity and gains a clear increase of internal energy. At this point a deeper understanding of the martial contents of the system becomes necessary, particularly in relation to the application-related aspects of the various form elements. Therefore one should practise Pushing Hands, check the single form elements for this, and learn both the discharge and the dissolving of energy. When the form has reached a quality of being able to withstand a frontal push, one will have mastered the necessary elementary aspects. At this point the student will gain more and more confidence if he keeps training hard. This usually results all by itself in an increased number of forms being trained day by day, and the exercises become refined for instance by use of a staff that is three metres long, or the sword, the sabre, the long-pole or the spear, or by learning about explosive force.

By training in a hard-working mode as described here for about two more years, reaching the fourth level of Taiji-*Gongfu* comes into sight. Within the third level single movements are more coordinated and the internal energy is flowing with much less friction, but it is still rather weak, and the coordination between movement and the function of the internal organs is not yet sufficiently elucidated. By training alone without being distracted, one should be able to achieve internal and external coordination. Confronted with a punch or during combat, it may be possible to keep up with an attacker's action and effect a change if his force is rather soft and slow. The learner should use any opportunity to bring his assailant into an unfavourable situation. He should avoid confrontation with a strong move from the attacker, yet counter-attack him if there is a weak point. It is recommended to control this gently.

Being on this level and meeting with an opponent who is stronger may cause the learner to find that his force of *peng*, of warding off, is still insufficient. It feels as if our position is pressed in or collapsing. The stance is not yet the way it should be: permanently centred and not to be surmounted due to its roundness. In this situation we cannot yet manoeuvre our body in the way we would wish. The student doesn't yet have at hand the principle described in the classical texts: 'Strike with your hands without allowing them to be seen. Once they do become visible nothing can be done any more about it.'

Giving way or throwing off still requires too much effort. The body is still too rigid. This condition is described as 30 per cent Yin and 70 per cent Yang; still the hard prevails too much.

THE FOURTH LEVEL OF GONGFU IN TAIJIQUAN

At the fourth level the progress from medium to small spiral movements should be mastered. This is the stage where we are nearing accomplishment, and this success is a very high level in *Gongfu*. By now the effective training methods should be mastered. The really important requirements of the forms should be understood and ready to be performed. One should have understood all the applications and martial concepts concealed within the movements. The flow of Qi inside the body should be 'smoothed out'. Every move should be harmonised with breathing. Every movement during the form should now be connected with the idea of an attacking opponent. Or: one should imagine being surrounded by a multitude of attackers. Every move within the forms should be performed in a continuing mode so that each stance and each section of the body are linked with each other at any time, so that the whole body will move as one. The movements of the upper and the lower body are related to each other, so that a continuous flow of energy exists between them. This flow is controlled from the waist. One should execute the form 'as if I was facing an opponent, though in fact no one is there'. Being confronted then in reality with an attacker, we should be calm, yet stay aware: 'as if no one was there, though the opponent stands in front of me'.

The training content of the forms resembles that of the third level. Theoretically the fifth level of Taiji-*Gongfu* can be achieved from here within about another three years.

In the martial abilities there is a considerable difference between the third and the fourth level. The third level aims at dissolving the opponent's force and avoiding conflicts that may arise within one's own movements. This involves taking an active role and forcing the opponent into passiveness. The fourth level not only enables the student to dissolve the opponent's force, but in addition gives him the ability to execute a targeted emission of force. By now the student has enough internal energy, and he is able to change and to adapt to the situation using energy and awareness while remaining flexible. Within the space of his movements the body now forms an integrated system. That's why the opponent's attack no longer poses a major threat. Once in contact with the opponent, the student won't have any trouble in changing along with the impact, thereby dissolving with ease the force that's targeting him. While perceiving the specific direction of the opponent's force, it becomes possible to follow it and to keep changing, so that any opposing action can be countered. The student is now capable of emitting the proper amount of force as well as continuously re-adjusting himself. He can predict the opponent's intention while acting calmly himself and precisely adjusting his own force. This allows him to hit the opponent in the most precise way.

Thus a person with these capabilities is described as 40 per cent Yin and 60 per cent Yang. This indicates being rather good in performing Taijiquan.

THE FIFTH LEVEL OF GONGFU IN TAIJIQUAN

The fifth level is the stage of proceeding from small circular movements to circular movements that are no longer visible, where one proceeds from mastering the form to 'invisible' execution.

The classical texts of Taijiquan say: 'With the gentle flow of energy, with the cosmic energy, one's own internal Qi moves in a natural way.

Moved by a solid form all through towards the invisible. So one will realize how marvellous the natural is.' The movements should by now be flexible and gentle. There should be a sufficient amount of internal energy.

Yet no matter how far the student may have advanced, it remains important to keep striving for the best. It is absolutely necessary to work hard day after day to achieve a flexible and adaptable body capable of manifold changes. The body should be fit to change internally and to distinguish between what's essential and what is not. This should be invisible from the outside.

Only then has the fifth level of Taiji-*Gongfu* been reached. In terms of martial skills the hard (*gang*) should accomplish the soft (*rou*). The form should be of ease, dynamic, elastic and lively. Every move and every moment of no emotion is consistent with the principle of Taijiquan. Every movement is launched from the entire body without any break. This means that every part of the body should be very sensitive and able to act immediately whenever necessary. This should go so far that every part of the body is capable of attacking like a fist whenever in contact with the opponent. The deliberate emission of power and its preservation should also be constantly alternating. The stance should be firm as if supported on all sides.

Therefore this level is described as: 'The only person capable of playing with Yin and Yang without being biased by neither of the two.' A person holding this degree of skill is considered a good master. A good master will make any movement consistent with the Taiji-principle which means that (the actual) movement has become invisible.

Having brought the fifth level of Taiji-*Gongfu* to perfection means that a strong connection and coordination between the spirit, the contraction and relaxation of the muscles, their movements and the functions of the internal organs has been established, one that will not be constricted or derailed even by a sudden and strong attack. Instead we remain flexible and agile.

However, even when we have reached this point, we should keep training continuously in order to reach new levels further beyond. Science aims beyond given limits. So does the science of Taijiquan: a whole lifetime is not enough to realise in entirety all the beauty and the power of Taijiquan.

Chapter 19

Interview with Grandmaster Chen Xiaowang

Published under the title 'Energy and Motion', DAO Special Edition Taijiquan 2000

'Taijiquan, in particular the Chen style, is characterised by spiral movements. The training is intended to generate energetic spirals also inside the body. What is the relation between internal and external spiral movements?'

When we begin our training, when we learn to perform the movements in the correct way, it has a stimulating effect on the spiral motion inside the body. Performing the movements correctly, doing the outer circling and spiralling movements within the form, is something that develops gradually, something you learn step by step. The space, the distance between the incorrect and the correct execution of the movements, is what we call 'temporary mistakes', mistakes that occur midway, obstacles so to speak. These mistakes, these obstacles on the trail are part of the normal course of learning Taijiquan; they belong to it and are part of the way of learning the Gong, that is: the artistry. Where this is not the case, where advancing doesn't occur gradually, without all these temporary obstacles, if one instead keeps training – perhaps for a long time – without meeting these obstacles on the way, then this does not indicate a case of being on the way towards learning about the art, but instead one is moving ahead in vain. This means that the obstacles are of use; they are necessary to the learning process.

At the start of training, when the movements of the form aren't yet performed correctly and the mistakes and obstacles in between are still quite numerous, the internal Qi, the energy that moves on spiral tracks inside the body, can't really begin to move with fluency. Later, however, when these temporary mistakes gradually become less, the Qi at a certain point will begin flowing inside. Internal and external movements will start to flow along with each other. One might say that Qi begins flowing when these mistakes are overcome by about 60 or 70 per cent. When the flow of internal Qi begins, it will likewise influence the external movements. In the beginning it is rather our external form that fuels the inner Qi's motion. As time passes and Qi really becomes fluent, this process is inverted so that the Qi inside supplies the power and controls the outer moves. We can compare this with a motor: in the beginning it needs a starter to make it run – which would be our outer movement – but once it has started running it will continue doing so without further need of an external drive.

The proportion changes so that it is energy inside that starts moving, and it's the outer movement which follows. Without the movement of Qi inside there will not be any external motion. This indicates a change in the relationship between outer movement and internal energy, which enables energy to take control. We achieve such a change by performing the Silk Reeling exercises. The art of the silk-exercises, the *Cansigong*, shows and defines the basic principles of movement in Chen-style Taijiquan, i.e. that first, the *Dantian* is the centre of all the movements; second, that when one part moves all other parts will move; third, that it is always one joint moving after the other, that movement is being transferred from one joint to the next. All types of motion inside Taijiquan, that is all forms as well as all movements during *Tuishou*, have their origin in this principle. This is expressed by the expression: 1000 movements – one principle. Once one has understood this principle, then it is indeed a very good method for learning any of the forms, exercises and applications in Qigong and in the martial arts.

'Can the various stages of this learning process be distinguished?'

This is a bit like in reading: when I see how you write German, it all looks right to me, because I cannot read German. If you wrote Chinese, however, I could of course recognise what is right and what is wrong, because I know Chinese very well. With Taijiquan it's the same: you can assess whether someone does something right or wrong only if you have the ability yourself.

'What about the relationship of spiral movements in nature, with man and with Taijiquan?'

The common ground is simply depicted by the Taiji-symbol of the two halves continuously merging, with a dot related to one entity being inside the other. This principle is to be discovered everywhere – within the greatest that we are able to imagine, namely the universe whose functions follow this principle, as well as with the earth; and also our own body functions. The movements inside our body change from Yin to Yang and from Yang to Yin. We can sense this while we breathe, by our digestion or by our metabolism. Change happens from solid to empty and from empty to solid, and when this is not the case, when something comes to a halt, we begin to feel pain, and something is unharmonious. We always strive for a flowing transition. In nature this is the same, for example with the weather. Why does the wind blow? Because in one place the pressure is high, in the other it is low, and between them there is wind. The wind balances the extreme variations in nature, in a way as a 'natural Qigong', so we can feel the motion of Qi within nature. It is similar while training Taijiquan: when we do the movements in a flowing way it feels comfortable, but when there's a block somewhere we sense it as an uncomfortable feeling of disturbance.

'Why do we strive for a way of moving in accordance with the principle of naturalness?'

Energy and movement as flowing in togetherness – when one is moving, all is moving – is sought after because problems occur when it's absent, when there is a part somewhere that doesn't move, that refuses to join. Then pain will be caused and other problems.

'What's the influence of practising Taijiquan on health?'

The natural principles which are omnipresent everywhere in nature and normally inside the human body as well, the principle that Qi is moving, that there are places which are full and others which are less so, that Qi ought to be flowing as unopposed as possible, during digestion for example or in metabolism and so on, this is what we call natural, what happens anyway, something we are born with, the way our body works – more or less well. By training Taijquan or the silk-exercises, we learn to activate the Qi. These exercises have been created by man, with the aim of driving our internal energy and the natural processes, to make them move in a better and stronger way. This way we may counterbalance certain weak points we might have, for example if Qi is lacking in one area, so it won't flow so well – just as if there is a river without enough water, the river will not be able to flow properly. We can take control and improve our fundamental constitution by way of proper training. The point is mainly to generate fluency.

'Can it be that training too much, in particular at the beginning when one's physical condition is not yet very good, may have a negative effect?'

Internal motion is continuous, and this is balanced over and over again, and when you train a lot you feel you are more hungry and have to eat more to keep the system working, and when you're too tired – once you're unable to absorb that much you simply get tired – you just can't train. It must be harmful to go beyond the personal limit of exhaustion without adequate replenishment. This is the principle given by nature, that is, not to push oneself beyond the natural limits, but instead to train just as much as one is able to without being shattered and exhausted. This way the personal energy and the internal motion can be stimulated slowly and in a soft way, so that Qi in turn will need less external drive. Consequentially less energy is needed each time to start training at all – just like our example of the motor.

'When Qi begins flowing by itself, when Qi in turn by way of its flow stimulates outer movement, will it remain that way or are there further changes?'

The fact is that in the beginning, when Qi does flow, the body becomes pervious and Qi may well drive the outer movement; this flow of Qi, however, is still very weak. It's like just having learnt how to drive a car and still being a bit insecure, driving wide at corners, for example, or taking too much space in order to park the vehicle, because one hasn't much control over the movements yet. It's the same with Qi. Though already flowing through yet still being thin and weak, this stream of Qi easily becomes lost again, for instance while receiving a push during *Tuishou*. Then the flow is interrupted again; this is because the movements being made are still so large that a fast reaction is not yet possible. Qi will gradually grow stronger inside the body, and the flow of Qi becomes more powerful so that it keeps flowing because the movements aren't so extreme any more. Movements will then become smaller and smaller, so that one actually no longer needs to move at all, and Qi will still keep flowing inside. During this evolution, cycles become smaller and smaller. In Chinese they say: 'A good performer in Taijiquan will do small cycles.' After a very long time of exercising, the movements may gradually diminish, and that indicates progress. Moving further ahead there could be a stage where no cycles would be made any more.

Being able at least to produce cycles or spirals with the movements of Qi following them is of course better than not having this skill at all. Being attacked and not having this skill at all simply results in being beaten. Being able to produce large circles and spirals at least enables one to dodge a blow, but one isn't yet fast enough to react prior to the opponent's next move. With the Qi flowing in smaller cycles and spirals and so producing enough force, one becomes capable of fighting back during an attack immediately. With growing ability, the flow of Qi increases and becomes more compact. The elementary image of Qi is that of something flowing, as with water that rises or does not rise, or exists only by a quantity of drops.

'Thank you very much for your explanations.'

Note: The interview was held and translated into German by Anina Seiler, TCM practitioner from Zurich, during a class in Hamburg.

Chapter 20

Sequences in Technique with Grandmaster Chen Xiaowang

The following pictures are a rarity, in that prior to the publication of the German edition of this book they had not been published before. They were taken in the early 1990s, in Australia. The attacker is impersonated by Howard Choy.

Figures 84–88 Striking Both Hands against the Foot (shuang bai lian)

Figure 84

Figure 85

Figure 86

Figure 87

Figure 88

Figures 89–93 Buddha's Guardian Pounding the Mortar (1) (jin gang dao dui)

Figure 89

Figure 90

Figure 91

Figure 92

Figure 93

Figures 94–98 Buddha's Guardian Pounding the Mortar (2) (jin gang dao dui)

Figure 94

Figure 95

Figure 96

Figure 97

Figure 98

Afterword

This book is absolutely incomplete. Each chapter is just a small bite, a small idea of the world that is opening to you with Taijiquan. Still, you and I are through with this book now and hopefully know much more than before. But in what way does it help?

I may feel that I know all these things now, at least in some way, but capability, skill – no, skills and abilities exist as little as they did before. Perhaps I can chat now with the wise-guys during the next armchair session of Taijiquan, or on some internet forum. However, knowledge alone won't help my health or my self-defence or anything else if I don't transform it into living reality. But how am I to do that?

By internalising it, by truly understanding, not just by knowing. The point is to understand in entirety, turning knowledge into a living part of myself instead of letting it remain a plain intellectual matter. And how's that going to work? By way of training.

So it's down to exercises, the big secret once again. Still, it's so easy just to talk about it. In the past while watching a good Kungfu movie – that is, when I was sitting in the cinema – I was full of zeal: 'The only thing I wanted to do was train, train, and train again...' That was in the evening. Drunk with enthusiasm I drove home and felt pretty gung-ho about the early morning training session ahead. Alarm clock set to five a.m. and off to bed. And then? As early as 5 a.m.? Poor me, do I have to get up now? Poor me, must I start training now? Traumatic images of Rocky emerged, Rocky before dawn, he cracks an egg and swallows it down raw, prior to racing up the streets of the city. And off I was back to sleep. So much for enthusiasm.

Cheng Man-ch'ing is quoted as saying: 'For every minute of theory, there is one hour of training.' Unfortunately things in most cases are just the other way round. I don't remember any more how often I've seen my favourite Kungfu movies. Over and over again. But let me be honest: of course I trained like a maniac. And I keep doing so. And that's precisely what I wish to suggest to you here and now as the very ethos of this book: train like a maniac!

Well. Not really that way; but please train as much as your time allows. It's definitely worth it. And to make it worth every single minute of your zeal, you ought to know exactly what in fact you are training. And you should have a good teacher who is capable of giving you proper correction and helping you improve.

If this book has been a help to you in attaining deeper knowledge of Taijiquan and given you a couple of tips for training, it has met its goal. And after that there is no way out: it's not the time to go to sleep yet. So get up and go outside. Train!

Jan Silberstorff,
Hamburg, February 2003

Glossary

Bagua The eight trigrams, combined term for Yin and Yang

Baihui Highest energetic spot of the body, top of head

Cansigong Silk thread exercises, silk-exercises

Cansijin Force of the silk thread, energy from the silk-exercises

Chenjiagou Residence of the Chen family in Wen County, Province Henan, PR China

Cun Chinese measure of 1.5 cm (used for one thumb's width)

Dantian Energy centre below the navel, centre of all movements in Taijiquan

Daodejing Opus of Laotse, Daoist classic, also: Tao Te King

Daoyin Old energetic gymnastic exercises, today filed under Qigong

Dumai Body meridian, runs from the palate across top of head and back to the Huiyin spot

Fajin Issuing force, energy

Fangshenshu Self-defence

Gong Work

Gongfu Time, effort, prowess, Chinese term for true artistry

He-Taijiquan Variety of Chen-style Taijiquan, emerged from Xiaojia

Hongtong-Beiquan Martial art from the district of Hongtong, Shanxi province

Huang Ting Jing Ancient classical work by Wei Huacun on internal energy work, attributed to Daoism

Huiyin-point Perineum

Kongjia Empty frame, term for moves without content

Kungfu Gongfu, today mainly used in the West as a term for Chinese martial art, see also *Gongfu*

Laogong Energetic spot in the centre of the palm

Laojia Erlu 2nd form, Old Frame of Chen-Taijiquan after Chen Changxing

Laojia Yilu 1st form, Old Frame of Chen-Taijiquan after Chen Changxing

Laotse Prime father of Daoism

Liang Yi 'The Two Phenomena', the primal polar powers

Meridian Energetic pathway in the human body

Mingmen Energetic gate in the lower back area

Nei san he The 'Three Internal Harmonies', term for internal context in Tiajiquan

Paochui Cannon-hammer, indicating the 2nd form of Chen-Taijiquan

Paoquan Cannon-fist, indicating the 2nd form of Chen-Taijiquan

Beijing Form Short form of Taijiquan, simplified government version from 1956

Pin Yin Standard Mandarin romanisation

Qi Chinese term for energy, related among others to Taijiquan

Qigong 'Working with energy', general term for internal exercises

Qi xie tao lu Chinese term for weapon forms

Renmai Body meridian, continues from Huiyin across front side of the body to palate

Rou Soft

Si Xiang 'Four Images', combined term for Yin and Yang

Shifu 'Father–teacher', traditional term for the teacher within a personal teacher–disciple relationship

Shigong Shifu's Shifu, i.e. 'Grandfather–teacher'

Taolu Coherent sequence of movements, form

Tuishou Pushing Hands, partner exercises of Taijiquan

Tuna Old energetic breathing exercises, today filed under the term of Qigong

Wai san he 'The Three External Harmonies', structure-oriented term in Taijiquan

Wushu Chinese term for martial art

Xiaojia Small Frame, variation of Chen-style Taijiquan by Chen Youben

Xinjia New Frame, indicates a variation of Chen-style Taijiquan by Chen Fake, also past term for Xiaojia

Yijing also I Ching, 'Book of Changes', classical work on theory of Yin and Yang, known also as casting oracle sticks

Yongquan Energetic point in the sole of foot

Zhanzhuang Standing Post, Standing Column, meditative standing exercise of Chen-style Taijiquan

Zhenqi 'True Qi', the encompassing energy

Appendix I: World Chen Taijiquan Association

GRANDMASTER CHEN XIAOWANG

Born in 1946 in Chenjiagou, PR China, Chen Xiaowang is the direct descendant of the Taijiquan founding family in the 19th generation, being the world's chief representative and inheritor of the Chen-

Figure 99 Grandmaster Chen Xiaowang

Taijiquan tradition. Grandmaster Chen Xiaowang who is also a world-famous calligrapher has received numerous awards and was officially nominated Bearer of National Treasures of the PR China. He regularly holds classes all over the world, and he is considered a living legend. His mission is not only the global distribution of Taijiquan, but also the preservation of the authentic school and teachings. The WCTA which he founded with the assistance of Jan Silberstorff is now the world's largest association of Taijiquan.

MASTER JAN SILBERSTORFF

Jan Silberstorff received his official Taijiquan training licence from the PR China to teach Taijiquan in China in 1989. In 1993 he became the first Western medallist in the official tournament of Chenjiagou, birth-place of Taijiquan. In the same year he became the first Western indoor student and family disciple of Grandmaster Chen Xiaowang and now is teaching as a 20th Generation successor of the Chen family. Together

Figure 100 Master Jan Silberstorff

they founded the World Chen Xiaowang Taijiquan Association and Jan became the leader of the German section, which is now the largest organisation of its kind. Jan is fluent in Chinese and lived in China for many years. In 1998 he was invited to be the first Westerner to perform in the official Singapore State Wushu Masters Event, which was broadcast all over Asia. From the International Wushu Federation of the PR China he got the highest Duan grade in Grandmaster Chen Xiaowang's Western Taiji community.

Jan has published three books, many articles, several DVDs, and has produced two TV series about Taijiquan. As a member of the 20th Generation of the Chen family, Jan currently teaches in 15 countries around the world.

WORLD CHEN TAIJIQUAN ASSOCIATION GERMANY

In the direct line from Grandmaster Chen Xiaowang (19th generation of the founding family of Taijiquan) and Master Jan Silberstorff (21st generation), WCTAG – being the German branch of the world association WCTA – teaches the Taijiquan of the family Chen from Chenjiagou (PR China), the legendary birthplace of Taijiquan. Taijiquan has been revived as a living and complete system, its elements being the traditional hand and weapon forms, *Tuishou* (pushing hands) and *Sanshou* (free martial application). The foundation for this is the authentic Qigong (energy work) of the Chen family, the Reeling Silk exercises.

Taijiquan was originally practised within the Chen family exclusively, until about 150 years ago when classes were open to the public. As a consequence of this, Taijiquan changed and various new schools (*Yang*, *Wu*, etc.) evolved from the Chen-style.

The wish of today's family inheritor of the original Taijiquan, as well as his personal disciple Jan Silberstorff and a staff of more than 100 teachers nationwide, is to spread Taijiquan worldwide, and to maintain the family nature of learning and passing on.

Seminars, weekly classes, international camps and educational journeys are continually organised by WCTAG, and the association is a focus point for information and events. Beyond this, WCTAG is constantly active in providing further educational and training material.

WCTAG is the German organisation of the global association World Chen Xiaowang Taijiquan Association (WCTA). It is a founding member of the German umbrella association for Qigong and Taijiquan (DDQT), and the General Education Guidelines (AALL) have been developed according to the educational concept of WCTAG.

In addition, WCTAG is also the German section of IAMTJQA, the Taiji Association of Chenjiagou, the birthplace of Taijiquan. It is a member also within the German Network for Taijiquan and Qigong and the European TCFE (Tai Chi Chuan Federation Europe). WCTAG is the largest self-contained Taijiquan association in Europe.

WCTA is the largest traditional Taijiquan association in the world. WCTA is represented in more than 35 countries worldwide. WCTAG is present in more than 80 cities in Germany.

To contact WCTAG and the author:

WCTAG
Rendsburgerstr. 14
D-20359 Hamburg
Germany
Tel.:/Fax: +40-40-3194224
Internet: www.wctag.de
Email: wctag@t-online.de

Figure 101   *Figure 102*

Appendix II: The Forms of Chen Taijiquan

THE 19-STEP FORM

chen shi tai ji quan shi jiu shi (WCTAG)

First section

1. *yu bei shi*	Preparation Stance
2. *jin gang chu miao*	Buddha's Guardian Steps Out of the Temple
3. *lan zha yi*	Tying the Coat
4. *shang bu xie xing*	Stepping Forward, Taking Oblique Position (End of the New Frame)
5. *shang san bu*	Three Steps Forward
6. *yan shou gong quan – zuo*	Hand Conceals Arm and Fist – left
7. *shuang tui shou*	Push with Both Hands (Small Frame)

Second section

8. *dao juan hong*	Step Back with Arms Rolled in
9. *shan tong bei*	Swiftly Dodging with the Back
10. *yan shou gong quan – you*	Hand Conceals Arm and Fist – right
11. *liu feng si bi*	Six Sealings, Four Closings (Small Frame)

Third section

12. *yun shou*	Circling Hands
13. *gao tan ma*	High Pat on Horse
14. *you deng yi gen*	Kick with Right Heel
15. *zou deng yi gen*	Kick with Left Heel

Fourth section

16. *ye ma feng cong you, zuo*	Wild Horse's Mane Parting – right and left (New Frame)
17. *yu nu chuan suo*	Jade Woman Casting the Shuttle
18. *jin gang dao dui*	Buddha's Guardian Pounding the Mortar
19. *shou shi*	Closing Stance

THE 38-STEP FORM

chen shi tai ji quan san shi ba shi (WCTAG)

First section

1. *yu bei shi*	Preparation Stance
2. *jin gang dao dui*	Buddha's Guardian Pounding the Mortar
3. *bei he liang chi*	The White Crane Spreads Its Wings
4. *san shang bu*	Three Steps Forward
5. *xie xing*	Taking Oblique Position
6. *lou xi*	Enfold and Raise Knee
7. *qian tang ao bu*	Neatly Pacing Forward in Diagonal Mode
8. *yan shou hong quan*	Hand Conceals Arm and Fist
9. *pie shen quan*	The Fist Follows the Turned-in Body
10. *shuang tui shou*	Push with Both Hands

Second section

11. *san huan zhang*	Change Palms Three Times

12. *zhou di kan quan*   Fist Showing under the Elbow
13. *dao juan gong*   Step Back with Arms Rolled in
14. *tui bu ya zhou*   Step Back and Strike with Elbow
15. *bai she tu xin*   The White Snake Pushes out the Tongue
16. *shan tong bei*   Swiftly Dodging with the Back
17. *qian tang ao bu*   Neatly Pacing Forward in Diagonal Mode
18. *qing long chu shi*   Blue-green Dragon Shoots out of the Water
19. *ji di chui*   Striking Downward

Third section

20. *er ti jiao*   Kicking with Both Feet
21. *hu xin quan*   Protecting the Heart with the Fist
22. *qian zao*   Taking up from the Front
23. *hou zao*   Taking up from the Back
24. *you deng yi gen*   Kick with Right Heel
25. *zuo deng yi gen*   Kick with Left Heel
26. *yu nu quan suo*   Jade Woman Casting the Shuttle
27. *lan zha yi*   Tying the Coat
28. *liu feng si bi*   Six Sealings and Four Closings

Fourth section

29. *dan bian*   Single Whip
30. *que di long*   The Dragon Bows to the Ground
31. *shang bu qi xing*   Step Forward, Forming the Seven Stars
32. *xiao qin da*   Small Catching and Hitting
33. *yun shou*   Circling Hands
34. *gao tan ma*   High Pat on Horse

35. *shuang bai lian*	Moving Both Hands towards Foot
36. *dang tou pao*	Directly Hitting the Head
37. *jin gang dao dui*	Buddha's Guardian Pounding the Mortar
38. *shou si*	Closing Stance

FIRST FORM, 'OLD FRAME'

chen shi tai ji quan lao jia yi lu (WCTAG)

First section

1. *yu bei shi*	Preparation Stance
2. *jin gang dao dui*	Buddha's Guardian Pounding the Mortar
3. *lan zha yi*	Tying the Coat
4. *liu feng si bi*	Six Sealings, Four Closings
5. *dan bian*	Single Whip
6. *jin gang dao dui*	Buddha's Guardian Pounding the Mortar
7. *bai he liang chi*	The White Crane Spreads Its Wings
8. *xie xing*	Taking Oblique Position
9. *lou xi*	Enfold and Raise Knee
10. *shang san bu*	Three Steps Forward
11. *xie xing*	Taking Oblique Position
12. *lou xi*	Enfold and Raise Knee
13. *shang san bu*	Three Steps Forward
14. *yan shou gong quan*	Hand Conceals Arm and Fist
15. *jin gang dao dui*	Buddha's Guardian Pounding the Mortar
16. *pie shen quan*	The Fist Follows the Turned-in Body
17. *qing long chu shui*	Blue-green Dragon Shoots out of the Water
18. *shuang tui shou*	Push with Both Hands

Second section

19. *zhou di kann quan*	Fist Appears under the Elbow
20. *dao juan gong*	Step Back with Arms Rolled in
21. *bai he liang chi*	The White Crane Spreads Its Wings
22. *xie xing*	Taking Oblique Position
23. *shang tong bei*	Swiftly Dodging with the Back
24. *yan shou gong quan*	Hand Conceals Arm and Fist
25. *liu feng si bi*	Six Sealings and Four Closings
26. *dan bian*	Single Whip
27. *yun shou*	Circling Hands
28. *gao tan ma*	High Pat on Horse
29. *you ca jiao*	Rubbing with the Right Foot
30. *zuo ca jiao*	Rubbing with the Left Foot
31. *zuo deng yi gen*	Kick with Left Heel
32. *shang san bu*	Three Steps Forward
33. *shen xian yi ba zhua*	The Immortal Takes Hold
34. *er ti jiao*	Kick with Both Feet
35. *hu xin quan*	Protecting the Heart with the Fist
36. *xuan feng jiao*	Foot Kick Like Tornado
37. *you deng yi gen*	Kick with Right Heel
38. *yan shou gong quan*	Hand Conceals Arm and Fist

Third section

39. *xiao xin da*	Small Catching and Hitting
40. *bao tou tui shan*	Enclosing the Head between Arms and Push Mountain
41. *liu feng si bi*	Six Sealings, Four Closings
42. *dan bian*	The Single Whip
43. *qian zhao*	Taking Up Forward
44. *hou zhao*	Taking Up Backward
45. *ye ma fen zhong*	Wild Horse's Mane Parting
46. *liu feng si bi*	Six Sealings, Four Closings

47. *dan bian* — The Single Whip
48. *yu nu chuan suo* — Jade Woman Casting the Shuttle

49. *lan zha yi* — Tying the Coat
50. *liu feng si bi* — Six Sealings, Four Closings
51. *dan bian* — The Single Whip
52. *yun shou* — Circling Hands
53. *shuang bai lian* — Moving Both Hands against Foot

54. *die cha* — Fall Down and Spread Legs
55. *jin ji du li* — Golden Rooster Stands on One Leg

Fourth section

56. *dao juan gong* — Step Back with Arms Rolled in

57. *bai he liang chi* — The White Crane Spreads Its Wings

58. *xie xing* — Taking Oblique Position
59. *shang tong bei* — Swiftly Dodging with the Back

60. *yan shou gong quan* — Hand Conceals Arm and Fist
61. *liu feng si bi* — Six Sealings, Four Closings
62. *dan bian* — The Single Whip
63. *yun shou* — Circling Hands
64. *gao tan ma* — High Pat on Horse
65. *shi zi jiao* — Holding the Arms Crossed and Slapping the Foot

66. *zhi dang chui* — Strike on Crotch
67. *yuan hou tan guo* — White Ape Offering Fruit
68. *dan bian* — The Single Whip
69. *que di long* — The Dragon Bows to the Ground

70. *shang bu qi xing* — Step Forward and Strike by Seven Stars

71. *xia bu kua gong* — Step Back and Spread Arms
72. *shuang bai lian* — Moving with Both Hands against Foot

73. *dang tou pao*	Straight Punch on the Head
74. *jin gang dao dui*	Buddha's Guardian Pounding the Mortar
75. *shou shi*	Closing Stance

SECOND FORM, 'OLD FRAME'

chen shi tai ji quan lao jia er lu (pao chui) (WCTAG):

First section

1. *yu bei shi*	Preparation Stance
2. *jin gang dao dui*	Buddha's Guardian Pounding the Mortar
3. *lan zha yi*	Tying the Coat
4. *liu feng si bi*	Six Sealings, Four Closings
5. *dan bian*	Single Whip
6. *hu xin quan*	Fist Shielding the Heart
7. *xie xing*	Taking Oblique Position
8. *hui tou jin gang dao dui*	Buddha's Guardian Turns Pounding the Mortar
9. *pie shen quan*	Fist Follows the Turned-in Body
10. *zhi dang (quan)*	Aiming with the Fist at the Belly
11. *zhan shou*	Knock off by Hand
12. *fan hua wu xiu*	Flower Turns with Dancing Sleeves
13. *yan shou gong quan*	Hand Conceals Arm and Fist

Second section

14. *yao lan zhou*	Turn Hip and Ward Off with Elbow
15. *da gong quan, xiao gong quan*	Strike with Full Arm
16. *yu nu chuan suo*	Jade Woman Casting the Shuttle
17. *dao qi long*	Step Back Riding the Dragon
18. *yan shou gong quan*	Hand Conceals Arm and Fist

19. *guo bian guo bian* — Wrapping the Fuse
20. *shou tou shi* — With the Head of a Beast
21. *pi jia zi* — Throwing out of the Form
22. *fan hua wu xiu* — Flower Turns with Dancing Sleeves
23. *yan shou gong quan* — Hand Conceals Arm and Fist

Third section
24. *fu hu* — The Tiger Lies on the Ground
25. *mo mei gong* — The Arm Brushes the Eyebrow
26. *huang long san tiao shui* — The Yellow Dragon Stirs the Water Three Times
27. *zuo chong* — Stamping Thrust Forward Left
28. *you chong* — Stamping Thrust Forward Right
29. *yan shou gong quan* — Hand Conceals Arm and Fist
30. *sao tang tui* — Leg Sweeping the Hall
31. *yan shou gong quan* — Hand Conceals Arm and Fist
32. *quan pao chui* — Universal Cannon Fist
33. *yan shou gong quan* — Hand Conceals Arm and Fist

Fourth section
34. *dao cha dao cha* — Spread Arms Twice and Strike
35. *you er gong, zuo er gong* — Two Arms Right, Two Arms left
36. *hui tou dang men pao* — Turning with Straight Hit on the Gate
37. *wo di da zhuo pao* — Punching from Bottom to Top
38. *yao lan zhou* — Turn Hip and Ward Off with Elbow
39. *shun lan zhou* — Elbow Follows and Strikes
40. *wo di pao* — Punch Downward
41. *hui tou jing lan zhi ru* — Turning the Body, Releasing the Rope Straight Down into the Well
42. *jin gang dao dui* — Buddha's Guardian Pounding the Mortar
43. *shou shi* — Closing Stance

FIRST FORM, 'NEW FRAME'

chen shi tai ji quan xin jia yi lu (WCTAG)

First section

1. *yu bei shi*	Preparation Stance
2. *jin gang dao dui*	Buddha's Guardian Pounding the Mortar
3. *lan zha yi*	Tying the Coat
4. *lui feng si bi*	Six Sealings, Four Closings
5. *dan bian*	Single Whip
6. *jin gang dao dui*	Buddha's Guardian Pounding the Mortar
7. *bai he liang chi*	The White Crane Spreads Its Wings
8. *xie xing ao bu*	Neatly Pacing Forward in Diagonal Mode Taking Oblique Position
9. *chu shou*	Begin to Enfold
10. *qian tang ao bu*	Neatly Pacing Forward in Diagonal Mode
11. *xie xing ao bu*	Neatly Pacing Forward in Diagonal Mode Taking Oblique Position
12. *zai shou*	Repeat Enfolding
13. *qian tang ao bu*	Neatly Pacing Forward in Diagonal Mode
14. *yan shou gong quan*	Hand Conceals Arm and Fist
15. *jin gang dao dui*	Buddha's Guardian Pounding the Mortar
16. *pie shen quan*	Fist Follows the Turned-in Body
17. *bei zhe kao*	Dodging with the Shoulder, Striking to the Back
18. *qing long chu shui*	Blue-green Dragon Shoots out of the Water
19. *shuang tui shou*	Pushing with Both Hands

Second section

20.	*san huang zhang*	Palms Changing Three Times
21.	*zhou di quan*	Fist Appears under the Elbow
22.	*dao juan gong*	Step Back with Arms Rolled in
23.	*tui bu ya zhou*	One Step Back, Striking with the Elbow
24.	*zhong pan*	Striking All Around from the Middle
25.	*bai he liang chi*	The White Crane Spreads Its Wings
26.	*xie xing ao bu*	Neatly Pacing Forward in Diagonal Mode Taking Oblique Position
27.	*shan tong bei*	Swiftly Dodging with the Back
28.	*yan shou gong quan*	Hand Conceals Arm and Fist
29.	*liu feng si bi*	Six Sealings, Four Closings
30.	*dan bian*	Single Whip
31.	*yun shou*	Circling Hands
32.	*gao tan ma*	High Pat on Horse
33.	*you ca jiao*	Rubbing Foot – right
34.	*zuo ca jiao*	Rubbing Foot – left
35.	*zuo deng yi gen*	Kick with Left Heel
36.	*qian tang ao bu*	Neatly Pacing Forward in Diagonal Mode
37.	*ji di chui*	Fist Strikes Downward
38.	*fan shen er ti jiao*	Turning the Body and Kick with Both Feet
39.	*shou tou shi*	With the Head of a Beast
40.	*xuan feng jiao*	Kick Like a Tornado
41.	*you deng yi gen*	Kick with Right Heel
42.	*yan shou gong quan*	Hand Conceals Arm and Fist

Third section

43.	*xiao qin da*	Small Catching and Hitting
44.	*bao tout ui shan*	Enclosing the Head between Arms and Push Mountain

45. *san huan zhang*	Palms Changing Three Times
46. *liu feng si bi*	Six Sealings, Four Closings
47. *dan bian*	Single Whip
48. *qian zhao*	Taking up from the Front
49. *hou zhao*	Taking up from Behind
50. *ye ma fen zhong*	Wild Horse's Mane Parting
51. *liu feng si bi*	Six Sealings, Four Closings
52. *dan bian*	Single Whip
53. *shuang zhen jiao*	Stomp with Both Feet to Make the Earth Quake
54. *yu nu chuan suo*	Jade Woman Casting the Shuttle
55. *lan zha yi*	Tying the Coat
56. *liu feng si bi*	Six Sealings, Four Closings
57. *dan bian*	Single Whip
58. *yun shou*	Circling Hands
59. *bai jiao die cha*	Move towards Foot, Fall Down and Spread legs
60. *zuo you jin ji du li*	Golden Rooster Stands on One Leg, left and right

Fourth section

61. *dao juan gong*	Step Back with Arms Rolled in
62. *tui bu ya zhou*	One Step Back, Striking with the Elbow
63. *zhong pan*	Striking All Around from the Middle
64. *bai he liang chi*	The White Crane Spreads Its Wings
65. *xie xing ao bu*	Neatly Pacing Forward in Diagonal Mode Taking Oblique Position
66. *shang tong bei*	Swiftly Dodging with the Back
67. *yan shou gong quan*	Hand Conceals Arm and Fist
68. *liu feng si bi*	Six Sealings, Four Closings
69. *dan bian*	Single Whip

70. *yun shou*	Circling Hands
71. *gao tan ma*	High Pat on Horse
72. *shi zi bao lian*	Holding the Arms Crossed and Slapping the Foot
73. *zhi dang chui*	Aiming the Fist at the Belly
74. *bai yuan xian guo*	White Ape Offering Fruit
75. *liu feng si bi*	Six Sealings, Four Closings
76. *dan bian*	Single Whip
77. *que di long*	The Dragon Bows to the Ground
78. *shang bu qi xing*	Step Forward and Strike by Seven Stars
79. *xia bu kua gong*	Step Back and Spread Arms
80. *shuang bai lian*	Moving Both Feet to the Foot
81. *dang tou pao*	Cannon Strike on Head
82. *jin gang dao dui*	Buddha's Guardian Pounding the Mortar
83. *shou shi*	Closing Stance

SECOND FORM, 'NEW FRAME'

chen shi tai ji quan xin jia er lu (pao chui) (WCTAG)

First section

1. *yu bei shi*	Preparation Stance
2. *jin gang dao dui*	Buddha's Guardian Pounding the Mortar
3. *lan zha yi*	Tying the Coat
4. *liu feng si bi*	Six Sealings, Four Closings
5. *dan bian*	Single Whip
6. *ban lan zhou*	Block on Both Sides with the Elbow
7. *hu xin quan*	Fist Shielding the Heart
8. *ao bu xie xing*	Neatly Pacing Forward in Diagonal Mode Taking Oblique Position

9. *sha yao ya zhou quan* — Stop with Hip and Press with Elbow

10. *jing lan zhi ru* — Releasing the Rope Straight Down into the Well

11. *feng sao mei hua* — Wind Sweeping the Plum Blossom

12. *jin gang dao dui* — Buddha's Guardian Pounding the Mortar

Second section

13. *bi shen chui* — Fist Shielding the Body
14. *pie shen chui* — Fist Following the Twisted Body

15. *zhan shou* — Knock off by Hand
16. *fan hua wu xiu* — Flower Turns with Dancing Sleeves

17. *yan shou gong quan* — Hand Conceals Arm and Fist
18. *fei bu ao luan zhou* — Flying Step and Break Through with Elbow (Like a Phoenix)

19. *yun shou* — Circling Hands
20. *gao tan ma* — High Pat on Horse
21. *yun shou* — Circling Hands
22. *gao tan ma* — High Pat on Horse
23. *lian zhu pao* — Continuous Firing
24. *lian zhu pao* — Continuous Firing
25. *lian zhu pao* — Continuous Firing
26. *dao qi lin* — Qilin Turns Around
27. *bai she tu xin* — The White Snake Pushes out the Tongue

28. *bai she tu xin* — The White Snake Pushes out the Tongue

29. *bai she tu xin* — The White Snake Pushes out the Tongue

30. *hai di fan hua* — Flower Turns at the Bottom of the Sea

31. *yan shou gong quan* — Hand Conceals Arm and Fist

Third section

32.	*zhuan shen liu he*	Turning the Body with Sixfold Sealing
33.	*zuo guo bian pao*	Wrapping the Fuse and Detonate – left
34.	*zuo guo bian pao*	Wrapping the Fuse and Detonate – left
35.	*you guo bian pao*	Wrapping the Fuse and Detonate – right
36.	*you guo bian pao*	Wrapping the Fuse and Detonate – right
37.	*shou tou shi*	With the Head of a Beast
38.	*pi jia zi*	Throwing out of the Form
39.	*fan hua wu xiu*	Flower Turns with Dancing Sleeves
40.	*yan shou gong quan*	Hand Conceals Arm and Fist
41.	*fu hu The*	Tiger Bends Down
42.	*mo mei gong*	The Arm Brushes the Eyebrow
43.	*you huang long san jiao shui*	The Yellow Dragon Stirs the Water Three Times – right
44.	*zuo huang long san jiao shui*	The Yellow Dragon Stirs the Water Three Times – left
45.	*zuo deng yi gen*	Kick with Left Heel
46.	*you deng yi gen*	Kick with Right Heel
47.	*hai di fan hua*	Flower Turns at the Bottom of the Sea
48.	*yan shou gong quan*	Hand Conceals Arm and Fist

Fourth section

49.	*sao tang tui (zhuan jing pao)*	Leg Sweeping the Hall (Explosive Twist of Lower Leg)
50.	*yan shou gong quan*	Hand Conceals Arm and Fist
51.	*zuo chong*	Stamping Thrust Forward Left
52.	*you chong*	Stamping Thrust Forward Right
53.	*dao cha*	Spread Arms and Punch

54. *hai di fan hua*	Flower Turns at the Bottom of the Sea
55. *yan shou gong quan*	Hand Conceals Arm and Fist
56. *duo er gong*	Grab for Something with Both Arms
57. *duo er gong*	Grab for Something with Both Arms
58. *Lian huan pao*	Connected Cannon Strikes
59. *Yu nu chuan suo*	Jade Woman Casting the Shuttle
60. *hui tou dang men pao*	Turning Round with Straight Hit on the Gate
61. *Yu nu chuan suo*	Jade Woman Casting the Shuttle
62. *hui tou dang men pao*	Turning Round with Straight Hit on the Gate
63. *Pie shen chui*	Fist Following the Twisted Body
64. *Ao luan zhou*	Break Through with Elbow (Like a Phoenix)
65. *Shun luan zhou*	Same-Direction Strike with Elbow (Like a Phoenix)
66. *Chuan xin zhou*	Stabbing the Elbow into the Heart
67. *Wo li pao*	Exploding from Inside the Cave
68. *Jing lan zhi ru*	Releasing the Rope Straight into the Well
69. *Feng sao mei hua*	Wind Sweeping the Plum Blossom
70. *Jin gang dao dui*	Buddha's Guardian Pounding the Mortar
71. *Shou shi*	Closing Stance

SWORD FORM

chen shi tai ji dan jian (WCTAG)

First section

1. *yu bei shi*	Preparation Stance
2. *tai ji jian chu shi*	Taiji-Sword Initial Stance
3. *chao yang jian*	Turn towards the Sun with the Sword
4. *xian ren zi lu*	The Immortal Showing the Way
5. *qing long chu shui*	Blue-green Dragon Shoots out of the Water
6. *hu xi jian*	Shielding the Knee with the Sword
7. *bi men shi*	Closing the Gate
8. *qing long chu shui*	Blue-green Dragon Shoots out of the Water
9. *fan shen xia pi jian*	Turning Around and Split Downward with the Sword
10. *qing long zhuan shen*	Blue-green Dragon Turns Around
11. *xie fei shi*	Diagonal Flying
12. *zhan chi dian tou*	Unfolding the Wings and Nodding with the Head

Second section

13. *bo cao xun she*	Parting the Grass and Searching for the Snake
14. *jin ji du li*	The Golden Rooster Stands on One Leg
15. *xian ren zi lu*	The Immortal Showing the Way
16. *gai lan shi*	Protect and Gate
17. *gu shu pan gen*	The Old Tree Winding Its Roots
18. *e hu pu shi*	The Hungry Tiger Bounces on his Prey

19. *qing long bai wei*	Blue-green Dragon Wags the Tail
20. *dao juan gong*	Stepping Back with Arms Turned in
21. *ye ma tian jian*	The Wild Horse Jumps Across the Creek
22. *bai she tu xin*	The White Snake Pushes out the Tongue
23. *wu long bai wei*	Black Dragon Wags the Tail
24. *zhong kui zhang jian*	Zhongkui Holding the Sword
25. *luo han xiang long*	The Lohan Defeats the Dragon
26. *hei xiong fan bei*	The Black Bear Turns Around

Third section

27. *yan zi zhuo ni*	The Swallow Picking in the Mud
28. *bai she tu xin*	The White Snake Pushes out the Tongue
29. *xie fei shi*	Diagonal Flying
30. *ying xiong dou zhi*	Eagle and Bear Fighting Each Other
31. *yan zi zhuo ni*	The Swallow Picking in the Mud
32. *zhai xing huan dou*	Grabbing the Stars and Tossing Them Back
33. *hai di lao yue*	Drawing the Moon from the Bottom of the Sea
34. *xian ren zi lu*	The Immortal Showing the Way
35. *feng huan dian tou*	The Phoenix Nods His Head
36. *yan zi zhou ni*	The Swallow Picking in the Mud
37. *bai she tu xin*	The White Snake Pushes out the Tongue

Fourth section

38. *xie fei shi*	Diagonal Flying

39. *zuo tuo qian jin*	Carrying a Thousand Pounds – left
40. *you tuo qian jin*	Carrying a Thousand Pounds – right
41. *yan zi zhuo ni*	The Swallow Picking in the Mud
42. *bai yuan xian guo*	White Ape Passing the Fruit
43. *luo hua shi*	The Falling Blossom
44. *shang xia xie zi*	Oblique Stabbing Upward and Down
45. *xie fei shi*	Diagonal Flying
46. *na zha tan hai*	Nazha Stretches towards the Sea
47. *guai mang fan shen*	The Giant Python Turns Around
48. *wei tuo xian chu*	Weituo Pounding the Mortar
49. *mo pan jian*	Moving the Sword in Horizontal Circles 'like a Millstone'
50. *shou shi (tai ji jian huan guan)*	Closing Stance (The Taiji-Sword returns to its original position)

SABRE FORM

chen shi tai ji quan dan dao (WCTAG)

1. *yu bei shi*	Preparation Stance
2. *hu xin dao*	Shielding the Heart with the Sabre
3. *qing long chu shui*	Blue-green Dragon Shoots out of the Water
4. *feng juan can hua*	Wind Tearing the Dried Flower
5. *bai yuan gai ding*	The White Cloud Conceals the Summit

6. *hei hu sou shan*	The Black Tiger Searches the Mountains
7. *su qin bei jian*	Suqin Carrying the Sword on the Back
8. *jin ji du li*	The Golden Rooster Stands on One Leg
9. *ying feng gun bi*	Taking up the Stab-weapon, Re-direct it and Dodge it
10. *yao zhan bai she*	Cutting through the White Snake's Hip
11. *ri tan san huan*	Drawing Three Rings around the Sun
12. *bo yun wang ri*	Driving the Clouds Away to See the Sun
13. *zuo bo cao xin she*	Ploughing the Grass and Searching for a Snake – left
14. *you bo cao xin she*	Ploughing the Grass and Searching for a Snake – right
15. *qing long chu shui*	Blue-green Dragon Shoots out of the Water
16. *feng juan can hua*	Wind Tearing the Dried Flower
17. *yan bie jin chi*	Wild Goose Twisting the Wings
18. *ye cha tan hai*	Yecha Stretches towards the Sea
19. *you fan shen kan*	Turning the Body and Performing a Strike – right
20. *zuo fan shen kan*	Turning the Body and Performing a Strike – left
21. *bai she tu xin*	The White Snake Pushes out the Tongue
22. *huai zhong bao yue*	Embracing the Moon and Move It to the Chest
23. *shou shi*	Closing Stance

POLE/SPEAR FORM

chen shi tai ji li hua qiang bai yuan gun (WCTAG)

First section

1. *qi shi*	Preparation Stance
2. *ye cha tan hai*	Yecha Stretches towards the Sea
3. *quan wu hua*	Full Turn (Dance of the Blossom)
4. *zhong ping qiang*	Punch on Mid-level
5. *ji san qiang*	Three Straight Spears
6. *shang ping qiang*	Spear on Upper Level
7. *zhen zhu dao juan lian*	Step Back and Roll in Pearl-embroidered Curtain
8. *xia ping qiang*	Spear on Lower Level
9. *dian tui yu lu qiang*	Jump across Leg, Row and Stab with the Spear
10. *zha qing long xian zhua*	Blue-green Dragon Showing the Claws
11. *shang buzhuo yi qiang*	Stepping Forward, Grabbing the Spear with One Hand
12. *cao di ci bian lang qiang*	Sweep the Ground, Stab and Block Side with Spear

Second section

13. *wang qian da liang qiang*	Move Ahead with Spear and Strike Twice
14. *huang long dian gan*	The Yellow Dragon Punctuates with the Rod
15. *lian zha yi qiang*	Sting with the Spear from Bottom to Top
16. *bang e wu hua*	Half Turn (Dance of the Blossom)
17. *yao qun lan qiang*	Hold Back the Crowd with Spear at Hip-level
18. *hui tou bang e wu hua*	Turning the Head and Doing a Half Turn

19. *shou an di she qiang*	Pressing a Snake to the Ground with a Spear
20. *tiao yi qiang*	Raising the Spear
21. *zha yi qiang*	Performing a Sting with the Spear
22. *yan liang qiang*	Concealed Double Attack
23. *zuo qi yi sao chao tian qiang*	Wave the Flag and Hold it Skyward – left
24. *you yao qi yi sao tie niu geng di qiang*	Waving the Flag and Plough the Earth as if with an Iron Bull – right
25. *hui tou ban ge wu hua*	Turning the Head and Doing a Half Turn
26. *xia di shui qiang*	Sink to Bottom like Dripping Water
27. *yan liang qiang*	Concealed Double Attack

Third section

28. *shang qi long qiang*	Climb on Dragon and Ride with the Spear
29. *wang qian jin bo cao xun she*	Advance, Poking the Grass and Searching for the Snake
30. *wang hou tui bai yuan tuo qiang*	The White Ape Retreats and Pulls the Spear after Him
31. *hui tou zha wu long ru dong*	Turn Around and Sting – the Black Dragon Goes to the Cave
32. *dian hui tui shou pipa shi*	Jump Back over Leg and Take Back the Pipa
33. *wang qian da liang qiang*	Move Forward with Spear and Strike Twice
34. *yao qi sao di tai shan ya luan*	Waving the Flag Sweeping the Ground, the Taishan Squashing the Egg
35. *ban ge wu hua*	Half Turn (Dance of the Blossom)
36. *ling mao pu shu*	Swift Cat Catching the Mouse

37. *zuo pu yi qiang*	Bounce upon with Spear – left
38. *you pu yi qiang*	Bounce upon with Spear – right
39. *fan shen hui tou ci qiang*	Turning Round Head and Body and Sting
40. *ti yi gen zi*	One Kick with Heel
41. *dan shou chu qiang*	Single-handed Outward Stab with Spear

Fourth section

42. *quan wu hua*	Full Turn (Dance of the Blossom)
43. *er lang dan shan*	Erlang Carries the Mountain on the Shoulder Pole
44. *ban ge wu hua*	Half Turn (Dance of the Blossom)
45. *xia liu feng qiang*	Stab Down by Six Tenth
46. *hui tou ban ge wu hua*	Turn Around Doing a Half Turn (Dance of the Blossom)
47. *yao zi pu an qun*	Sparrow Hawk Bouncing upon the Quail
48. *tiao yi gen zi*	Raising Pole and Heel
49. *zha yi qiang*	Sting with the Spear
50. *quan wu hua*	Full Turn (Dance of the Blossom)
51. *er lang dan shan sao yi qiang*	Erlang Carries the Mountain on the Shoulder Pole
52. *ban ge wu hua*	Half Turn (Dance of the Blossom)
53. *mei nu ren zhen*	The Fair Lady Inserts the Thread into the Needle Eye (and: *yu nu chuan suo* – Jade Woman Casting the Shuttle)
54. *ci chuang hong men qiang*	Sting Like an Assassin

Fifth section

55. *hui tou sao yi qiang*	Turning Around and Sweeping with the Spear

56. *quan wu hua*	Full Turn (Dance of the Blossom)
57. *hu xi qiang*	Shielding the Knee with the Spear
58. *yan liang qiang*	Concealed Double Attack
59. *cang long bai wei*	Dark-green Dragon Wagging the Tail
60. *wang qian sao yi qiang*	Advance and Sweep with the Spear
61. *wang qian zai sao yi qiang*	Advance and Sweep Again with the Spear
62. *wang zuo sao yi qiang*	Sweep with Spear to the Left
63. *wang you sao yi qiang*	Sweep with Spear to the Right
64. *ban ge wu hua*	Half Turn (Dance of the Blossom)
65. *tai gong diao yu*	Taigong while Fishing
66. *hui ma qiang*	Turn Around Performing a Counterpunch
67. *shou shi*	Closing Stance

HALBERD FORM

chen shi tai ji da dao (WCTAG)	
chun qiu da dao –	'Springtime – Autumn Halberd
qing long yan yue dao	the Halberd of the Green-blue Dragon that Veils the Moon'

First section

1. *guan sheng ti dao shang ba tiao*	General Guan Raises the Halberd and Occupies the Bridge
2. *bai yun gai ding cheng ying hao*	The White Cloud Conceals the Peak (and the Hero Appears)

3. *ju dao mo qi huai bao yue* — Raising the Halberd, Circling the Banner like a Millstone and Embracing the Moon

4. *shang san dao xia sha xu chu* — Triple Forward Move of the Halberd, Scaring Xu Chu to Death

5. *xia san dao jing tui cao cao* — Triple Forward Move of the Halberd and Force Cao Cao Back

6. *bai yuan tuo dao wang shang kan* — White Ape Dragging the Halberd and Hacks to the Top

7. *quan wu hua* — Full Turn (Dance of the Blossom)

Second section

8. *yi peng hu jiu di fei lai* — The Tiger Jumps in Circles on the Spot

9. *fen zhong dao nan zhe nan dang* — Parting the Mane and Ward off Forward and Back

10. *shi zi dao pi kan xiong huai* — Forming a Cross with the Halberd and Splitting the Heart

11. *mo yao dao hui tou pan gen* — Circling the Hip 'Like a Millstone', Turning the Head and Winding the Roots

12. *wu hua sa shou wang shang kan* — Turn Body and Hack to Top

13. *ju dao mo di huai bao yue* — Raising the Halberd, Circling the Banner 'Like a Millstone', and Embrace the Moon

14. *wu hua sa shou wang xia kan* — Turn Body and Hack to Bottom

15. *luo zai huai zhong you bao yue* — Sink to the Centre of the Chest, Again Embracing the Moon

Third section

16. *quan wu hua shua dao fan shen kan* — Full Turn, Brushing with the Halberd, Turn Again and Back

17. *ci hui yi ju xia ren hun*	Sting Backwards so to Shatter the Human Soul
18. *wu hua wang zuo ding xia shi*	Body Turning, Placing the Halberd Exactly to Bottom Left
19. *bai yun gai ding you zhuan hui*	White Cloud Concealing the Peak, Turn Around Again
20. *wu hua fan shen wang shang kan*	Turn Body and Hack to Top
21. *zai ju qing tong kan si ren*	Raising the Halberd Again, Seeing a Dead
22. *wu hua wang you ding xia shi*	Body Turning, Placing the Halberd Exactly to Bottom Right
23. *bai yun gai ding you zhuan hui*	White Cloud Concealing the Peak, Turn Around Again

Fourth section

24. *di jiu tiao pao meng hui tou*	Hand Over the Alcohol, Raising the Robe with the Stick and Rapidly Turning Around
25. *hua dao zhuan xia tong pan gan*	Turn Around with the Halberd, Grab it at the Bottom of the Pole
26. *wu hua shuang jiao shui gan zu*	Turning the Body, Boldly Holding up Someone with the Feet
27. *hua dao zhuan xia tie man zhuan*	Turn Around with the Halberd and Lock the Iron Gate
28. *juan lian dao tui nan zhe bi*	Roll in the Curtain, Step Backwards, Block and Close
29. *shi zi dao wang ju qi*	Forming a Cross with the Halberd, then Raise
30. *fan shen zai ju long tan shui*	Turn the Body and Raise Again – the Dragon Stretches to the Water

DOUBLE SWORD FORM

chen shi tai ji shuang jian (WCTAG)

1. *shuang jian qi shi*	Double Sword Preparation Stance
2. *luo hua liu shui zhao yang jian*	Guiding the Sword of the Morning Sun
3. *shuang shen mei nu wang yue*	Turning the Body, Contemplating the Moon Like the Beautiful Lady
4. *ye cha tan hai*	Yecha Stretches towards the Sea
5. *hei xiong fan bei zhao yang jian*	The Black Bear Turns Around, and Hold Sword of the Morning Sun
6. *zhuan shen feng huang shuang zhan chi*	Turning the Body, Spreading the Wings Like the Phoenix
7. *shang san jian*	Three Swords Forward
8. *gu shu pan gen*	The Old Tree Winding Its Roots
9. *ri tao san huan*	Drawing Three Rings Around the Sun
10. *hei xiong fan bei zhao yang jian*	The Black Bear Turns Around, Hold Sword of the Morning Sun
11. *zuo luo han xiang long*	Lohan Defeats the Dragon – left
12. *you luo han xiang long*	Lohan Defeats the Dragon – right
13. *zhuan shen hu die xi shui*	Turning the Body and Absorb Water Like a Butterfly
14. *hei xiong fan bei zhao yang jian*	The Black Bear Turns Around, and Hold Sword of the Morning Sun
15. *zuo luo han xiang long*	Lohan Defeats the Dragon – left
16. *you luo han xiang long*	Lohan Defeats the Dragon – right

17. *zhuan shen er lang dan shan*	Turn the Body and Carry the Mountain Like Erlang
18. *hei xiong fan bei zhao yang jian*	The Black Bear Turns Around, and Hold Sword of the Morning Sun
19. *zhong kui zhang jian*	Zhongkui Holding the Sword
20. *gu shu pan gen*	The Old Tree Winding Its Roots
21. *fan shen xia pi jian*	Turn the Body and Slice Down with the Sword
22. *hei xiong fan bei zhao yang jian*	The Black Bear Turns Around, and Hold Sword of the Morning Sun
23. *zuo fan shen xia pi jian*	Turn the Body and Slice Down with the Sword – left
24. *you fan shen xia pi jian*	Turn the Body and Slice Down with the Sword – right
25. *zhuan shen zhoa yang jian*	Turning the Body Holding the Sword of the Morning Sun
26. *zuo you mo pan jian*	Drawing Circles Like a Millstone with the Sword, left and right
27. *ba wang quan ding*	Tyrant Holding the Trident in his Hand
28. *hu xi jian*	Shielding the Knee with the Sword
29. *bai shi tu xin*	The White Snake Pushes out the Tongue
30. *zuo feng huang shuang zhan chi*	The Phoenix Spreads his Wings – left
31. *you feng huang shuang zhan chi*	The Phoenix Spreads his Wings – right
32. *zhan shen zhao yang jian*	Turning the Body Holding the Sword of the Morning Sun
33. *lian huan ci hu*	Subsequently Stabbing the Tiger
34. *zuo you shuang wu jian*	Making Both Swords Dance – left and right

35. *zuo pan long jian*	The Dragon Winds – left
36. *you wo hu jian*	The Tiger Lays Down to Sleep – right
37. *shi zi gun xiu qiu*	The Lion Rolls the Clothball
38. *ba yun wang ri*	Towering Beyond the Clouds and Seeing the Sun
39. *huai zhong bao yue*	Embracing the Moon in Front of the Chest

DOUBLE SABRE FORM

chen shi tai ji quan shuang dao (WCTAG)

First section

1. *shuang dao qi shi*	Double Sabre Preparation Stance
2. *quan wu hua zhao yang dao*	Full Turn (Dance of the Blossom), Holding the Sabre of the Morning Sun
3. *qie san dao zhao yang*	Triple Cut with the Sabre of the Morning Sun
4. *yi dao yu bu*	Jump with the Sabre
5. *yan bie jin chi*	The Wild Goose Turns her Golden Wings
6. *shang san dao*	Three Steps Forward with the Sabre
7. *gu yan chu gun*	Lonesome Wild Goose Leaving the Flock

Second section

8. *yi dao zhao yang*	The Sabre of the Morning Sun
9. *zuo cha hua*	Put in the Flower – left
10. *you cha hua*	Put in the Flower – right
11. *hu die xi shui*	Butterfly Absorbing the Water
12. *yi dao zhao yang*	The Sabre of the Morning Sun
13. *zuo cha hua*	Put in the Flower – left
14. *you cha hua*	Put in the Flower – right

15. *fu hu*	Tiger Lying on the Ground
16. *yi dao zhao yang*	The Sabre of the Morning Sun
17. *zhong kui zhang jian*	Zhongkui Holding the Sword

Third section

18. *gu shu pan gen*	The Old Tree Winding Its Roots
19. *fan shen kan*	Turning the Body, Performing a Strike
20. *yi dao zhao yang*	The Sabre of the Morning Sun
21. *zuo jiao xiang*	Turning the Neck – left
22. *you jiao xiang*	Turning the Neck – right
23. *liang dao zhao yang*	Two Sabres of the Morning Sun
24. *liang dao zuo zhuan xiang*	Turning the Neck with Two Sabres – left
25. *you zhuan xiang*	Turning the Neck – right
26. *ba wang ju ding*	Tyrant Raising the Trident
27. *luo han xiang long*	The Lohan Defeats the Dragon

Fourth section

28. *you pian ma dao*	Sabre Cutting the Horse in Two – right
29. *zuo pian ma dao*	Sabre Cutting the Horse in Two – left
30. *bai shi tu xin*	The White Snake Pushes out the Tongue
31. *zuo pu you pu*	Counterstrike Left, Counterstrike Right
32. *shang bu qi xing*	Step Forward Striking with Seven Stars
33. *xia bu kua gong*	Step Backward and Spread Arms
34. *yi dao xia shi*	Sabre Splitting to the Bottom
35. *shou shi*	Closing Stance